Italian Fascism, 1915–1945

This book is dedicated to the memory of my mother and father.

Contents

Acknowledgement

I am particularly grateful to Tony Mason, who offered to read the chapters of the original edition as they were written, and did so speedily, giving not only comment and encouragement but also good advice on how to make the text more manageable and readable.

List of Abbreviations

AOI	*Africa Orientale Italiana* [Italian East Africa]
CIL	*Confederazione Italiana del Lavoro* [Italian Confederation of Labour (Catholic trade union organization)]
CGL	*Confederazione Generale del Lavoro* [General Confederation of Labour (Socialist trade union organization)]
CLNAI	*Comitato di Liberazione Nazionale per Alta Italia* [Committee of National Liberation of Northern Italy (the organisation coordinating the political and military activities of the anti-Fascist Resistance)]
CONFAG	*Confederazione dell'Agricoltura* [Confederation of Agriculture (the umbrella organisation of landowners and farmers associations)]
CONFINDUSTRIA	*Confederazione dell'Industria Italiana* [Italian Industrialists Confederation]
EOA	*Ente Opere Assistenziali* [Agency for Welfare Activities (Fascist party social welfare organisation)]
ERR	*Ente Radio Rurale* [Rural Radio Agency]
FIOM	*Federazione Italiana Operai Metallurgici* [Italian Federation of Metalworkers (CGL-affiliated national metalworkers trade union)]
FISA	*Federazione Italiana Sindacati Agricoltori* [Italian Federation of Farmers' Syndicates (Fascist union of farmers)]
GIL	*Gioventù Italiana del Littorio* [Italian Youth of the Lictors (Fascist party youth organisation)]
GUF	*Gioventù Universitaria Fascista* [Fascist University Youth (Fascist students organisation)]

INCF   *Istituto Nazionale di Cultura Fascista* [National
              Institute of Fascist Culture]
IRI   *Istituto per la Ricostruzione Industriale* [Institute
              for Industrial Reconstruction]
MVSN   *Milizia Volontaria per la Sicurezza Nazionale*
              [Voluntary Militia for National Security]
ONMI   *Opera Nazionale di Maternità ed Infanzia*
              [National Mother and Child Agency]
ONB   *Opera Nazionale Balilla* [National Balilla
              Organisation (Fascist children and youth
              organisation)]
OND   *Opera Nazionale Dopolavoro* [National
              Afterwork Organisation (Fascist leisure and
              recreational organisation)]
OVRA   *Organizzazione per la Vigilanza e la Repressione
              Antifascista* [Organisation for the Surveillance
              and Repression of Antifascism (the Interior
              Ministry's secret police branch)]
PCF   *Parti Communiste Français* [French Communist
              Party]
PFR   *Partito Fascista Repubblicano* [Republican
              Fascist Party]
PNF   *Partito Nazionale Fascista* [National Fascist
              Party]
PPI   *Partito Popolare Italiano* [Italian Popular Party
              (Catholic)]
PSI   *Partito Socialista Italiano* [Italian Socialist Party]
RSI   *Repubblica Sociale Italiana* [Italian Social
              Republic]

Modern Italy

Introduction: Locating Fascism

What is 'new' about this revised edition of *Italian Fascism 1915–1945*, which was first published in 1995? Well, the title, for a start. The Fascist movement was formed in 1919. But the starting date for the book has been pushed back to 1915 to reflect the origins of Fascism as a political movement in the interventionist campaign to bring about Italy's entry to the First World War, Mussolini's own transition from Socialist to 'Fascist' during the period of interventionism and the war itself, and the importance of the war experience to setting Fascist goals and 'values'. This will emerge more emphatically in Chapter 1, as will an attempt to deal with what some intellectual historians see as the emergence of a kind of 'prehistoric' generic fascism and Italian Fascism from the pre-war European matrix of non-conformist ideas and movements.

This mainly historiographical introduction is also new and should have appeared in the first edition. The historiography of Italian Fascism deserves a book of its own, and, thankfully, the Australian historian, Richard Bosworth, has already written one.[1] Although obvious and self-evident, it is worth reminding the British, American, and even Australian, readers of this book, that their countries have not lived through the breakdown of democratic politics, and fascist dictatorship leading to war, defeat and foreign occupation, as people did in Italy and Germany between 1918 and 1945. Coming to terms with their countries' recent nightmarish past was, and to some extent still is, an open wound, or at least a raw nerve, for Italians and Germans since 1945. This has meant that historical narratives and interpretations of Italian Fascism and German Nazism have always had a political edge and relevance far greater than, for instance, the argument among British historians about both the morality and practicality of the British government's 'appeasement' of the fascist dictators in the late 1930s, opened up by A.J.P. Taylor's book on the origins of the Second World War.

It is still meaningful to talk of Italy's post-1945 democratic parliamentary Republic being founded and legitimised on the fact and ensuing myth of a politically broadly based democratic anti-Fascist alliance, including the Communists, which coalesced in the period of the armed resistance to Mussolini's revamped Fascist regime and its German ally and patron between 1943 and 1945. The attempt to validate the present and future democratic politics of the country by reference to the break with its nasty Fascist recent past reinforces the sense that the history of Fascism written after its demise in 1945 has always been 'political' and 'contemporary'. This was all the more the case when, as we shall see, the so-called 'revisionist' historians in the 1970s and 1980s claimed that their studies were 'scientifically' objective and not politically inspired. In the context of the then current historiography of Fascism, for historians to lay claim to an apolitical objectivity in their treatment of Fascism was a very 'political' stance, indeed.

The strength of Richard Bosworth's book is the way he relates the historiography of Fascism to changes in contemporary Italian politics, culture and society since 1945. I can scarcely replay his book, here. It will have to be enough to say that, basically, historians of the Fascist period in Italy, as of the Nazi period in Germany, want to find out how to locate Fascism, in two senses. Historians explore where to place Fascism in the country's recent national history, an approach which necessarily takes them back into pre-First World War liberal Italy, and forward into post-1945 democratic and republican Italy, to examine the origins, impact and consequences of Fascism. They also attempt to situate Italian Fascism among other fascist or apparently fascist movements in inter-war and wartime Europe, exposing their similarities and differences in an effort to decide whether fascism was, indeed, a European-wide generic political phenomenon.

The debate over fascism as a generic phenomenon will probably run as long as there are historians of fascism, and locating Fascism in this sense is not the main aim of the book. However, the basis for a comparison between Italian Fascism and German Nazism should emerge from my treatment of the Axis and then political and military alliance between the two fascist powers, and of the Fascist race measures in Chapter 6.

So it may be as well to come clean now about where I stand on the matter of generic fascism. I see Italian Fascism as the 'first' fascism of many. But since one has to accept that what makes inter-war and wartime fascism historically and historiographically significant is Nazi Germany, it was not so much a model for other fascist movements, as an example. For instance, both the French fascist movement of the 1920s, *Le Faisceau*, and German Nazism in the early 1920s tried to emulate what so impressed them about Mussolini's movement in Italy, its ability to build a mass movement on anti-socialism and its coup technique, the way it took power. Even Hitler recognised Mussolini's 'primacy' in these respects, and they were the basis of Hitler's continuing respect and support for Mussolini, even when Fascist Italy was considered to be an under-performing and demanding ally of Nazi Germany.

Fascism as a general European phenomenon was the product of, and alternative to, the widespread European crisis of the post-First World War political and economic order, based on liberal parliamentary democracy and capitalism domestically, and the League of Nations internationally. Fascist movements came in two waves accompanying the most acute crisis points. These were the immediate aftermath of the First World War, marked by the threat from the left following the 1917 Bolshevik Revolution in Russia, and ethnic and territorial conflict in Central and Eastern Europe before, during and after the Versailles settlement of 1919–20, and the Great Depression of 1929–33, an economic recession of such dimensions that it appeared to be the structural and terminal crisis of malfunctioning capitalist economies and polities. Springing up in this context, the various fascisms, from Italian Fascism onwards, were radical hyper-nationalist cross-class movements with a distinctive militarist organisation and activist political style. In a climate of perceived national and international danger and crisis, they sought the regeneration of their nations through the violent destruction of all political forms and forces which they held responsible for national disunity and divisiveness, and the creation of a new national order based on the moral or 'spiritual' reformation of their peoples, a 'cultural revolution' achievable only through the 'total' control of society, and on class collaborative, regulatory forms of socio-economic organisation, often of a corporatist nature. So it seems that Italian Fascism cannot be isolated historically as only an Italian phenomenon. It was part of one general European response to a general European crisis of liberal democracy which matured in the wartime and inter-war years. The reasons why Italian Fascism was the first of the only two fascist movements to come to power in inter-war Europe and why it did so at the time that it did, might well, of course, be 'Italian' or specific to Italy.

The other issue of location, the placing of Italian Fascism in recent Italian history, is very much a concern of this book. Interpretations of Fascism appeared as soon as it became a force in Italian politics in the early 1920s, usually put forward by political activists on the Socialist and democratic left who opposed Fascism and wanted to understand it so that they could fight it more effectively. From the start, there were those who argued that Fascism was to be seen as a nasty and regrettable aberration or mistake, which one of Italy's most famous intellectuals, Benedetto Croce, called a 'parenthesis' in Italian history, a 'gap' in Italy's development which had little relation to what happened in Italy before or afterwards. Others, alternatively, thought that Fascism was, in the famous description of an anti-Fascist writer of the 1920s, the autobiography of the nation, a movement and regime which revealed and was the near-inevitable outcome of the flawed social, economic and political development of Italy from the mid-nineteenth century *Risorgimento* onwards, the national political and cultural revival which culminated in the territorial unification of the country in 1870.

These two sets of arguments about Fascism lead in interesting and divergent directions. The 'parenthesis' view literally puts the Fascist period into brackets, separating it off from what came before and what came after. From this perspective, Italy under its liberal political leadership between 1870 and 1915, and particularly under Giovanni Giolitti, Prime Minister in the early 1900s, was developing gradually into a modern industrial nation with parliamentary institutions, keeping, in other words, to the 'normal' pattern of development of Western European countries. This development was brutally interrupted by the coming to power of Fascism in 1922, the outcome of the impact of the First World War on Italian and European society, which included the Bolshevik Revolution in Russia in 1917 and the prospect it raised of socialist revolutions throughout Europe. Normal service was resumed with the military defeat of Fascism by 1945, when the country was once again able to progress along the road of parliamentary democracy.

The 'revelation' line of argument certainly does not underestimate the importance of the First World War for the rise of Fascism, but lengthens the perspective on the events of the immediate post-war years in Italy. So the crisis of the liberal system of government in Italy was not just down to the effects of the war. It went further back to the imperfect process of national unification and the 'abnormal' liberal politics of the pre-war period, when Italians were not made to feel citizens of their own nation and a huge gap had opened up between the mass of the people and their supposedly liberal state and political system. Chapter 1 shows that this is basically my reading of liberal Italy.

The Marxist version of the 'revelation' view emphasises that the distribution of power between the social classes remained basically the same from liberal to Fascist Italy. The political forms certainly changed from the liberal to the Fascist state. But the dominant social and economic interests behind both were the rich and already powerful. Reactionary agricultural and industrial employers had set up and financed the Fascist movement to destroy working-class organisations and to reverse the political and socio-economic gains of the organised working class in a post-war crisis of such severity that it became clear that the old liberal politicians were not up to the job. The real and lasting basis of the Fascist state was the permanent repression of the rights and interests of Italian workers.

Each of these viewpoints throws, in turn, a different light on the post-1945 situation in Italy. If Fascism was a 'parenthesis', a horrible historical accident, then it was definitely 'over' and most unlikely to recur. However, if Fascism was the 'revelation' of Italy's recent past, then it could also be a 'revelation' of Italy's present and future, and the post-1945 Italian Republic, dominated until recently by the Catholic Christian Democratic Party, could carry the same 'defects' as liberal Italy. If conditions were as 'right' as they were in the early 1920s, then the threat of Fascism might re-emerge and had to be guarded against. This was why one of the anti-Fascist groups, *Giustizia e Libertà* (Justice and Liberty), whose exponents had practically invented the 'revelation' thesis, and which had participated in the armed resistance against Fascism from 1943, and whose successor, the Action Party, led the first post-war Italian government, was so insistent that there should not be a restoration of the pre-Fascist Italy of 1922, but a complete recasting of the country's institutions after the defeat of Fascism.

Most interpretations of Italian Fascism have tended towards one or another of these two positions, and in the 1970s the 'revelation' view was more widely held by historians. From the mid-1970s, however, the 'parenthesisers' staged something of a comeback, largely as a result of the controversy in Italy aroused by the work of an Italian historian, Renzo De Felice, who died recently, whose views sparked off the nearest thing in Italy to the 'Historians Controversy' over Nazism in Germany at about the same time. De Felice's lifework was a mammoth unfinished biography of the Fascist dictator, Benito Mussolini. This turned out to be a very controversial, influential and at the same time problematic re-reading of Mussolini and Fascism. Approaching from an apparently neutral but disguised conservative nationalist viewpoint, De Felice produced a more sympathetic portrait of Mussolini and the regime he personified than the ones conveyed in the then still largely anti-Fascist historiography of Fascism. Precisely because of his claimed neutrality towards who and what he was studying and of his approach to Fascism as 'history', belonging in the past, De Felice also opened or re-opened a debate about the function and practice of history, and more pointedly for contemporary Italians, about whether Fascism was still to be taken as a matter of current political concern and controversy.

Although the ramifications of the controversy provoked by De Felice's work have affected the way all Italian and non-Italian historians of Fascism handle its history, there is not much evidence of this in English language general histories of Fascism. The recent book on Anglo-Italian diplomatic relations by the independent scholar, Richard Lamb,[2] reproduces in all its, I think, mistaken glory, the De Felician line on Mussolini's foreign policy. John Whittam, in his otherwise sensible, pragmatic and low key narrative history of Italian Fascism,[3] calls De Felice, to my mind unbelievably, 'the maestro', in his annotated bibliography, and lists all seven volumes of De Felice's biography of Mussolini to show he has read them. But, along with Alexander De Grand, whose really excellent survey history is now in its third edition,[4] he acknowledges some kind of intellectual debt to De Felice without noticeably incorporating his work into the text.

There are understandable reasons for this, to do with the inordinate length of De Felice's standard bearing biography of Mussolini, and the amount of time De Felice has taken to write it. Starting in the mid-1960s, by 1990 De Felice had published the seventh volume of his mammoth, but still incomplete, 'life and times' biography of Mussolini, which in total was about 6000 pages of dense text, the equivalent of a page to every three days of Mussolini's life. An eighth volume, taking the reader up to January 1944 in another 700 pages of text, was published posthumously in 1997. This multi-volume biography has all the appeal of an encyclopaedia and thankfully, for English readers, has so far not been translated from the original Italian, and is probably untranslatable.

The biography is appallingly written history, whatever you feel about the length, and while largely jargon-free, has an opaque and convoluted style which sometimes defeats or obscures understanding with its never-ending sentences tumbling onwards into clause, sub-clause, and sub-sub-clause. He promised us a one volume *précis*, but this and the completion of the biography up to Mussolini's killing in April 1945 were pre-empted by his death.

So what follows is an attempt to go where no English language history has gone before and to locate De Felice in the post-war historiography of Italian Fascism. The De Felician controversy was ignited not so much by the four volumes of the book which had appeared by 1974, as by the publication of an interview with De Felice in 1975.[5] It was here, and in the follow-up anniversary interview, published in 1995,[6] along with intervening newspaper articles and interviews, that De Felice felt he could speak more clearly than in the actual biography about his treatment of Mussolini and Fascism.

The political and cultural contexts are important in order to understand the impact and resonances of De Felice's work. The first interview book came out after a time of the 'opening to the left' in Italian politics, with the post-war Christian Democrat-dominated coalition governments being broadened out to include politicians from the Socialist Party, and there existed the real possibility of the Communist Party entering formally into the arc of government in a so-called 'Historic Compromise', following its effective political exclusion during the Cold War years of the late 1940s and 1950s. Never at least disguising his anti-communism, De Felice felt that he had to challenge what he saw as the established anti-Fascist academic culture of his own country and its reading of the Fascist past, which condemned Fascism as a repressive, unpopular and warlike dictatorship, and corresponded to the post-war Italian Republic's declared foundation on anti-Fascist principles and on the 'popular' anti-Fascist Resistance of 1943–45.

This was something of a paranoic reaction. It is hard to see exactly what anti-Fascist cultural establishment De Felice felt was inhibiting the expression of anything other than the official anti-Fascist line, when at least to the early 1960s Italian politics and cultural production were frozen into a Cold War mould, where the hegemonical force was the conservative and anti-Communist Christian Democrat Party. Even if one accepts the passing hegemony of Marxist and fellow-travelling intellectuals for a time in the 1970s, hardly any of the university professorships in history were held by men of the left; they were very much like De Felice, in fact.

Anyway, De Felice thought that this official anti-Fascism made for bad history, since it led people to make political and ideological comparisons between Italy's present and recent past. He claimed to be writing non-political, neutral, value-free, interpretation-free, 'objective' and 'scientific' history; old-fashioned history, methodologically, in other words. By now, every historian's alarm bells should be ringing. The study of archive documents, for De Felice, is like an archaeological dig, and can never be 'political' or 'contemporary', because the source material belongs to the past, far removed from the 'contemporary' world. But the historian, of course, does belong to the contemporary world, and there is bound to be some kind of interaction between the historian living in his or her world and the historical evidence being investigated. Any serious historian who claims absolute objectivity, letting the facts speak for themselves, as if history is one damned thing after another, is either being naïve or behaving suspiciously.

Behind this apparently non-judgemental line lay the 'parenthesis' approach: Italian Fascism was unique, distinctive, specific and it was finished with, a phenomenon which existed and could only exist in the 1919–45 period, and therefore to be studied as 'history', not to serve some anti-Fascist political and ideological purpose. The sheer overwhelming length and detail of the biography are, in themselves, a demonstration of De Felice's belief that you first have to write Fascism's history and only then can you interpret it.

De Felice has always publicly denied that his Mussolini biography was sympathetic to the dictator and Fascism, though his critics in Italy accuse him of rehabilitating Fascism, and his 'anti-anti-Fascist' history has been welcomed in Italian right-wing and neo-Fascist circles. Perhaps one should not judge historians by the uses which others make of their histories. But De Felice himself has argued that the contemporary irrelevance of the old political conflicts between Fascists and anti-Fascists, no longer credible with the passing of time and his own 'historicisation' of Fascism, made it a nonsense to continue treating the Italian neo-Fascist movement, the *Movimento Sociale Italiano* (Italian Social Movement), as a pariah in political life.

The conservative, anti-left 'agenda', declared or not, of De Felice's work became clearer in the transformed Italian and international political climate of the early 1990s. The dramatic changes to the Italian party political system, under the weight of the collapse of international communism and of political corruption scandals, included the disintegration of the previous poles of the system, the Christian Democrat and Communist parties. The disappearance of the old political certainties has inevitably strained the anti-Fascist wartime Resistance legitimacy of the immediate post-war settlement which led to the foundation of the democratic parliamentary Republic. The beneficiary of the system collapse, Silvio Berlusconi, the monopolist media entrepreneur, soccer club owner, founder and leader of a new political party named after one of the politeir soccer chants, *Forza Italia!* (Come On, Italy!), and currently Italy's Prime Minister, has included the MSI, now re-branded as the *Alleanza Nazionale* (National Alliance), in his government coalition, a demonstrable mark of his often-expressed belief that Fascism is 'over' and now 'only' 'history'. De Felice's 'post-Fascist' viewpoint in a sense matches the 'post-Fascist' stance of the present neo-Fascist movement, an important and now apparently legitimate and credible political force from the early 1990s, a sign for some that Italy has finally moved on from the Fascist/anti-Fascist divisions of the recent past.

Since De Felice did not write off Fascism as 'bad' or 'evil', and thought that it was an 'historical fact' to be analysed 'on its own terms' and without making any prior judgement, he started taking seriously Fascist sources and what Fascists at the time said they were doing. As an historian of Fascism, I see this recourse to Fascist sources as De Felice's most important contribution to the study of the Fascist regime. As a result of his researches and those of his 'school', we now have a far better understanding of what Fascists and Fascism intended to do. This serves to body out Fascism as an autonomous political phenomenon with its own 'agenda', when it has long been interpreted as a secondary force functional to some other more significant trends, a by-product of capitalism in crisis or of 'modernisation'.

Picking up on De Felice's Fascist sources takes the historian onto dangerous ground. Sometimes justifiably, De Felice has been criticised for an over-literal and naïve reading of 'biased' sources, which came close to passing off Fascist propaganda as the reality. His critics thought that such a failure to distinguish Fascist words from their deeds showed a lack of historical judgement and an inability to see behind the words for the 'real' meaning of Fascism. I have attempted in this book not to fall into the same trap of being seduced by the sources, and to show a proper historical awareness of the gap which existed in Fascist Italy between intention and performance. But my own feeling is that as historians we are more likely to be able to reconstruct what Fascism wanted to do, and less likely to be able to assess the impact of what they actually did, given that the very nature of a 'totalitarian' system affected people's responses to it and the way these responses were expressed and recorded. There is more on this in Chapter 4.

It is often difficult to work out the De Felician line from the thousands of pages of the biography, and its very detail and length induces him to be internally inconsistent. I have rather taken objection to his allegedly 'objective' approach to the writing of history. But there are many other more specific matters which have led to argument among historians. De Felice's contribution to the debate about these particular issues will be incorporated into the text as and when these issues arise, and it will then, I hope, be made clear the extent to which I follow or, more often, disagree with the De Felician line. But it may be as well to signpost some of these issues here: Fascism as the movement of 'emerging' middle classes (Chapter 1); the degree to which the Fascist regime was 'consensual' in the 1930s (Chapter 4); Fascist foreign policy (Chapters 5, 6); Fascist colonial policy in East Africa (Chapter 6); the Fascist race laws (Chapter 6); the Italian 'civil war', 1943–45 (Chapter 8); and Fascism's 'legacy' to post-war Italy (Conclusion).

There is a greater emphasis in this book on the nature and development of the Fascist regime than on Fascism's origins and rise to power. What drives the analysis in Parts II and III is a view of the 'primacy of foreign policy', and making an explicit connection between the regime's internal and foreign policies, between Fascist 'totalitarianism' and wars of conquest and expansion. Italian Fascism was, essentially, about war, both on its own society and against other societies, and perhaps only an anti-Fascist reading of Fascism leads to this conclusion.

Part I
The Conquest of Power, 1915–29

1 The War, the Post-war Crisis and the Rise of Fascism, 1915–22

1. POLITICS AND SOCIETY IN POST-UNIFICATION ITALY

The national elections of November 1919 were the most significant in Italy since the political and territorial unification of the country in 1870. They were the first elections to take place under conditions approaching mass political democracy. All adult males had the vote. The electoral law of August 1919 introduced proportional representation with large multimember constituencies replacing the pre-war first-past-the-post, single-member constituency system.

These elections precipitated a crisis in the country's parliamentary system. Italy's first experience of mass democratic politics converged with a period of uninterrupted political, social and economic disturbances arising from the impact of an internally divisive war and a difficult transition from war to peace. Much of this opening chapter looks at how the elections provided the context for the emergence and rise of Fascism, initially an effect and then a cause of the political crisis they opened up.

The emergence of mass democracy was a dramatic challenge to the practice and management of oligarchic liberal parliamentary politics which had developed from unification to the eve of the First World War. From 1870 to the granting of near-universal adult male suffrage in 1912, national parliamentary institutions were raised on a narrow base of political participation. The electoral system reflected very real concerns among the country's rulers – the liberal nationalist minority drawn from the educated and propertied middle class and the liberal aristocracy – about the survival and cohesion of the newly unified state. They faced initially endemic disorder and criminality in the south, which was worsened by the impact of unification. For the southern peasants and artisans, the new nation-state was a predatory one, imposing northern Piedmontese institutions and economic policies. These brought higher taxes, conscription and internal free trade, which destroyed previously protected southern industry. Banditry and crime in the south had always fed on peasant hostility to the exactions of the state. There was also the longer-term problem of the Catholic church's official hostility to the Italian nation-state, based on the Papacy's claim that unified Italy had usurped its central Italian possessions, which were seen as the guarantee of the church's independence in the fulfilment of the universal mission to minister to all Catholics.

The evolution of parliamentary politics both mirrored and reinforced the mutual isolation of 'legal' Italy, the Italy of parliament, government and the state apparatus, and 'real' Italy of the mass of the population. 'Real' Italy was politically excluded by the limited franchise and the Pope's *non expedit* decree of 1874 banning Catholics from participating in national politics as either 'electors' or 'elected'. From the 1880s, governments were cobbled together through a process of *trasformismo*, which sprang from the practice of prime minister-designates co-opting their apparent political rivals into government and making in turn their parliamentary followings part of the new governmental majority. In blurring political differences, *trasformismo* at best represented a kind of liberal parliamentary consensus for the defence of liberal institutions and the political hegemony of the liberal political class against those forces, Catholic, democratic and Socialist, which threatened the disintegration of the state. At worst, *trasformismo* perpetuated government by corrupt parliamentary oligarchies.

One of the essential lubricants and guarantors of *trasformismo* was the promise of ministerial office, which opened up patronage, favours and influence to parliamentary supporters of the government and their small electorate. The other was the political and electoral interference of the prefects, the most important state officials in the provinces, who essentially brokered the relationship of interest linking government, parliamentary deputy and electors. Single-member constituencies and a limited franchise obviously facilitated the operation of the system, which was particularly effective in delivering the southern vote. Deputies representing the south and the islands were the basic voting fodder for the parliamentary majorities of successive governments.

The workings of the parliamentary and electoral system became both cause and effect of the widening gap between the country and its formally liberal political institutions. *Trasformismo* certainly entrenched, if

it did not create, the disparity between the political and economic development of northern and southern Italy. The price exacted by the southern
deputies for their parliamentary support was that government should
maintain and not challenge existing socio-economic structures and control
of local government in the south, to which the deputy and his electors were
inextricably linked. This effectively precluded any reform of the *latifundia*,
the large, poorly farmed estates prevalent in many areas of the south.
The backwardness of the south was essentially built into the functioning of Italy's parliament.

'Transformistic' practices also reduced parliament to a political
cipher and helped to make the government and the state administration,
rather than parliament, the focus of meaningful political activity. Managed elections and a largely docile parliamentary majority composed of
southern deputies trading votes in parliament for government favours
made for 'bland parliamentary dictatorships'[1] and the relative absence
of political conflict in parliament over *issues*. Such a situation similarly
inhibited, by making unnecessary, the formation of party organisations
among liberals at either the constituency or the parliamentary level.
Since elections could be made and parliamentary majorities created so
easily, liberal deputies had no need for party ties or support. They
rather gathered themselves loosely in regionally based parliamentary
groups and around leading politicians likely to be heads or members of
governments.

Parliament, in other words, was not the centre of political activity of
the country at large, but represented the interests of the liberal political
class. An electoral and parliamentary system based on a limited suffrage,
the fixing of elections and *trasformismo* could not reflect and represent
divisions and conflicts within the nation as a whole. As a result oppos-
itional movements to the left and right organised largely outside
parliament and did not even really see parliament as a channel for the
articulation and resolution of their interests and grievances. Catholic,
Socialist and later, nationalist programmes were systematically opposed
to parliamentary forms of government and were alternatives to them. If
there was an inherent 'crisis of the liberal state', then this was it: the
problem, intensifying with the growth of socialism from the 1890s, of
how to integrate popular forces into the political and parliamentary
processes of the nation.

The issue was confronted by Giovanni Giolitti, Prime Minister at various
points between 1903 and 1914. He attempted to narrow the growing
alienation of parliament from country by harnessing or neutralising

popular movements whose strengths and interests were extra- and anti-parliamentary, without undermining the political hegemony of liberal élites. He encouraged a limited *de facto* abrogation of the papal veto on Catholic political participation by getting Catholics to vote with and for liberals against Socialists in 'clerico-moderate' electoral alliances. By introducing social reforms, and urging the prefects to soften the use of the wide discretionary powers given to the police in illiberal and repressive legislation, he sought to strengthen reformists against revolutionaries in the Socialist Party. To this end, Giolitti also adopted an unprecedented stance of governmental neutrality and mediation in labour disputes of an economic rather than political nature.

Giolitti's flexibility had its limits: his openness towards some Catholics and some Socialists was still a form of *trasformismo* and did not imply any fundamental changes in liberal parliamentary and electoral practice to accommodate new popular forces. Giolitti had a reformist strategy in the industrialising and developing north. This complemented and was made possible by the continuation of the customary methods of coercion, patronage and clientelism used to control southern politics and ensure the support of southern deputies for the government in office.

Characteristically, Giolitti's concession of near-universal adult male suffrage in 1912 was part of a package to co-opt reformist Socialists into his government. Its democratising impact in the 1913 general elections was contained by the usual Giolittian holding operation: an anti-socialist electoral pact with the Catholics, and the clientelistic management of elections in the south. Giolitti's pre-war reformism was finally broken and discredited by Socialist opposition to participation in government and to the Libyan War of 1911–12, which saw the revolutionary wing triumph over the reformists at the 1912 party congress. 'Red Week' in June 1914, marked by an antimilitarist general strike and a series of local popular insurrections, seemed to indicate the futility and danger of meeting social unrest and revolutionary agitation with Giolittian reformist methods.

This essentially political analysis of what happened in post-unification Italy points to a flawed process of national state formation after 1870. Such a view implicitly runs counter to Croce's more optimistic reading of Italy's pre-war political development which has the effect of making Fascism an aberrant interruption of that development rather than an outcome of its imperfections. The alienation in liberal Italy of the mass of the people from the men and institutions which governed them would later be used by the Fascist regime to justify its positioning of itself in recent Italian history as the force 'completing' the *Risorgimento* and 'making' Italians through the masses' subordination to a powerful state. By 1914, the problem of the popular masses' involvement in national political affairs was evident enough, but not that its resolution would take the form of Fascism.

Yet some historians do seem to take matters in this direction, and in so doing, distance themselves even further from the Crocean idea of Fascism as 'parenthesis', and from the view that the real catalyst to the emergence of Fascism in Italy was the experience of the First World War. The French intellectual historian, Zeev Sternhell, has tried to argue that as an ideology, fascism originated in pre-war France. He says that it emerged before the outbreak of the war as a fully-fledged, coherent ideology synthesising the two apparently polar ideological opposites, nationalism and socialism, the 'socialism' coming mainly from an anti-materialist reworking of Marxist socialism by the French thinker, Georges Sorel, and the revolutionary syndicalists he influenced. Sternhell has extended from pre-war France to pre-war Italy the view that fascism had a history before it had a name, that a fascist ideology existed before any political movement embodying that ideology, appearing to suggest that a similar germination of 'fascist' ideas occurred in liberal Italy. Sternhell's work is congruent with, though not necessarily identical to, a set of studies of the early twentieth-century intellectual and cultural antecedents to Italian Fascism, which indicate similar connections between ideas developed before the war and those of Fascism.

What can be made of these interesting and problematic developments in the study of the historical origins of Fascism? It does seem logically and historically odd to separate the ideology from the movement and to suggest that there was an already fully articulated ideology searching, as it were, for a movement. A Fascist movement and Fascist ideology presumably co-existed; they appeared at the same time as each other. Only when Fascism emerged as a political movement did the ideological synthesis happen and become an observable phenomenon. But this does not rule out the fertilisation of the Fascist movement by ideas emerging in the pre-war period.

There was a European-wide cultural and intellectual 'revolt' in the 1890s and early 1900s. In Italy, as in France, this ranged a significant minority of the country's educated 'intelligentsia' against the then dominant ways of thinking about and perceiving the world which assumed that everything was knowable through the use of human reason, rejecting metaphysical speculation for the 'truth' of empirically proven and tested 'facts'. The intellectual non-conformists, in Italy as elsewhere, resented what they saw as the boring materialism and lack of 'soul' of their emerging urban, industrial, 'scientific' mass societies, and drew on the findings of the new social sciences, themselves, of course, signs of the dominant rationality of knowledge, which were exposing the basic irrationality, and psychological and emotional drives to much of human behaviour and actions.

Two significant intellectual and political influences on non-conformist opinion should be mentioned here, since practically every fascist leader of the inter-war period, including the 'first' fascist, Benito Mussolini, read them or read about them in some form or another, and cited them as having an impact on their political thinking and conduct. Gustave Le Bon's work on the psychology of crowds seemed to demonstrate that what inspired people as a mass to collective action were their emotions and feelings, not rational discourse and argument. The way for a politician to reach people, then, was by tapping into their subconscious will and soul, not by trying to convince them of the logic of his case. Georges Sorel, reacting against what he condemned as reformist Socialist parties' capitulation to democratic parliamentary politics and in order to recover socialism's revolutionary 'soul', emphasised the need for violence in smashing the bourgeois order, which denoted the will to act, the force of people's emotional attachment to socialist revolution. He thought that the same mobilising and energising function would also be achieved by the use of political 'myths', that is, visionary and inspirational sets of core beliefs felt in the popular subconscious and conveyed by word and images. As adapted by Mussolini and other fascists, the popular pull of the 'myth' was its capacity to evoke a mass response and inspire political action, not necessarily in its objective 'truth' or 'reality'.

The counter-cultural 'revolt against reason' was fed into the activities of several political or cultural movements and personalities in pre-war Italy. They all specifically targeted the Giolittian 'system' as the embodiment of the safe, small-minded 'little Italy' (*Italietta*), consigned to being an international nonentity in a 'social Darwinist' world of the growing global economic, military and imperial rivalry among the world's industrial and industrialising powers at the turn of the twentieth century. The Italian Futurists, attempting to bridge politics and culture, played politics as art, celebrating in iconoclastic public displays and gestures the dynamism, speed and exhilaration of the modern machine age, condemning everything that was 'past', old, established and traditional. Their glorification of violence and of the 'beauty' of war as the supreme arbiter of individual and national worth was shared in a rather more placid way by intellectuals writing for a pre-war journal in Florence, *La Voce*, who looked to war and empire to realise the then inadequate spiritual and cultural national consciousness-building among Italians. The self-dramatising hyperbolic nationalist poet, Gabriele D'Annunzio, the Nietzschean hero figure personified, gave his presence and his poetry to every nationalistic campaign going, in his one-man mission to 'educate' the Italian people into a national consciousness.

The personal, political and ideological connections between these cultural movements and personalities, and Mussolini and Fascism, were undeniable. The Futurists joined the early Fascist movement in 1919–20, and even though many of them were alienated by the movement's apparent move to the right, its founder and leader, Filippo Tommaso Marinetti, stayed on to become an important, even iconic, figure in the cultural politics of the Fascist regime. D'Annunzio was both Mussolini's ally and his only serious rival for leadership of the nationalist camp after the First World War. Mussolini read and collaborated on *La Voce* before the war, while still a socialist leader, and incorporated some of its counter-cultural approaches into his idea of revolutionary socialism.

This, perhaps, is the point. The pre-war 'revolt against reason' provided ideas on which post-war Fascist leaders and the movement drew on setting out their political stall as Fascists. You might also be able to say that some of a generation of university-educated young men were influenced by pre-war intellectual and cultural developments which pushed them in nationalistic directions and opened them up to the appeal of the post-war Fascist movement. But in the end, Sternhell's argument for an ideological fascism emerging by 1914 is not persuasive in the case of Italy, nor indeed, in the case of France. Whatever Mussolini's pre-war contacts with *La Voce*, you cannot plausibly transform Mussolini, or indeed *La Voce*, into an 'ideological' fascist or even prehistoric 'proto-fascists', at this point in time. Neither can we use the same labels to categorise in 1914 the revolutionary syndicalists who joined the Fascist movement at its founding in 1919, and the Nationalists who eventually merged into the Fascist Party in 1923, shortly after Mussolini came to power. The syndicalists' ideological transition from revolutionary syndicalism to 'national syndicalism' by 1918 was the result of their reading of the First World War experience in Italy. It was during the war that Mussolini and the Nationalists came closer together on both internal and international issues. What bridged Mussolini's stance as a revolutionary socialist in 1914 and his re-invention as the first fascist in 1919 was the First World War. As for those pre-war disaffected young middle-class would-be intellectuals, they were also the combatant generation, and their service as front line junior officers during the war was probably as, if not more formative, than exposure to the counter-cultural ideas of the decade before the war. It was, in other words, the war experience which was decisive in making some, and by no means all, of the pre-war critics and opponents of *giolittismo* into Fascists.

2. THE WAR IN ITALY

The first democratic elections in Italy's history were held in an exceptional atmosphere, characterised by a generalised, diffused but genuine popular mood of discontent and desire for profound change in Italian politics and society. The immediate post-war mood of *diciannovismo* or '1919-ism' was generated by the experience of wartime mobilisation and its impact on a scarcely unified nation. It was this mood which the early Fascist movement, founded in March 1919, was intended to tap, targeting a particular constituency created by the war: radicalised ex-soldiers, the war veterans.

Most Italians, even by 1914, did not have much sense of identity with or attachment to the nation-state and its political institutions. This was the legacy of Italy's unification process which liberal parliamentary government had recognised, guarded against but failed to resolve. In this context, Italy's involvement in the First World War was the first great collective and national experience for literally millions of Italians, especially the largely peasant conscript army. But partly because of imperfect nation forming since unification and partly because of the way Italy entered the war in 1915 and the way that war was conducted, the Great War did not bring about national integration and unity. There was no *union sacrée*, no temporary national and political truce for the duration of the war. Italy's wartime experience was extremely divisive; it increased popular alienation from the liberal parliamentary state while heightening expectations of transforming it. Italy's national war was 'waged in an atmosphere of civil war'.[2]

The decision to renounce the Triple Alliance which bound Italy to Austria-Hungary and Germany, and to enter the war in May 1915 on the side of France and Britain, was itself internally divisive. There was a heterogeneous majority in parliament made up of Giolittian liberals, Socialists and Catholics who wanted Italy to remain neutral and not intervene in the conflict, which seemed to match the mood in the country at large. Intervention was therefore a kind of coup against the will of parliament. Its neutralist majority was not only pressurised by the extra-parliamentary agitation of a vocal, equally heterogeneous coalition of interventionists, but was also obliged to endorse a *fait accompli* engineered by the right-wing liberal Prime Minister, Antonio Salandra, and the king, which deprived parliament of a say in decision-making. Salandra had secretly negotiated the terms of the Treaty of London under which Italy was to enter the war without consulting parliament or Giolitti, the leader of the largest group of deputies in the Chamber. The king as head of state had backed this up by circulating fellow heads of state in France and Britain on Italy's commitment to war.

This barely constitutional charade indicated how Italy's entry into the war was as much an act of domestic as foreign policy. This was the case not only for Salandra and the king but also for the unlikely combination of interventionists in 1914-15. The war, from their varying perspectives, was a chance to bury the Giolittian model of liberal reformism which had dominated Italian politics for much of the decade before 1915.

Salandra's royal coup was the conservative liberal option in action, enhancing the authority and powers of king and government as against parliament. The interventionist democratic left of Radicals, Republicans and Social Reformists wanted a war against Austria to complete national unification, but in a Mazzinian sense, as a contribution to a new international order premised on free, equal and democratically run nations. Such a stance linked Italy's legitimate territorial claims to the democratic renewal of Italy's political institutions. For the Nationalists, it was a war of expansion. An imperialist war necessitated a centralised, unitary organisation and mobilisation of human and material national resources, which approximated to and validated their own pre-war vision of an anti-parliamentary and post-liberal authoritarian corporatist order.

Finally, the spectrum of interventionism took in groups on the revolutionary left. Some revolutionary syndicalists were joined in one of the interventionist organisations, the *fasci di azione rivoluzionaria*, by a small group of Socialists and ex-Socialists including Benito Mussolini. Their break with the Socialist Party was precipitated by its pacifist, internationalist and neutralist position, a unique stance when socialist movements elsewhere were rallying behind the national war effort.

The interventionist revolutionary syndicalists partly interpreted the war in a rather conventional way. They thought the Italian proletariat should join the struggle against German imperialism and militarism, whose victory would mean the end of those political freedoms making working-class organisation possible at all. They also shared with Mussolini the intuition that the war would be revolutionary in other less predictable ways, that *somehow* it would change things. As an important leader of the dominant revolutionary faction and editor of the party newspaper *Avanti!*, Mussolini was obliged to defend the PSI's strictly neutralist stance. What most appeared to gall Mussolini was that this position confined revolutionaries to the sidelines. It meant that Socialists did nothing except passively spectate on a general European conflagration which might well destroy existing political alignments and create revolutionary opportunities.

This kind of political adventurism was at least consistent with some aspects of Mussolini's individualistic and idiosyncratic conception of revolutionary socialism which he had revealed during his career as a Socialist organiser and propagandist up to 1914. Mussolini's socialism was a unique and personal cauldron of innate rebelliousness and anti-establishment feeling, opportunism and the attempt to assimilate Marxist class struggle with a reading of European and Italian critiques of rational culture and its political counterpoints in liberal democracy and reformist socialism. Blending Marx with Friedrich Nietzsche, Henri Bergson, Georges Sorel and Gustave Le Bon produced a view of socialism at odds with the more deterministic and orthodox Marxism of even his fellow intransigents in the PSI. Mussolini saw the party as a dynamic revolutionary élite, whose main task was to form a revolutionary consciousness in the proletarian masses, to prepare them psychologically for revolution through propaganda and direct action. Mussolini's view of the party as a revolutionary élite, his instrumentalist conception of political ideals as 'myths' whose value lay in their ability to mobilise enthusiasm and commitment, and his emphasis on action and will shaping events, all testified to his exposure to the general European and Italian cultural and intellectual reaction against reason. They represented common ground in Mussolini's political and cultural development, and helped to make intelligible his political journey from socialism through interventionism to Fascism.

The divisions opened up in the country by the way Italy went to war were widened at both the political and social level by the prolongation of the war. It was imperative that the government achieved some kind of lasting political and social truce in order to prosecute the war more effectively. Yet a lengthening war worked to destroy the conditions for such a truce. The PSI was the one party that remained officially com-mitted to peace and neutrality throughout the war, a position defined rather ambiguously as 'neither support nor sabotage'. Such a formula in fact covered and rationalised both the party's anti-war stance and the reality of the party's and affiliated labour organisations' actual involve-ment in the war effort. Nevertheless, industrial labour was obviously crucial to sustaining greater production as the war continued, but its voluntary co-operation could not be guaranteed because of the PSI's stance. This contributed to a harsh factory regime being imposed on workers, who were put under military discipline in war-related industries. Food shortages in the industrial cities were accelerating inflation, eating away at the wages of even the highest-paid skilled workers in the engin-eering sectors. Food riots which erupted in Turin in summer 1917 had a definite anti-war edge.

In a war which accentuated rather than sublimated class and political divisions, military defeats fed back immediately and directly into internal political and social tensions. The military disaster at Caporetto in October–November 1917 left the Austrian and German armies occupying Italian territory. It was seen by the government, military and interven-tionists as not so much a defeat of the army but as a failure of the nation to unite behind the war effort. Blaming Caporetto on internal pacifism, subversion and defeatism justified tighter government controls on the labour movement and the Socialist Party in the last year of the war. The PSI, then, was attracting simultaneously both greater government repression and popular support, arising from their opposition to the war and exploitation of discontent at its economic and social costs.

The party's maximalist revolutionary position was reinforced by the suggestive example and model of the 1917 revolutions in Russia, especially the October Bolshevik Revolution, which indicated that violent proletarian revolution was imminent, inevitable and would arise, as in Russia, from the war-induced crisis of the bourgeois capitalist state. 'Doing as in Russia'[3] confirmed the PSI in its fundamental hostility to the liberal state. The programme adopted in September 1918 called for the creation of a socialist republic and the dictatorship of the proletariat.

Caporetto and its aftermath heightened the isolation of the PSI from the nation. It also accelerated the 'nationalisation' of the interventionist, ex-socialist and ex-revolutionary syndicalist left. Its exponents joined committees of national defence set up after Caporetto to rally people behind the faltering war effort and take action against the internal 'sabo-teurs' of the nation. The recovery from the Caporetto defeat helped to convince Mussolini that 'nation' was more important than 'class', both as a cause to fight for and as a force capable of engaging and mobilising people.

The government's need to recover from the defeat, and rally the home and fighting fronts to continue the war brought about significant changes in how it projected the war and war aims, particularly to the combatants in the trenches. The expectations of a better world which fuelled '1919-ism' were in part the product of the social and national content which the government and military gave to the war in the period from Caporetto to the armistice in November 1918. 'The liberty of tomorrow is the discipline of today', according to the founder of the army's new education and propaganda units.[4] The soldiers' commitment to and sacrifice for the nation in war was unambiguously linked to the rewards they could expect for that service in the post-war renewal of society.

The most tangible recognition of national service for peasant infantrymen was, of course, land. The government set up a special agency for ex-servicemen in January 1919, which aimed, among other things, to facilitate the transfer of land to returning soldiers. Without waiting for the government, the slogan 'land to the peasants' was translated directly into action in the post-war land occupations of the south, carried out by demobilised war veterans making good the wartime promises to them. In more general terms, the attempt throughout 1918 to make the war signify something to those who were fighting it, laid the basis of the myth of 'combatantism' (*combattentismo*). Several post-war movements, including Fascism, were to draw on this. Because soldiers had fought for the nation, they had won the right to remake the nation and become its new ruling class. In 1919 the interventionist democratic left revamped an old Republican idea for the calling of a popularly elected Constituent Assembly which would redraft the country's constitution and political system. This was exactly the kind of proposal inspired by the collective experience of war and indicated even in this legalist format how that experience had diffused the conviction that the country could not be governed as before. The government's own attempt to give a meaning to the war in 1918 had mortgaged the future of the liberal state and the liberal political class.

The Fascist version of the combatant 'myth' was an idealisation of the war experience. But like all effective 'myths', it had enough of a basis in the real experience of trench warfare to appeal to at least some combatants. There was a considerable and sharply felt physical and psychological distance between the miserable and dangerous existence of soldiers and their junior officers in the front line trenches, and the more comfortable and safer lives of both their families and other civilians way behind the lines on the 'home front' and their senior commanding officers in military bases to the rear of the actual fighting. As a result, front line troops and officers came to see themselves as a breed apart, bonded and banded together against the 'shirkers' and 'sharks' of the 'home front' and their indifferent and incompetent commanders by an experience of trench warfare not felt nor comprehended by others. The 'mateyness' and comradeship emerging from a terrible shared experience of danger and deprivation were glorified as the fraternity of a trench 'community', which for some Italian soldiers was taken as the birth of a new 'national' society, the basis and model for changes in their own society after the war. Ex-combatants were due a special place and status in post-war society, even a leadership role, because of their sacrifice and commitment to the national cause during the war.

This 'myth' of the war was actually built on the experience not of the rank and file conscript soldiers, who were only too glad, once the war was over, to return to civilian life, but rather on that of the young educated middle-class junior officers who were volunteers and conscripts, and not career soldiers. These junior officers shared the trench existence of the units they commanded and for some it was their first prolonged contact with Italians drawn from other social classes and other regions. Trench life was egalitarian, in the sense that officers and men faced the same squalid and dangerous daily grind, and also hierarchical, in the sense that officers commanded and led their troops. This egalitarian and simultaneously hierarchical trench community was perceived as the microcosmic meritocratic society of the post-war future; the ideal of the relationship between élites and popular masses to be forged after the war.

There was another more specialised group of combatants in the Italian army who extended their wartime camaraderie, their elitism and their militarised violence into the post-war world. These were the *Arditi*, or 'Daring Ones', special assault troops who were trained separately, armed differently, with dagger and grenades, uniformed differently, and treated differently to the human cannon fodder of the trenches, and who saw much more personal, face-to-face combat than the soldiers in the trenches. Their sense of being a special élite fighting force was carried over into the formation of their own veterans' association after the war, which was subsidised and cultivated by Mussolini and his newly founded Fascist movement. The *Arditi* came to personify the Fascist will to action and to use violence not only as a means to end all political arguments, but also as a 'value' in itself, a mark of manhood, superiority and worth, and patriotism, since the violence was directed at the nation's 'enemies'.

The last year of the conflict seemed to be bearing out the gamble behind revolutionary interventionism, that the war would become a 'revolutionary war'. The trajectory taken by the syndicalists during the war and particularly from 1917, completed their revision-cum-repudiation of Marxism. They had come to see Italy's problems as being nationally specific, which could not be addressed in the orthodox universal Marxist terms of capitalist crisis and class conflict. Italy's unique problems of economic underdevelopment and national disunity were brought into sharp focus by the country's mobilisation for war. The issue was not so much capitalism, as the chronic mutual alienation of state and society, leading to popular antipathy to national political institutions, which was both cause and effect of an unrepresentative parliamentary system and a corrupt and unproductive liberal political class. The now 'national syndicalist' alternative to parliamentary democracy was a state in which a community of producers would participate in political life through their membership of economic organisations. Such a system would not only stimulate the greater production of national wealth to the benefit of all producers, including workers, but would also ensure a more meaningful and continuous form of political involvement because it was related to people's economic activity. The proletariat had failed to seize the 'revolutionary' opportunities of war, and the PSI had now adopted a Bolshevik-style socialist revolution which was irrelevant to the resolution of Italy's unique problems of economic growth and national integration. Hence, the anti-parliamentary revolution would be led by a new élite of ex-combatants, formed in and by the war.

Expelled from the PSI in late 1914 for rejecting neutrality, Mussolini's own definitive break with revolutionary socialism also matured in the period from Caporetto to the end of the war. Mussolini had started his own newspaper, *Il Popolo d'Italia*, in November 1914, with the money from the French government and some Italian interventionist industrial concerns, who also saw the value of Mussolini's defection in dividing socialism. 'Who pays?' was the derisive cry from the PSI which Mussolini had now abandoned. The suggestion that he was 'bought off' has fed the view of Mussolini as an unprincipled opportunist. But his break with the PSI was a real political gamble and not a good career move, personally or politically. He had given up an influential position within the Socialist Party for an uncertain political future, which became a political isolation lasting until 1920, when 'events' rescued his political career.

Emblematic of Mussolini's position in 1918 and through into the Fascism of 1919 was the change in the masthead of his daily newspaper, *Il Popolo d'Italia*. A 'socialist' daily up until the edition of 1 August 1918, thereafter it became the 'paper of combatants and producers'. These were all-inclusive and elastic categories which did not conform to the usual class and political divisions. Their use represented Mussolini's attempt to make something of the disruptive effects of war on existing political alignments and affiliations and of the experience of wartime mobilisation.

The personal and political opportunism was self-evident. Both Mussolini and the interventionist syndicalists had to accept that they had only managed to draw a small minority of workers into a 'revolutionary war'. Their conclusion that the proletariat was no longer the revolutionary class rationalised this failure. *Combattentismo* and 'productivism' were themes through which to appeal to new potential constituencies thrown up by the war. In December 1917 Mussolini had anticipated the emergence of a 'trenchocracy' (*trincerocrazia*) of worker-soldiers and peasant-soldiers, who because of their involvement in the wartime struggle to save the nation could become the proponents of 'an anti-marxist and ... national socialism'.[5]

As for the 'national syndicalists', Mussolini's commitment to the 'producers' and to 'productivism' was similarly connected to the war experience, where the priority was production at almost any cost to meet the escalating demands of the war economy. The maximisation of production in the national interest required the end to class conflict and the co-operation of organised groups of all producers, from workers to technicians and entrepreneurs. There would obviously be a place in the national community of producers for the worker-as-producer. But Mussolini's gloss on 'productivism' emphasised the creation rather than the distribution of wealth. This implied continuing social and economic inequality and an unavoidable 'natural' hierarchy among producers on the basis of experience, competence and responsibility, of the relative weight and importance of each producer to the productive process. 'Productivism' could be read as a charter for capitalist entrepreneurs. It certainly brought Mussolini closer to the Nationalist position and to the concerns of the war industrialists who were financing both the Nationalist press and *Il Popolo d'Italia*.

Mussolini's conversion to 'productivism' was also linked to the increasingly nationalistic and imperialist foreign policy stance that he adopted in the course of 1917–18. The muscle for a policy of national independence, let alone one of national expansion and grandeur, had to come from economic and particularly industrial growth. 'Productivism' also had an anti-political thrust. It confronted a parasitical political class with the superior national role of the producer, and intimated as an alternative to the liberal parliamentary state a syndicalist or corporative model of social and political organisation capable of achieving the cross-class unity of producers. By the armistice in 1918, Mussolini had brought together in 'combatantism', 'productivism' and imperialism the ingredients of the first fascism.

The extent to which Fascism was the product of Italy's war experience should now be clear. Mussolini's political evolution from revolutionary socialism to 'national socialism', and that of the interventionist revolutionary syndicalists to 'national syndicalism', occurred during and as a result of Italy's mobilisation for 'total' war. In order to fight a war of unprecedented dimensions, the government, as in other belligerent countries, was obliged to organise, regulate and mobilise the country's economic and human resources, and in so doing, intervene across the normal divide between public and private activities. Individual liberties and the accountability of the executive organs of government to parliament were necessarily suspended in the face of the national emergency and in the name of an efficiently managed national war effort. Here was the 'nation at war', an incomplete working model of a new state system, which would inform the creation of the Fascist so-called 'totalitarian' state from the mid-1920s. The temporary wartime regime of 1915–18, combining repressiveness and popular mobilisation, was, in retrospect, almost a dry run for the Fascist state. Finally, the myth of 'combatantism', of a new national society and a new national élite in the making, gave Mussolini's Fascist movement its ready-made political constituency of war veterans created in and by the war, and validated the use and 'morality' of violence.

3. '1919-ISM' AND EARLY FASCISM

The first *fascio di combattimento* (combat or fighting group) was formed at Milan in March 1919, just before a meeting called to launch the movement. By the summer, *fasci* had been set up in about seventy towns and cities, mainly in the north. There was no real break in continuity either in aims or personnel between the revolutionary interventionism of 1917–18 and the *fasci* of 1919. The movement quite consciously aimed to keep alive and exploit the wartime divisions between those who had wanted and fought the war and those who had not. The Fascist programme was put together by the summer of 1919 and broadly corresponded to the general tenor and content of Mussolini's speeches to the Milan meeting in March. It combined nationalism, patriotism and an anti-PSI stance with a collection of radical, anti-clerical and democratic social and financial policies. These included proposals for a political system democratised by universal suffrage and proportional representation and enhanced by a form of occupational corporate representation; an eight-hour day, minimum wage and social insurance legislation; and a heavy progressive tax on capital and confiscation of excessive war profits. A call for workers' control of industries and public services was tempered by 'productivist' concerns for efficient management.

Argument about whether this programme was tendentious to the left or right perhaps misses the point. The amalgamation of radical and nationalist ideas was determined by the perceived outlook and expect-ations of the constituencies it was meant to attract: left interventionists and ex-servicemen. The workers' demands in the programme addressed 'the workers who were returning from the trenches', a recognition of the 'rights of those who had fought in the war'.[6] Their rights, in other words, were due to them as combatants not as workers. Combatants included anybody and everybody who had been soldiers and could not be defined by the usual class and party loyalties. The Fascist programme attempted to catch the anti-establishment and subversive feel of '1919-ism' and meet the aspirations of an unpredictable new 'class' formed in the war.

The adoption of the term *fascio* and Fascism's definition of itself as an anti-party movement were important in this respect. Denoting a repudi-ation of existing political structures and a discredited ruling class, *fascio* conveyed the idea of a loose grouping of people who, whatever their background, could act together to achieve common objectives. There was a transitoriness to this, because the movement could dissolve once its aims were realised. But being a movement rather than a party, the 'cauldron in which elements from all parties found a place'[7] was designed to encourage recruitment. It was common even after the formal constitution of a party in 1921 for Fascist members to be associated at the same time with other political organisations. Being a kind of pool for men of different backgrounds enabled the anti-party to pose as a national movement superior to and transcending other political and class loyalties – much the same effect which was sought by the claim to represent combatants and producers. As 'the church of all the heresies', the anti-party was permitted complete flexibility in tactics and programme and was not tied to the discipline and previously agreed principles of a party.

The *fasci* were therefore made for action, 'organs of creativity and agitation that will be ready to rush into the piazzas'.[8] Again in Mussolini's own words, the programme of the *fasci di combattimento* was in the name. They were combat organisations which would get things done pragmatically and resolve problems by acting decisively, and would not be inhibited from action by any ideological preconceptions. The war experience was the self-evident reference point for Fascism's activism and no-nonsense military approach, expressed most obviously in the recourse to violence as the way of settling political arguments.

The connection between the pre-war anti-Giolittian 'revolt against reason', interventionism, the war and early Fascism's activist style could be seen most clearly in the high profile in the Milan *fascio* and some other *fasci* of the Futurists and their associates among the ex-servicemen, the *Arditi*. Modern cultural iconoclasts, the Futurists embraced violence and destruction as regenerative forces of change in both art and politics, were among the most vociferous of interventionists, volunteered for military service, and contributed much of the anti-establishment flavour of the 1919 Fascist programme. The *Arditi*, some of them Futurists before the war, and covered in a glamorised aura of violence by their much-publicised wartime exploits, were the least likely of Italy's war veterans to take easily to demobilisation and civilian life.

Arditi became Mussolini's hired bodyguards on the formation of the Milan *fascio*, helped to organise armed units within the *fasci* in summer 1919 in support of Gabriele D'Annunzio's planned coup in Fiume, which many of them actually joined, and were used in the general squadrist militarisation of the Fascist movement from late 1920 to early 1921. Even though the Fascist movement became the Fascist Party in 1921, it retained throughout important characteristics of the anti-party of 1919, above all its activism and ideological relativism. These traits were embodied in squadrism in 1921–22, and its pretensions to be the only really national above-party political force.

Fascism claimed to represent the war generation but managed to attract only certain groups of it. The *Associazione Nazionale dei Combattenti* (National Servicemen's Association), founded in 1919, became the most important war veterans' organisation. It was particularly strong among the peasant conscripts and middle-class, lower-rank officers of the south and the islands, where its regional and local associations for a short period after the war tried to change the area's landholding and political structures in the name of the new men and new spirit formed in the trenches. The ANC shared with Fascism the anti-political and anti-system thrust of '1919-ism'. But certainly, nationally and with some exceptions locally it resisted both Fascist and Nationalist attempts to turn it in ultra-nationalistic and subversive directions. The mixed or separate ex-servicemen's electoral lists of those who stood in the 1919 elections usually had a democratic and reformist slant.

Instead, the Milan *fascio* and the early *fasci* recruited among the self-styled élite of ex-servicemen such as the *Arditi* and the volunteers, and among officers rather than enlisted men. In university and garrison towns and cities like Bologna, Padua and Florence, some young army officers resuming their studies while awaiting demobilisation founded or joined the first *fasci*. Elsewhere, Nationalist or Republican university and secondary students' associations were sometimes the nucleus of the *fasci* in northern provincial capitals, which for much of 1919 and 1920 showed signs of life only during the school and university terms.

Some revolutionary and democratic interventionists gravitated naturally to the *fasci*. The 1919 *fasci* in Venice and Cremona, for instance, practically re-created the local anti-PSI interventionist coalition of reformist ex-Socialists, Radicals and Republicans. The Milan *fascio* itself, which effectively assumed the leadership of the movement as a whole, included ex-socialists like Mussolini and revolutionary syndicalists like Michele Bianchi and Cesare Rossi, whose connections went back to the *fasci di azione rivoluzionaria*.

This rather motley collection of professional political activists and syndicalist organisers drawn from the interventionist and 'nationalised' left, and Futurist intellectuals and *Arditi*, together with some democratic interventionists and a spattering of patriotic students and ex-army officers, made up most of the limited early constituency of Fascism. Mussolini's Fascist-Futurist list which stood in Milan in the November 1919 elections won barely 5000 votes of the 270 000 cast in the constituency. This signified Fascism's failure to unify and represent even left interventionism. It marked the broader political failure of groups specifically formed on the basis of the war experience and the aspirations of the ex-servicemen to exploit the post-war mood for change.

4. THE 1919 ELECTIONS

It was clear from the 1919 election results summarised below that the major beneficiaries of '1919-ism' were the two post-war mass parties: the PSI and the Catholic Popular Party or PPI (*Partito Popolare Italiano*). The great majority of peasant and proletarian combatants had voted for these parties as the radical alternatives to the 'old Italy'.

The regional distribution of votes and parliamentary seats was extremely revealing. The PSI and PPI performed best in the north and the centre of the country. Only 10 of the PSI's 156 seats and 24 of the PPI's 100 seats were won in Italy south of Rome. The electoral strength of the liberal groupings lay precisely and overwhelmingly in the south and the islands. Ex-servicemen's candidates stood in most southern constituencies as a self-declared regenerative force challenging the traditional clientelism and jobbing of southern politics, and 15 of the 20 elected were in southern seats. But veterans' associations were only politically significant in Sardinia, and to a lesser extent in the Abruzzi and the Molise, where they inspired democratic regional autonomy movements.

It was apparently one of the freest votes ever, since the Prime Minister in 1919, Francesco Nitti, had formally declared that there would be none of the usual governmental interference in the electoral process. The PSI and the PPI had made the most of the premium placed on party organisation and a party platform by a list and multi-member constituency

	Elections		
	1913	1919	1921
PSI	52	156	139 (includes 15 PCI)
PPI	(28 Catholic)	100	108
Liberals and allies	400	220	239 (includes 36 Fascists)

form of proportional representation. In the pre-war single-member and simple majority system, personalities without a party organisation could still win the day. This had happened again in the south and the islands in 1919 even under the new electoral system, as clientelism persisted and the two mass parties were weaker and less organised there.

The parliament elected in 1919 was, therefore, a hybrid. Nearly half the Chamber of Deputies was made up of liberal groupings who had no permanent party organisation behind them and no precise and binding commitment to a party programme. The other half were deputies belonging to parties who were tied both to a party platform and an extraparliamentary party executive. The post-war Italian parliament was the meeting ground of modern party politics and the traditional liberal politics of personality, and the clash of two worlds played a part in the paralysis of parliamentary government between 1919 and 1922.

The electoral triumph of the PSI and the PPI in 1919 created a completely new parliamentary context for the resolution of political and social conflicts. Parties with mass constituencies had achieved levels of parliamentary representation proportional to their actual strength in the country. This destroyed the possibility of automatic liberal parliamentary majorities. As Charles Maier says, the 1919 elections marked the end of liberal parliamentary hegemony.[9] The 1919 election results and those of 1921, which showed a basically similar configuration of political forces, made coalition government essential. But it was difficult to achieve stable parliamentary majorities for governments in the period 1919–22.

To a great extent, this was due to the attitude of the largest single group in parliament, the PSI. Consistent with its revolutionary maximalist position, the PSI refused to participate positively in the workings of the parliamentary institutions of the bourgeois state which it was committed to overthrow, and would not collaborate in parliament or outside with bourgeois parties. Its role in parliament was a spoiling one. It would vote against governments because governmental instability hastened the bankruptcy of state institutions. But it would never be available itself as a partner or supporter of coalition governments. The Socialist parliamentary group contained a high proportion of reformists, probably about sixty deputies. But although the reformist Socialists disagreed with the party's maximalist stance, they were not prepared to break ranks out of a sense of party patriotism and unity. Only in August 1922 did the parliamentary reformist Socialists indicate their willingness to enter or support a coalition government, in circumstances that, as we shall see, made their gesture both futile and counter-productive.

The liberals were never a unified parliamentary bloc before or after the war. The decline in their position at least in northern and central Italy reflected an inadequate electoral and party organisation for mass democratic politics, and political divisions opened up by the war, with neutralist liberals competing against interventionist liberals in many constituencies. Giolitti's alienation from right liberals over the war made agreement among liberals in parliament problematic, at least in 1919–20. By the time of the May 1921 elections, many of these war-derived divisions among liberals had been superseded by the need for unity against socialism, and ex-interventionist and ex-neutralist liberals stood together in Giolitti's governmental electoral lists. Nevertheless even the establishment of the Liberal Party in October 1922 could not disguise the previous and continuing fragmentation of the liberal deputies in unstable parliamentary groupings based on personalities and regional affinity. Significantly, the main groupings of southern liberal deputies did not even join the Liberal Party.

The amorphousness of liberal parliamentary politics assumed real significance once it was clear after the 1919 elections that liberals could not govern alone and the PSI would not govern with any other party. Stable parliamentary majorities were possible only if liberals and the PPI could reach some workable and lasting accommodation. Such a situation gave the youngest and most inexperienced political movement, the PPI, the pivotal role in post-war parliamentary politics.

The foundation of the PPI in January 1919 marked the full integration of Catholics into the political life of the country. The Pope's revocation of the *non expedit* in 1918 decoupled Catholic participation in national politics from the issue of the loss of the papacy's temporal possessions in 1870 and from the exclusive identification of Catholics with the defence of the Church's interests. The PPI was to be independent of the Vatican and of the church's network of Catholic laypeople's organisations, Catholic Action: a 'party of Catholics', but not a 'Catholic party'. Unlike the PSI, the PPI was a legalist and constitutionalist party, though committed to political reform. Proportional representation had been one of the first demands of the PPI not only because it would secure the party more seats in parliament. In the conception of Luigi Sturzo, the Christian Democrat Sicilian priest who led the party, proportional representation would help to clean up and modernise Italian politics by encouraging the formation of parties and open competition between them on the basis of programmes. In this way also parliament could become the focal point of Italian political life, since under a reformed electoral system it would be truly representative of the popular will.

The PPI's progressive and reforming programme had a distinctively Catholic emphasis on decentralisation, freedom of association, small peasant proprietorship, class collaboration and corporate representation, and the vitality of those 'natural' institutions like the family linking the individual to society and the state. The party was formally a confessional, but it was clearly inspired by Catholic principles: it was a Catholic democratic alternative to both liberalism and socialism. Sturzo's desire for the PPI to be independent of the church was genuine enough, though his own position was difficult, since he was a priest subject to ecclesiastical discipline. The party programme also included, if it did not highlight, a commitment to the freedom and independence of the church, or in other words the defence of the church's interests. Again, the church's parochial structure, although naturally enough not coinciding with constituency boundaries, was a ready-made way of bringing in the Catholic vote. Many parish priests in the north and the centre were active supporters of the party and anyway involved in the web of Catholic social and economic organisations which covered the Catholic peasant heartland of Venetia and Lombardy. So, the PPI was not identified with the church, at least in its own eyes if not those of its political opponents. But it definitely had relations with the church and could not fail to be affected by the attitudes and priorities of the ecclesiastical hierarchy and the Vatican.

Despite aconfessionality, it was mainly a common religious affiliation which encouraged Catholics to vote for the PPI. Its appeal to Catholics across class differences, apparently one of the sources of its electoral strength, was at the same time its point of vulnerability. The party was, in fact, itself a coalition of wide-ranging and often incompatible interests with different conceptions of the party's role. At one extreme was a combative union organisation whose spokesmen, the PPI deputy and labour organiser, Guido Miglioli, saw the party as a class party representing the 'Christian proletariat'. At the other extreme were conservative Catholics, behind whom were important banking, industrial and landowning interests, who took a 'clerico-moderate' view of the party. They were open to right-wing political alliances and concerned that the party should be unashamedly Catholic and confessional in its identification with and defence of the church.

As a cross-class party, the PPI would be particularly subject to centrifugal pressures at times of serious social and political conflict, which in fact existed for most of the period between 1919 and 1922. There were strong pressures from within the party and from the Vatican for the revival of 'clerico-moderate' electoral alliances against socialism, which Sturzo resisted to preserve the PPI's independence, but was unable to prevent in all cases. Equally, the PPI left was urging co-operation with even the PSI against Fascism in 1921 and 1922. But symptomatically, tentative discussions between the PPI leadership and the reformist Socialists were inconclusive, once the 'clerico-moderates' in the party declared their opposition to any such PPI–PSI understanding. Inactivity and procrastination bought party unity, but reconciling the PPI factions clearly inhibited the party's ability to be politically decisive and affected its availability for coalitions. Government crises were often confused and prolonged by the PPI struggling to come to terms with its own internal tensions. This was especially so in 1922, when the sheer exasperating inconclusiveness of the attempts to form governments undermined parliament's credibility and helped to ease the way for Fascism's entry into government.

The PPI was generally unwilling to take the responsibility for forming and leading coalition governments, because it was an inexperienced party and did not feel that its weight in parliament justified such action. However, the party's internal volatility meant that it could only with difficulty perform the pivotal stabilising role in parliament indicated by its commitment to parliamentary democracy and its electoral performance. Coalitions between the PPI and liberals were inherently fragile, contributing to the paralysis and inactivity of government. Behind this instability lay policy differences which intertwined with different approaches to parliamentary government, a measure of the sudden impact of political democracy and of the liberals' reluctance to adapt to the change.

Nitti, Prime Minister of three successive governments between June 1919 and June 1920, refused to adopt agrarian reform as a condition of PPI parliamentary support. His successor, Giolitti, Prime Minister between June 1920 and July 1921, whose government included PPI ministers, similarly reneged on promises of female suffrage, proportional representation in local elections and state recognition of Catholic schools, which were meant to guarantee PPI backing. Besides the anti-clericalism of many liberals, these land and democratic reforms were difficult to accept, because they might damage liberals' electoral and political position, particularly in the south, even more the repository of liberal strength after the 1919 elections.

Binding programmatic commitments were also anathema to the usual liberal practice of the prime minister-designate cobbling together a coalition based on a loose alliance of parliamentary groupings, whose interests lay not so much in determining government policy as in gaining access to office and the patronage accompanying it. In contrast, the PPI insisted on prior agreement between prospective coalition partners for governments with a clear legislative programme, whose composition would be related to the parliamentary representation of each partner and whose continuation would depend on the enactment of the agreed policies. This formal and rather inflexible stance directly related governments and their policies to the balance of parties in a popularly elected parliament.

By bitter experience, the PPI could not help concluding that to enter a government was to abandon its programme. This certainly influenced the PPI's opposition to the mooted return to power of Giolitti in 1922 and thereby prolonged the government crises of that year. The PPI and the liberals never achieved a lasting accommodation because of this mismatch between modern party politics and *trasformismo*. In this way, post-war parliamentary politics reflected all too accurately the fundamental political, social and economic divide between the north and the south of the country. The liberals had been defeated by the two mass parties in 1919. But because of the PSI's indifference and hostility to parliament, and the PPI's inability and reluctance to find a parliamentary role, they still had to govern.

5. THE *BIENNIO ROSSO* AND FIUME

The 1919 elections, then, destroyed the axiomatic liberal control of parliament and dramatically ended the isolation of parliament from the nation, though not necessarily in a way that strengthened parliamentary institutions or facilitated stable parliamentary government. Italy anyway faced a post-war crisis of such dimensions in the so-called *biennio rosso* or 'Red Two Years' of 1919–20 that it would have tested the resilience of any political system.

The *biennio rosso* was a period of intense, widespread and almost continuous political, social and economic unrest in both town and countryside from spring 1919 until late 1920, peaking during the spring to the autumn of 1920. It was only from the autumn of 1920 that Fascism began to emerge as a mass movement, and the significance of this juncture can scarcely be overestimated.

The unrest of 1919–20 overlapped with and to an extent was caused by a post-war economic crisis, the effects of which were felt well into 1922. This crisis sprang from the economic strains imposed on a relatively poor country by the waging of a prolonged and expensive war which Italy quite literally could not afford to fight. As a result, the war was financed in ways which both mortgaged the country's economic future, postponing to the end of the war painful decisions about how its costs were to be met, and transferred national wealth unfairly. Government indebtedness increased to staggering proportions, both towards its own citizens who had loaned money to the government through wartime Treasury bonds, and towards the richer Allies, particularly the United States, who had supplied on credit the food, fuel and raw materials on which the country's economy relied also into the post-war period.

A production-at-any-cost mentality fuelled largely uncontrolled and ever-increasing expenditure of public funds on wartime economic mobilisation. The government paid for it by printing money, a characteristic device for financing growth without the means to do so. The inevitable outcome of expanding wartime demand and an increase in note circulation was an inflationary spiral which sustained a mainly artificial and speculative industrial boom. This favoured the rise of a few giant combines such as Fiat, Ansaldo and Ilva to the positions of prominence in the war economy. The war manufacturers' quick and high profits were speedily reinvested not only in new plants but also in buying shares in other companies, as they created unwieldy horizontal and vertical industrial empires covering mining, shipping and transportation, electricity generation, engineering and heavy industries.

The inflationary spiral continued through 1919 until mid to late 1920, fed by rising prices for post-war food and raw material imports and the declining value of the Italian currency abroad, as Allied war credits and support for the lira ended. Wartime and post-war inflation had mixed social effects. It certainly hit urban and rural property owners who lived from rent, especially when rental and leasing contracts were frozen for the duration of the war, and those with savings or fixed incomes, and all consumers. However, for those who owed money or wanted to borrow money – and this included the government of course – inflation constantly reduced the value of the debt. People who had given their savings as well as their sons to support the war effort undoubtedly resented the impact of inflation. It gave a cutting edge to the widespread sense of middle-class grievance against those who had apparently exploited their patriotic sacrifice, the 'sharks' and the 'shirkers'. These were the war profiteers and the industrial workers, perceived to be the beneficiaries of an economy of high prices and correspondingly high wages. This is perhaps the point to keep in mind when looking at the effect of post-war inflation on the discontent behind the 'Red Two Years'. A particularly sharp rise in food prices precipitated the strikes and popular demonstrations of July 1919. But generally, union agitation in 1919 and at least in the first half of 1920 for better pay, improved work conditions and fringe benefits was contained within the inflationary cycle, their costs passed on by the employers in higher prices.

Much of the agitation of 1919–20 was of such a conventionally reformist and defensive character, to put up hedges against inflation. But this was not necessarily how it was perceived by either side, because of the feverish climate of '1919-ism', of great expectation of change generated by the war and European revolution. Economic disputes were often given a political and revolutionary aura, certainly by the Anarchists and Anarcho-syndicalists, where they were influential in the labour movement in Liguria, Tuscany and the Marche, and also by the PSI, if only as a competitive reflex. Some of the major incidents of the *biennio rosso* had a definite though passing insurrectionary feel, such as the food riots of July 1919, the general strike in Turin and Piedmont in April 1920, and the June 1920 army mutiny in Ancona against transfer to Albania, which was supported by a general working-class mobilisation in the region reminiscent of 'Red Week' in 1914. Expectations were being raised beyond the demand for higher wages or the eight-hour day or social insurance schemes, all working-class gains of 1919–20, to the transformation of society. The aims and conduct as well as the revolutionary rhetoric of some of the agitation bore this out.

The unrest of the *biennio rosso* took different forms in the rural south and the islands than it did in the industrial towns and cities and the countryside of northern and central Italy. In the south, it had a traditional shape: occupations of the *latifundia*. Spreading initially from Lazio in the spring to the autumn of 1919, coinciding with the demobilisation of Italy's peasant army, land occupations resumed in spring 1920 and were particularly intense in the autumn of 1920, affecting parts of Sardinia, Sicily, Calabria, Campania and Apulia.

The Socialists, who were weak or non-existent in most of the south, did not usually lead or organise the occupations, except in Lazio and

Apulia. Instead, the occupations were sometimes led by Catholic peasant leagues and more often by men belonging to the local ex-servicemen's associations. They were recently demobilised peasants taking action themselves to realise the wartime promises of land. The occupations of 1919–20 were rolled back or contained effectively enough by the combined repressive and mediating actions of the police and prefects. Their action was facilitated by the readiness to negotiate and compromise of the improvised veterans' co-operatives. This stance reflected the PPI's inter-class approach and composition, and the continuing hold of the old clientelistic relationship between landlord and peasant. In general, land occupations in the south resulted in peasant co-operatives accepting rental and lease agreements rather than confiscation, division and ownership, and ironically contributed to the absorption of ex-servicemen's associations into the clientelistic fabric of local southern politics.

In the agricultural areas of the north and the centre, and exceptionally in the southern region of Apulia, Socialist, and sometimes also Catholic, labour and peasant organisations led often extended and bitter campaigns against landowners and employers for better wages and tenancy agreements. The Catholic peasant leagues affiliated to the 'white' union federation, the CIL (*Confederazione Italiana del Lavoro*), founded in 1919, had 1.25 million members in 1920, recruiting mainly among waged workers on contract, sharecroppers, and small proprietors and tenant farmers of Liguria, Lombardy and Venetia. Even more dramatically, the socialist agricultural union federation, *Federterra*, had nearly doubled its pre-war membership to almost half a million by the autumn of 1919 and had 900 000 members in 1920. It not only expanded in its traditional areas of strength among the *braccianti* or landless labourers of Emilia and Apulia, but also attracted previously unorganised and quiescent rural groups, such as the *mezzadri* or sharecroppers in Tuscany and Umbria.

It is important to realise that the immediate post-war agrarian disputes were most intense in the areas of commercialised or capitalist farming in Apulia, the Po basin provinces of Lombardy, Venetia and Emilia, and central Tuscany. With the exception of Tuscany, the struggles of the *biennio rosso* were a culmination of nearly two decades of class conflict engaging entrepreneurial farmers, landowners and organised labour.

In Tuscany, the post-war outbreak of peasant discontent shocked landowners by its novelty and scale. The idealised cosy and co-operative relationship between landowner and *mezzadro*, harmoniously sharing both the costs and proceeds of the farm's production, had steadily disintegrated since the late nineteenth century. Landowners produced for the market and in the effort to maximise profits, strained the sharecropping system to its social and economic limits, by throwing more of the expenses of production onto their peasant tenants and by squeezing their share of the produce. The wartime and post-war promises of land and social justice completed the radicalisation of the sharecroppers: a massive agricultural strike ending in July 1920 and involving half a million of the 710 000 peasants in the region won a new *mezzadria* contract. This agreement gave an above half share of the proceeds to the tenant, and transferred a higher proportion of production costs onto the landlord, who felt that this destroyed the very viability of the commercialised sharecropping system. Worse still for the landowner was that tenants' security of tenure and a voice in farm management could be construed as an erosion of his rights of ownership.

This was the real point at issue in the prolonged and vicious labour disputes in the Po Valley provinces and Apulia, which again concluded in victories for the peasant leagues in the summer and the autumn of 1920. Drainage and land reclamation schemes, and high investment in the Po Valley from the 1880s had helped to create a productive capitalistic agriculture. This was, typically, medium-sized livestock and dairy leaseholding farms in Cremona and Mantua, and large estates leased or owned by commercial farmers, who employed an army of landless proletarians for the harvesting of wheat and increasingly important industrial crops such as hemp, tomatoes and sugar beet, in Ferrara, Bologna, Rovigo, Padua and parts of Brescia. The farming system of Bari and Foggia in Apulia was different in that it was monocultural and unmodernised, based on the extensive cultivation of wheat for market, which made even higher wages a direct threat to relatively low profitability. But otherwise, the working of the estates by landless agricultural labourers enrolled in combative socialist leagues, the only labour organisations of any substance in the south, gave the same pattern and tempo to class conflict here as in the Po Valley.

Employers in these commercialised farming zones were reluctantly prepared to concede higher wages and a shorter working day, at least as long as the inflationary spiral continued. But what they bitterly resisted and resented was *Federterra's* demand to control the supply of labour and employment, and the Catholic leagues' call for peasant co-management of farms and even the right to buy out farmers. They saw these claims as an unacceptable challenge to property and management rights.

Control of labour was the key in the *braccianti* zones of the Po Valley, because there were always too many labourers chasing too little work.

Rural overpopulation had created structural underemployment. A surplus of labour allowed employers to drive down wage levels and restrict workers to alternating periods of activity during sowing and harvest, and enforced idleness particularly during the winter months. The *braccianti* contracts, including the important Paglia–Caldo agreement concluded in Bologna in October 1920, invariably obliged employers to recognise the employment offices run by *Federterra* as the exclusive source of the supply of labour and imposed year-round employment quotas on all farmers, large and small, the number of workers usually being related to farm size. The labour quotas not only guaranteed the allocation of work for the union's members. They were *Federterra's* wedge into farm management, because the farmer's loss of control over the number of men he might want to employ and the duration of their employment affected other decisions about the amount of land to cultivate, the use of machinery, even the type of crop.

Federterra tried to organise a single peasant union, including sharecroppers and small tenant farmers as well as *braccianti*, and gained a much improved *mezzadria* contract also in 1920. But the interests of the agricultural proletariat remained the most important in the leagues. These were expressed not only in *Federterra's* aim to 'socialise' land and have it worked on collective tenancies by co-operatives of agricultural labourers, but also in the shape of the unitary union organisation itself. An absolute labour monopoly was so crucial yet so precarious in the overpopulated countryside, that it could only be maintained by the discipline and control of the whole agricultural sector, including small peasants who had to be prevented from exchanging labour and thereby avoiding the quota. The system had to be watertight to function at all. This accounted for the coercive aspects of the leagues' attempt to secure and retain the labour monopoly through fining, boycotting, and sabotaging the crops, livestock and property of those farmers employing non-union labour and those 'blackleg' workers who agreed to work for them.

The agricultural employers' economic defeats coincided and dovetailed with damaging setbacks in the autumn 1920 local elections, after which the PSI ran nearly one-third of all communal and almost a half of all provincial councils in Italy. Anti-Socialist coalitions won most of the major cities. But the real political damage was done in the provincial capitals and small towns of northern and central Italy, where the Socialist rural vote swept away the liberal and centrist politicians who usually represented landholding interests. In Siena province, 30 of 36 local councils went Socialist, as did 149 of 290 communes in Tuscany as a whole. In Emilia, the cradle of rural socialism, the PSI won control of a staggering 223 of 280 municipal councils, and in the province of Bologna alone, 54 out of 61.

The PSI had campaigned on a revolutionary platform, saying that they intended to take over the local sources of power of the bourgeois state and convert them into instruments of proletarian control, to enact a series of parochial revolutions. The Socialist town hall projected itself as a class administration waging the class war. The economic power of *Federterra* was now buttressed and complemented by the PSI's political control of the local seats of government. Socialist councils used their powers to raise taxes on wealth and property, increased spending on public services and works, favoured workers' co-operatives in municipal contracts and subsidised consumer co-operatives to undercut the private retail and distribution trades. A whole swathe of middle-class interests in town and country, from farmers to manufacturers, builders, landlords, professional men, shopkeepers and tradesmen, felt under attack from these municipal 'dictatorships of the proletariat'. 'There are occasions when I don't know whether I'm in Russia or in Italy',[10] complained a large commercial farmer to his Bolognese agrarian association in the spring of 1920. In retrospect, such fears seemed exaggerated, and many historians have challenged the 'myth' that Fascism 'saved Italy from Bolshevism'. But in late 1920, after the propertied classes had suffered disastrous economic and political defeats in north and central Italy, this was exactly the perception of recent events. At a local and provincial level the Socialist revolution was being inaugurated; it was already under way.

In the industrial centres, what alarmed employers most was the way working-class agitation sometimes went beyond wage demands to pose a challenge to ownership and managerial authority on the shop floor. By far the most significant and revolutionary development was the factory council movement in the mechanical and automobile plants of Turin. Building on the experience of wartime elective factory grievance commit-tees, the factory councils were elevated as the Italian equivalent of the soviets by the group of young Socialist (later Communist) intellectuals and labour organisers whose mouthpiece was Gramsci's review *L'Ordine Nuovo* (*New Order*). The councils were organs of factory demo-cracy which wanted far more than a say in plant management. Sharing the revolutionary syndicalist belief that through organising themselves workers acquired discipline, expertise and responsibility, the councils were seen both as executives of revolution and embryos of the post-revolutionary proletarian management of modern industry.

It was no wonder that industrialists resisted so intransigently the recognition of these factory councils, which was the real issue behind the general strike in Piedmont in April 1920. The council movement explicitly rejected both the reformism of the union federation, the CGL, and of the metallurgical workers' union, the FIOM, and the phony revolutionary position of the PSI maximalists, who in Gramsci's view were failing to exploit the 'revolutionary situation' of the *biennio rosso*. The councils operated at plant level, representing both union and non-unionised workers, and challenged the writ of the FIOM as much as the employers. This probably explained why the CGL and PSI leadership isolated the movement by refusing to extend the regional strike into a national one.

While workers' discontent touched the foundations of property and management, the government's attitude to it sharpened employers' perception of a crisis *of* capitalism. Nitti had come to government in June 1919 with the intention of effecting the transition from war to peace as rapidly as possible and governing through a liberal reformism in the pre-war Giolittian mould. Bringing the war to a definite end linked both domestic and foreign policies. The speedy conclusion of a peace settlement would help to secure continuing economic aid from the other ex-Allied powers, without which Nitti thought Italy could not survive economically, let alone recover. It would also justify and make possible the quick demobilisation of the troops and of the war economy, relieving the state of some of the enormous costs incurred in fighting the war.

Nitti inherited a disastrous international situation from the previous liberal government led by Vittorio Emanuele Orlando and Salandra. At the Versailles Peace Conference they had isolated Italy by adopting a policy that was both contradictory and self-defeating. Effectively taking up the Nationalist position on war aims, they demanded the fulfilment of the terms of the Treaty of London and in addition the annexation to Italy of the Adriatic industrial port of Fiume, which had a mixed Italian and Croat population and was occupied by Italian troops at the end of the war. By dubiously invoking the principle of national self-determination for Fiume and simultaneously denying it in the name of national power and expansion in the case of the Treaty of London, Italy alienated its wartime Allies. France and Britain had signed the Treaty of London but were not bound by the Italian claim to Fiume. The United States wanted free city status for Fiume. It had not been party to a secret treaty which bargained away other people's territory and was just the kind of deal running counter to President Woodrow Wilson's projected new order based on open diplomacy, the recognition of nationality and internationalism.

The Italian delegation withdrew in protest from Versailles in April 1919 to a wave of patriotic feeling deliberately whipped up by the government, and as promptly squandered by its ignominious return to the Conference and continued failure to secure Fiume. This was a policy which created the sensation that Italy was losing the peace. Patriotic sentiment was transformed into nationalistic grievance at a victory in war now being 'mutilated' by Italy's Allies and by the government's inability to protect Italy's national interests.

Nitti was in an impossible position. But in his anxiety to settle the Fiume question in a fashion that restored good relations with the United States, he took little account of national feeling and the way it could now be directed against the government. His decision to evacuate the city and hand it over to inter-Allied military command precipitated the coup already being organised by the Nationalists. Led by D'Annunzio, the hypernationalist soldier-poet, a band of war veterans and mutinous soldiers occupied Fiume in September 1919, with the clear connivance of the army stationed in the border zones, to prevent the city passing out of Italian military control and to bring down Nitti's government.

It is arguable whether the occupation was the 'decisive step' in the 'crisis of the liberal state'.[11] Nitti did not fall and the coup did not spread beyond the border area, although Nitti's lack of action against it certainly showed that some sections of the armed forces were seditious and could not be trusted to uphold state authority. Embarrassingly for over a year D'Annunzio behaved as if Fiume was the model and inspiration and point of departure for the overthrow of the Italian state. But in retrospect, the Fiume spectacle probably had more importance for the development of Fascism than as a real threat to the integrity of parliamentary government.

For a time Fiume absorbed the energies of Mussolini and the Milanese leadership in fund-raising and support, and emptied some provincial *fasci*, particularly in the north-east, as student and ex-officer members commuted to join in the great adventure. The Charter of Carnaro, the corporative constitution concocted for the city by D'Annunzio and his revolutionary syndicalist advisors, exercised a strong influence on many Fascists seeking an alternative blueprint to the liberal parliamentary order. For the Venetian Fascist leader, Pietro Marsich, D'Annunzionism was Fascism in action, both in its commitment to a violent coup against the parliamentary system and in its concrete implementation of a post-liberal corporative state. D'Annunzio's acclamatory and military style of personal government enacted in public spectacle and ritual anticipated some aspects of the charismatic rapport between leader and masses idealised later in Mussolini's regime. More immediately, even though Mussolini's eventual ditching of D'Annunzio ruptured relations with the *Arditi* Association, many ex-*Arditi* stayed in or joined the *fasci* and carried over into the Fascist squadrist campaigns of 1920–22 the violence, activist style and *braggadocio* they had displayed in the showcase of Fiume.

In a tacit political understanding with Giolitti, Nitti's successor as Prime Minister, Mussolini accepted or did not oppose the Italian–Yugoslav Treaty of Rapallo of November 1920 making Fiume a free city and the government's forcible ejection of D'Annunzio and his followers from Fiume a month or so later. Giolitti's combined diplomatic and armed resolution of the Fiume question by late 1920 effectively liquidated war and post-war foreign policy issues as a source of internal political conflict and division. The PSI's opposition to the war and its post-war condemnation of the futility and irrelevance of Italy's national claims gave a patriotic edge to anti-socialism. But it was above all the domestic impact of the *biennio rosso* which was the crucial test of Italy's political system. Fascism was from the start nationalistic and imperialistic and stood for the revision of the peace settlement, a stance confirmed at the second Fascist congress of May 1920. But Mussolini's abandonment of D'Annunzio, which outraged many Fascists, neutralised a political rival operating on much the same ground, and at the same time recognised that Fascism's opening to national politics lay in exploiting the internal social conflicts of the *biennio rosso*.

That opportunity came because parliament reflected in its composition the divisions in the country and the mood for change, but was unable to channel and meet post-war agitation, whose resolution was as a result extra- and anti-parliamentary. The non-cooperation of the Socialists and the volatility of the liberal-PPI parliamentary accords meant that it was difficult for both the Nitti and Giolitti governments to sustain reform programmes, which in any case did not synchronise with popular expectations of radical change.

Nitti's sober and low-key injunction to 'produce more and consume less' might well have been the appropriate economic medicine for a poor country trying to recover from an expensive war. But it was singularly out of line with '1919-ism'. Nitti's reforms never kept pace with the dynamic escalation of the disturbances of 1919–20. The Visocchi decree of late 1919 allowed the temporary occupation of uncultivated land, a provisional and expedient measure to contain the effects of land invasions already taking place. But while certainly alarming landowners, it hardly assuaged the land hunger behind the southern agitation and in fact encouraged new waves of occupations. Social welfare and eight-hour day legislation, and state-subsidised bread prices scarcely matched the scope of urban and agrarian working-class agitation which was questioning managerial and property rights on both farm and factory. State neutrality in labour disputes, whether a manifestation of the government's reformist tendencies or a rationalisation of the inadequacy of police resources in face of the scale of working-class agitation, led employers to believe that the government by its inaction was contributing to their defeats.

The perceived inability or unwillingness of government to defend property against revolutionary expropriation marked Giolitti's handling of the climactic events of the *biennio rosso*, the occupation of the factories in September 1920. It was initially a defensive measure in a dispute between the metalworkers' union, the FIOM, and industrialists over a new labour contract, designed to pre-empt a general employers' lockout. The occupations involved over half a million workers, mainly but not exclusively in the industrial triangle of Milan, Genoa and Turin, and were soon contesting rather more than better pay and conditions. Barricading themselves inside the occupied factories, workers led by factory councils attempted to manage the plants and continue production. Giolitti responded to what appeared to be a violation of property and managerial rights by re-enacting his pre-war reformist policies and approach. He refused employers' demands to evict the workers by force and followed up this initial neutrality with a government-mediated agreement between the FIOM, CGL and *Confindustria*, the national industrial employers' organisation. The agreement led to the workers' evacuation of the factories after nearly a month's occupation.

The problem was that it was 1920 not 1904 when Giolitti had used similar tactics in the first national general strike. For both sides of the original dispute, the occupation of the factories appeared to be a 'revolutionary' occasion. Employers had seen their factories taken over and operated by workers. The government had not only done nothing to reverse this usurpation of ownership and management. It had mediated an agreement to end the occupations which apparently recognised and would eventually legalise workers' control of production, even though the reformist FIOM and CGL saw such control as a union say in management rather than as a challenge to ownership, and the promised labour legislation was never passed through parliament. The government was perceived to be abetting and not resisting 'revolution'. The outcome of the occupations similarly disillusioned and demoralised the workers. For this reason they should be seen as the end point of the agitation of the *biennio rosso* and the summation of its failure.

The PSI had talked revolution both nationally and locally. Particularly in the provinces and communes of north and central Italy, it had even acted symbolically and substantially to suggest that a socialist revolution was not only imminent but actual. It draped the red flag from the town hall and used its local government powers to 'expropriate' the propertied classes through high taxation and support of consumer and producer co-operatives. But the PSI leadership had no national strategy to achieve revolution and convert the party's local centres of power into the political control of the country as a whole, either by organising a coup or working through parliament, where it was still the largest single party after the 1921 elections.

In part, the party thought that it did not need a strategy to gain power and that it could deterministically wait on revolution while bourgeois society broke up from within under the impact of the post-war crisis. In part, also, the PSI lacked a strategy because the combination of revolutionary rhetoric and revolutionary inaction precariously bridged and disguised the very real tensions in the socialist movement. There was an unresolved conflict over aims and approach between the revolutionaries or 'maximalists' who were strong in the party executive and among party members, and the reformists who were strong in the PSI parliamentary group, the major unions and the CGL, and generally in the party-affiliated network of economic and social organisations. There was a sense in which the party leadership felt that it could not push for too drastic action without the backing of the mass of workers, who were organised and led by unions that were more interested in reform than revolution. The relationship was rather clumsily formalised in an agreement that the PSI would take the lead in agitation having a political direction or resonance and that the unions would handle conflicts of an economic character.

In practice this was another recipe for doing nothing. Some of the disturbances of the *biennio rosso* were both economic and political, or were economic disputes which developed a political, even 'revolutionary' significance. The factory occupations were a case in point, since at first they represented the escalation of an industrial dispute and then raised fundamental issues of ownership and control of production which were to be resolved by government and parliament. In a mutual waiving of responsibility, the PSI leaders effectively let themselves be guided during the crisis by the union leaders who classed it as an economic dispute and precluded its extension under party direction, which would have given the occupations a definite insurrectionary edge. But even as a reform which stopped short of expropriating employers, a workers' control bill needed a PSI commitment to parliament and some kind of political relationship with government. This, of course, was exactly why Giolitti had proposed such an outcome as part of a typical 'transformistic' operation to the left. The self-fulfilling cycle of impotence was complete: a maximalist PSI would accept no favours from the bourgeois state it wanted to destroy and would certainly not work to achieve reforms through parliament. The PSI's behaviour during the occupations, as during the *biennio rosso*, exactly matched Mussolini's own acute prediction of the party's dilemma that it was incapable of carrying out reform or revolution.

Irrespective of whether a socialist revolution was a realistic proposition or not during the *biennio rosso*, the effects of the PSI achieving neither reform nor revolution were immense. The party's unwillingness or inability to translate talk of revolution into action disheartened workers who had lived through a repeating cycle of having their expectations of change raised and then disappointed; even the occupations of the factories had not led to revolution. Labour militancy ebbed after the end of the occupations, a decline in combativeness accelerated by the impact of the short but sharp deflationary economic recession which reached Italy in late 1920 and early 1921, and lasted throughout 1921. This was basically a crisis of overproduction. It was brought about by greater European and US competition, and falling internal demand arising from the demobilisation of the war economy, as government cut back on orders and credits to industry and in Giolitti's case, introduced taxes on excessive wartime profits and higher personal and corporate taxation. Prices and production fell as a consequence and employers met the costs of recession and Giolitti's fiscal policies by laying off workers and reducing wages.

Though labour agitation fell away from late 1920, it did not shake the perception among both agricultural and industrial employers of a crisis of capitalism being reached at the same juncture. Converging in the autumn of 1920 were actual or imminent cuts in profitability threatened by government tax demands and the recently conceded high-wage labour contracts which no employer would want to respect as the recession started to bite; industrial and agricultural labour settlements won by mass union action, which as in the Bologna Paglia–Caldo pact and the factory occupations appeared to be direct attacks on property rights in the name of workers' control and at the same time were spectacular demonstrations of the state's inability to protect property and order; and sweeping gains by Socialists in local government elections across the provincial capitals and agricultural towns if not the large cities of north and central Italy, which installed a string of self-styled municipal revolutionary 'republics'.

The negative achievement of the political and socio-economic gains of workers during the *biennio rosso* was to create a traumatic fear of 'Bolshevism' among groups which had most to lose in a socialist revolution. As Errico Malatesta, the Italian Anarchist, put it, 'if we do not go on to the end we shall pay with bloody tears for the fears we are now causing the bourgeoisie'.[12] Socialism provided the platform for the counter-reaction of Fascism. It created the fears on which Fascism grew, and almost literally set the stage for Fascism.

6. THE FASCIST REACTION

There were signs well before the autumn of 1920 that the Fascist movement would find its vocation as an anti-socialist reaction. The movement's national congress in May 1920 confirmed an opportunistic drift to the right, now that the PSI was clearly the major political beneficiary of '1919-ism'. The new programme accentuated the inter-class appeal of corporate representation and of 'productivism'. The anticlerical and republican thrust of 1919 Fascism was sufficiently diluted by the leadership to cause the departure of many of the Futurists and Republicans who had founded and joined the first *fasci*.

Also, in the spring and the summer of 1920, the movement experienced its first real local, political and organisational success in the border region of Venezia Giulia and more particularly in the port of Trieste. Here the *fascio* was organising the city's Italian population against the 'Bolshevised' Slavs. Such a potent mix of nationalism and anti-socialism was never repeated elsewhere, but the Trieste experience anticipated much of what was to happen more generally from late 1920. Aided by the Italian military garrison occupying Trieste under the terms of the Armistice, the *fascio* had set up armed and mobile paramilitary squads which attacked the premises of Slav organisations in the city.

It was clear that from at least the summer of 1920 the Fascist leadership wanted to generalise the formation of militarised units in the *fasci* and instructed their leaders to make this an organisational priority. Significantly in terms of timing and function, the first meaningful contact and collaboration between many *fasci* and the local political and socioeconomic establishment coincided with the municipal elections of October–November 1920. Clearly anticipating services to be performed in the forthcoming elections, Leandro Arpinati reformed the Bologna city *fascio* in September on the basis of an approach for an anti-Bolshevik force of 300 men from the Association of Social Defence. This was a lobby of local industrialists, tradesmen and farmers, formed in April to protect property and order during the strikes and popular agitation of the *biennio rosso*. Similar arrangements were simultaneously being made in, for instance, Venice, Leghorn and Brescia, often accompanied by the reconstitution or indeed formation of *fasci*. Such was the case in Ferrara, where after several false starts the *fascio* was founded formally only in October 1920. Fascist activity in these local elections helped to make them credible as the virile activist vanguard of a broad middle-class front against socialism.

Again important in timing and purpose, the incidents which sparked off a more general anti-socialist reaction occurred as an immediate result of the Socialist victory in the elections. In a quite deliberate and premeditated repudiation of the election result, the Bologna *fascio* provoked violent incidents disrupting the official inauguration of the Socialist mayor and city council on 21 November 1920. As the Fascists hoped, the disorder eventually justified the suspension of the council and the nomination of a prefectural commissioner to administer the city. Similar incidents took place in neighbouring Ferrara in December and in both provinces made the *fascio* the focus of middle-class hostility to the socialist political and economic control of the town and its rural hinterland.

Fascism, then, emerged as a mass movement from the autumn of 1920 when it began to benefit from the class and patriotic reaction to socialism. The movement expanded above all in the towns and countryside of north and central Italy, especially in Tuscany, rural Piedmont and the Po Valley provinces of Emilia, Lombardy and Venetia, where the post-war social and political conflicts had been most bitter and intense, and socialism appeared to be at its strongest. In much of the south and the islands, Fascism was almost completely absent or insignificant before late 1922, except for Apulia, a part of eastern Sicily and some of the major cities like Naples and Bari, confirming the symbiosis between

Fascism and socialism. Although the central committee had encouraged the militarisation of the *fasci* and thereby helped to equip Fascism for its anti-socialist role, the expansion of the movement from late 1920 occurred largely independently of the leadership in Milan. Fascism's growth was not the fruit of Mussolini's charismatic and dynamic leadership. It was financed, led and controlled locally, and the movement became an aggregate of provincial Fascisms shaped by their local settings. The provincialism and diversity of Fascism was important, but the movement developed with a broadly similar pattern and momentum, though at a varying tempo.

The crucible of Fascism in the northern countryside was the Po Valley, and the model of 'agrarian Fascism' was provided in Ferrara. Here, Fascism inserted itself into the long-standing and bitter class conflict exacerbated by the agitation of the *biennio rosso* between agricultural employers and landless labourers organised in *Federterra*. The nucleus of the squads formed within the *fascio* of the main town were ex-army officers and students, with both the taste for action and adventure, and some experience and expertise in organised violence. They carried out the first reprisals in the surrounding countryside. These 'punitive expeditions' were effective because in planning and execution they combined mobility and concentration of armed force against largely unarmed and unknowing opponents. The squads leapfrogged from commune to commune, simultaneously attacking socialist organisations and founding rural *fasci*.

The Fascist squads were directly financed and equipped by local farmers' and business associations, which in some places actually founded *fasci* with a clear anti-socialist function and set up the sons and relatives of their members as squadrist commanders. They began a systematic campaign to destroy by violence and pressure the organisational fabric of socialism, physically smashing up party and union premises, intimidating and humiliating socialist organisers and leaders, importing and protecting 'blackleg' labour, enforcing tax boycotts against Socialist councils as a prelude to their dissolution by the prefect or imposed resignation. This was a campaign by landowners and commercial leaseholding farmers to put a definitive end to working-class agitation and organisations by force, and restore more congenial labour and contractural conditions. Cowed and intimidated *braccianti* were recruited into new syndicates, not formally Fascist even by name, but led by ex-revolutionary syndicalists in the *fascio* and clearly linked to it. The employers renegotiated with them, to the exclusion of Socialist and

Catholic organisations, labour contracts which reversed or diluted the gains of 1920. This was a process with a built-in and accelerating momentum, as the pillars of socialist power in the countryside – the unions and the town halls – were brought to the point of disintegration by squadrist coercion and intimidation, and the sanction of unemployment. Unprotected in their persons or their jobs by the PSI and *Federterra*, the large number of day labourers pressurised into joining the new syndicates at least had immunity from violence and some prospect of employment.

The Fascists also won a rural lower-middle-class base in parts of Emilia, Lombardy and Venetia among sharecroppers, small tenant farmers and small peasant proprietors. Some of these had recently improved their position and extended their holdings or purchased land by taking advantage of wartime demand for agricultural products and inflationary reductions in rent and mortgage payments, as well as the panic selling in 1919–20 by landowners fearing Socialist expropriation. Rural Socialism threatened these newly acquired gains, as it did the interests of those *mezzadri* and tenant farmers who were initially organised by *Federterra* in the successful campaign for the revision of rental contracts in 1920. The Socialist goal of a collectivised agriculture where everyone would be a landless worker, evidently sacrificed actual and aspiring peasant proprietors. More immediately, *Federterra's* labour market monopoly was applied to large and small farmers alike, and all had to employ their quota of *braccianti*. Fascist protection against the leagues under the slogan of 'the land to those who work it' was accompanied in some Po Valley areas, starting with Ferrara, by a modest but much-publicised redistribution through the agency of the *fascio* of land made available by the landowners for the settlement of *braccianti* on sharecropping contracts. Forcibly challenging the labour monopoly of *Federterra*, and ruthlessly exploiting the contradictions of the PSI's land policy and the heterogeneity of its rural coalition of 1920, the *fasci* had managed to bring together both large landowners and leaseholders, and smaller farmers in an anti-socialist alliance.

The Fascist land policy of June 1921 would strain to reconcile the interests of large and small farmers and formalise the alliance under the slogans of 'agrarian democracy' and 'productivism'. It was regarded as socially desirable to make sharecroppers out of landless labourers and thereby build a fence against agrarian socialism. But no general redistribution of land was envisaged, and the commercial estates were inalienable and indivisible because they were efficient and productive.

The policy basically reworked that of the Bolognese association of commercial farmers since 1919. It foreshadowed the formation of the Fascist 'integral syndicate' in Bologna and other Po Valley provinces from late 1921, a single organisation for all farmers and landworkers which located the 'productivist' larger farmers within a wider 'community' of 'producers'.

In a matter of four months the squadrist offensive in Ferrara led by Italo Balbo, the opportunistic young Republican ex-army officer in the pay of the agrarian association, had turned the province around by the spring of 1921. Most Socialist councils had been forced to resign, and the syndicates, which had no members in February 1921, were 40 000-strong in June. No other situation was reversed so rapidly or so dramatically. Bologna province counted six *fasci* in March 1921 when the large-scale squadrist attacks began, and forty-three by October with a membership of about 12 000; in Padua, the single city *fascio* existing in March had become sixteen *fasci* and over 5000 members in June, almost all located in the Po basin. The disproportionate size of the Bologna city *fascio*, about 5000-strong, indicated the importance of the initial impetus which the provincial capitals gave to the expansion of the movement.

Elsewhere the pace of growth was slower. This was in part because of the resilience and even resistance of workers' and peasants' organisations, in part because a less-differentiated rural social structure did not allow the Fascists to recruit allies outside the big farmers against the Socialist leagues as effectively as in the Po Valley. The reliance on violence was correspondingly greater and the class interests it served all the more exposed. In central Tuscany, where *mezzadria* predominated, it was almost a straight fight between the *fasci* and squads sponsored by the agrarian association and the sharecroppers' organisation. In the wheat-growing areas of Apulia, the lack of any intermediate peasant groups meant that the action of the employer-backed squads against the *braccianti* leagues was not mitigated by any Fascist land policy, however demagogic, and even the syndicates had little weight. Generally outside Ferrara, agrarian Fascism finally broke the back of Socialist rural organisations during the winter to the spring of 1921-22, often with the help of battle-hardened squads from neighbouring provinces and usually employing the methods of the Ferrara model: squadrism, syndicalism and the destabilisation of local government.

In what became the Fascist strongholds of the Po Valley and Tuscany, the violent defence of both urban and rural middle class and propertied interests met in Fascism. Squadrism linked the Fascism of town and country in very obvious ways. It was usually the city *fascio* which first exported organised violence to the countryside. Any attempt to defeat socialism would have to confront the complementary urban and rural sources of its power in these areas, the agricultural unions and political control of the local council. Again, social and economic activities in town and country were inextricably interlinked. Many people had interests in both urban and rural areas, and much of local industry, trade, finance and the professions were concerned with servicing the needs of agriculture, or processing and refining agricultural products and employing peasant labour. Such connections evidently made industrialists and bankers as concerned as farmers about agricultural wage levels and general agricultural profitability and any threat to it.

The movement's counter-revolutionary alliance of threatened urban and rural interests therefore reflected this characteristic interpenetration between town and country. But even where this did not exist, Fascism took a basically similar form as an anti-socialist reaction, because industrial and agricultural employers faced the same kind of problems at broadly the same juncture and adopted the same violent solutions. Local industrialists founded Fascism in the small manufacturing towns and ports along the Ligurian coast and in the Tuscan mining and industrial towns, using the same complementary tactics of squadrist violence and syndicalism and with the same motivation as 'agrarian Fascism'. So, the Carrara *fascio* was led and organised in the interests of the marble quarry owners and traders, but over 75 per cent of its 1600 members were workers, mainly blacklegs recruited to the squads by the local Fascist boss, Renato Ricci.

There were, however, more nuanced attitudes to Fascism among industrialists than was usually the case with farmers. Smaller-scale provincial industrialists and manufacturers funded and supported their local *fasci* at source. Some big industrialist concerns, particularly those that had expanded frenetically during the war like Ansaldo and Ilva, were consequently most exposed to the effects of the transition to a peacetime economy and Giolitti's confiscatory tax policies. They continued to fund Mussolini and *Il Popolo d'Italia*, as they had in fact done during the war and afterwards. Their connections to the Milanese leadership of Fascism rather than to the provincial movements might have reflected some concern over the apparently limited horizons and objectives of squadrism.

But this was a caveat scarcely worth making in Tuscany where industrialists large and small, including managers of the Ansaldo businesses in the region, enthusiastically backed Fascism. The reservations which existed were found to be more among the large entrepreneurs of the major industrial cities of Lombardy and Piedmont, including Gino Olivetti, Giovanni Agnelli and other Turin businessmen. For some of these industrialists the impact of the recession from late 1920 through 1921 was softening up labour without the need for recourse to Fascist squads. Their violent and crude methods of restoring industrial peace were anyway often seen as undermining the continuity of production and destructive of good relations with the workers and their unions in the factory. As a result the Fascist syndicates, elsewhere the appendages of squadrism, found it difficult to make much headway among workers of the big industrial centres, a situation that persisted long after Mussolini came to power in October 1922.

7. GIOLITTI AND FASCISM

The take-off of Fascism as a provincial mass movement coincided with what turned out to be the final government led by Giolitti. While it would be an exaggeration to say that his government directly supported or connived at Fascism's violent anti-socialist offensive, Giolitti certainly tried to extract political advantage from it. As was clear from his moderate tactics during the occupation of the factories in the autumn of 1920, Giolitti hoped to revive his pre-war transformism to the left by bringing the PSI's non-revolutionary wing into the orbit of a reformist, centrist, liberal ministry. But at the PSI congress in January 1921 the party's reformists were not expelled nor did they leave the party, whose executive, however, remained in maximalist hands. As a result it was the extreme left factions that seceded to form the Communist Party. Nevertheless in Giolitti's view the reformists might be induced to leave a weakened PSI, since its official but nominal revolutionary stance was simply drawing onto itself Fascism's counter-revolutionary violence.

Using Fascism as a kind of political stick to weaken socialism would soon prove to be an ambiguous and risky strategy. But it was consistent with Giolitti's parallel attempt to co-opt Fascism by including it in a very broad anti-socialist electoral coalition to contest the general elections called for in May 1921. The so-called National Bloc governmental electoral lists ranged from groups on the democratic left and centre, through centre and rightist liberals to the Nationalists and the Fascists. It was formed to bring about a centrist majority in the new parliament at the expense of the PSI and the PPI, which faithful to the Sturzo line officially rejected any involvement in old-style electoral anti-socialist alliances between Catholics and liberals and generally stood on its own ticket. Giolitti expected to 'tame' Fascism and make it like any other political movement by getting it to participate in and thereby accept electoral and parliamentary politics. Parliamentary representation within a projected broad coalition of liberal interests would at least contain the level of squadrist violence and reduce the necessity for it by indicating that there were alternative ways of resolving political conflict and exerting political influence.

Trasformismo was no more successful on the right than it was on the left. The 1921 elections produced no fundamental changes in the make-up of parliament. The vote of the two mass parties remained largely intact, though the PSI turnout fell dramatically in those areas of Tuscany and the Po Valley where squadrism was most active and Fascist intimidation made a mockery of free elections. The increased representation of groups likely to provide a parliamentary majority for a liberal government was largely accounted for by the Fascists winning thirty-six seats in the National Bloc. But almost immediately the newly elected Mussolini made it clear that the Fascist deputies would not be parliamentary fodder for liberal governments.

Fascist inclusion in the National Bloc exposed the equivocation and confusion of Giolitti's strategy. Their presence in the governmental coalition lists conditioned even more the attitude to Fascism and squadrist violence of the prefects and the police forces responsible to them. These were the very agencies of the state which were expected to respond and adapt to shifts in political opinion and influence in their provinces, and favour where they could the election of 'government' candidates. The considerable Fascist violence and intimidation during the election campaign was now legitimate in the eyes of the local state authorities when carried out by a movement which was a member of the governmental electoral slate. Connivance at continued Fascist violence could now be construed as official policy.

It was common enough during 1920-22 for civilian and military policemen (the *carabinieri*) to fail to prevent or repress Fascist crimes of violence. The effect, of course, was to give squadrists immunity from detection and prosecution and allow them to act outside the law with impunity, a situation that helps to explain the one-sidedness of the 'civil war' against 'Bolshevism'. In many cases the relationship between provincial squadrist Fascism and the local state authorities was something approaching complicity. In much of Tuscany, for example, policemen, *carabinieri* and regular army officers not only turned a blind eye to the depredations of the squads – which was common practice almost everywhere – but were also in some cases active in the squads, sometimes even joining them or planning joint operations and supplying intelligence, equipment and transport. What seemed to evolve was an undisguised rapport between Fascism and local state officials, from the prefect and police chief to the policemen on the ground, though generally complicity was more marked among the lower ranks of the police forces.

A shared class and patriotic hostility to the perceived threat of socialism goes some way to accounting for the sympathies Fascism could draw on among provincial state officials. The operational difficulties of policing during the *biennio rosso* also contributed to the effective immunity enjoyed by squadrism. Often apparently overwhelmed by the scale, scope and longevity of workers' agitation, and anyway enjoined by central government to be 'neutral' in labour disputes, Fascism appeared to an embattled force to be a legitimate and necessary civilian auxiliary which would help the police restore law and order. In these circumstances, Giolitti's quite explicit directives of April 1921 to the prefects of Tuscany and Emilia-Romagna, the storm-centres of squadrism, that violence should not be allowed to mar the election campaign made a nonsense of his own decision to include Fascists in the National Bloc. As a result such contradictory orders were largely ignored on the ground. The prefects' failure to ensure the impartial application of the law against all lawbreakers deprived the government of the conventional means to contain squadrism. This was because members of the state's own apparatus of coercion were accomplices or accessories to illegalities committed in the name of a patriotic reaction against socialism. In some areas the state had already lost the monopoly of force, on which the rule of law depended, to an armed faction dispensing its own form of justice.

Fascist inclusion in the National Bloc also enhanced Fascism's respectability and support among provincial liberals, traditionally the political representatives of local landowning and commercial interests in Tuscany and the Po Valley, at the point when the movement anyway was spearheading and benefiting from a general middle-class reaction to socialism. The National Bloc confirmed and strengthened the often close co-operation between the *fascio* and local liberal associations; many leading provincial Fascists and their influential sympathisers were simultaneously members of the liberal clubs. Giolitti's removal of the prefect of Padua for his inaction in the face of Fascist violence was one of several instances of provincial state officials being disciplined for ignoring central directives on the maintenance of law and order. The prefect's justification was that the *fasci* contained too many important people in the province, including liberals who led the agrarian association, for him to take action against them. This response laid bare the effects of an ambiguous central government policy towards Fascism. So Giolitti had attempted to create at a national and parliamentary level a stable coalition including Fascists which accommodated and neutralised the movement, the classic 'transformistic' manoeuvre. But the effect was rather to accelerate the growth and increase the strength of the movement outside parliament through its alliance with provincial liberal leaders and its collusion with the exponents of state authority.

The assumption behind Giolitti's effort to 'transform' Fascism in the National Bloc, and which continued to inform his attitude to it after the May 1921 elections, was that Fascism was or could easily become a normal political movement like any other. The Fascist agreement to end violence, the so-called Pact of Pacification encouraged by Giolitti's successor as Prime Minister, Ivanoe Bonomi, in August 1921, and the decision of the national Fascist congress in November to make the movement into a party appeared to confirm Giolitti's prognosis. The summer and the autumn of 1921 saw the first great internal crisis of Fascism, and its resolution in fact made clear how different it was from the other political parties.

8. THE TRANSITION FROM MOVEMENT TO PARTY

The Pact of Pacification and the establishment of the Fascist Party were interrelated aspects of the same crisis of identity over the political aims and methods of Fascism. In the view of Mussolini and the Milanese leadership of the movement, socialism was being defeated by squadrist violence which had served its purpose. It should therefore be contained and run down as the 'Bolshevik' threat receded and before it became politically counterproductive. Continuing and excessive violence would make Fascism the cause of instability and disorder, alienating those middle-class sympathies aroused by the battle against socialism and perhaps precipitating the formation of an anti-Fascist coalition in parliament.

After the elections of May 1921, of course, the movement was represented in parliament and almost automatically had to give itself a national political strategy. The creation of a party implied a centralised and national organisational structure and the definition of long-term political aims in a formal programme. Fascism would be thus equipped for a more conventional phase of political activity in which it could compete for power in a parliamentary framework and not simply exhaust itself as a necessary but contingent anti-socialist reaction. Other related pressures were pushing Mussolini in the same direction, including the very rapid expansion of the movement, which grew from about 21 000 members in late 1920 to nearly 250 000 a year later. More crucially, the various provincial Fascisms were organisationally and financially independent of the movement's central organs. The transition from movement to party was Mussolini's attempt to control and organise provincial Fascism from the centre and make of it a national political force.

Mussolini's manoeuvre was only partially successful. Opposition to the pact and to the formation of the party came from the strongholds of squadrist Fascism in Emilia, Venetia, Tuscany and Piedmont. Eventually Mussolini and the provincial Fascist leaders were able to compromise by trading off repudiation of the pact against acceptance of the party. The pact pledged both Socialists and Fascists to put an end to violent reprisals and respect each other's economic organisations. One good reason for rejection was that it undermined the positions of local political and economic power being conquered by the movement and the employers who backed it through the squadrist offensive from late 1920. If violence was discontinued the squadrists would lose their reason for existence and their leaders the lever of control to dominate local affairs. The Fascists were intervening with violence in deeply divisive social conflict and employing it against one class in the interests of the opposing class, and this made control inherently precarious. A position acquired by force could only be maintained by force or the continued threat of force; coercion had its own momentum and rationale.

The pact, if acted on, would also reprieve Socialist unions. Once allowed to organise freely again, they would not only agitate to restore the labour and contractural conditions of 1920, but would also compete for a following with the Fascist syndicates, whose members had joined mainly unspontaneously because of the twinned pressures of intimidation and unemployment. For both employers and Fascists the pact threatened the disintegration of the syndicates, which by organising workers whom the squads had forced out of Socialist unions, were the way to make the squadrist defeat of socialism permanent and definitive.

Concern for the survival of the syndicates indicated that there was more at stake for Fascism than just the defence of class interests which undoubtedly lay behind squadrism. Many of the young provincial leaders of 'agrarian' Fascism, including Roberto Farinacci in Cremona, Balbo in Ferrara, Dino Grandi and Gino Baroncini in Bologna, and Augusto Turati in Brescia, were syndicalists of varying degrees of conviction. They had been influenced by the ex-revolutionary syndicalist organisers and propagandists active in interventionism and early Fascism and by D'Annunzio's ephemeral corporative experiments in Fiume. The credibility of the Fascist syndicates was in many ways vitiated by their connections to squadrism and the favour of employers. But in 1922 and 1923, for instance in the provinces of Bologna, Cremona, Padua, Brescia and Siena, the squads took action against recalcitrant employers who were failing to observe labour and rental agreements made with the syndicates and to give precedence in employment to workers registered in the Fascist unions. The disciplining of employers as well as workers pointed to the evident need of the syndicates to hold their membership together by demonstrating they could stand up to the bosses.

It was also indicative of the Fascist syndicalist view that workers would have their interests defended in a projected national syndicalist order whose aim, in the words of Grandi, one of the major exponents of 'agrarian' Fascism opposing the pact in the summer of 1921, was 'making the masses adhere to the national state'.[13] The first essential step in the 'nationalisation' of the Italian proletariat was the destruction of the influence and organisations of the anti-national and unpatriotic PSI. This was to be followed by the re-education of workers in 'national' organisations like the syndicates and their subsequent integration into a national community of all producers through corporations of workers and employers. They would be the basis of a new system of economic and political relations which would be at once more productive and participatory. This national syndicalism with its Mazzinian overtones of 'making Italians' incorporated anti-socialism into a more ambitious formulation of a new state which would challenge and replace the existing liberal parliamentary system.

The whole anti-establishment and anti-parliamentary thrust of the Fascist movement was therefore contradicted by the pact and the party proposal, which aimed to redirect the movement's activities to more conventional political and parliamentary activity. To Marsich, the Venetian Fascist leader, a parliamentary route would destroy the essence of Fascism. It would involve the movement working through a system it regarded as corrupt and wanted to supersede, and compromising with the transformistic and timeserving liberal representatives of the bourgeoisie.

Fascism would in such circumstances be no more than a conservative anti-socialist reaction. Characteristically Marsich's response to the pact was to mobilise the squads of Venetia for the occupation of the 'unfascistised' town of Treviso, which quite deliberately signalled squadrist Fascism's opposition to a parliamentary road as both means and end. Power should be achieved not through parliament but against it by the squads carrying out a revolutionary coup.

The seriousness of the provincial Fascist opposition could not be lost on Mussolini when Balbo, Grandi and Marsich met D'Annunzio in August 1921. The approach proved to be inconclusive, but clearly demonstrated that even secession from the movement or the choice of a new leader with more congenial aims and methods were possibilities. In face of the public rejection of the Pact of Pacification by provincial Fascism, Mussolini resigned from the movement's Central Committee but not from the movement itself. It was really a case of 'reculer pour mieux sauter' and Mussolini clearly had to take some account of the nature of provincial Fascism if he was to establish himself as the movement's recognised national leader. At the Rome congress of early November 1921 the movement formally transformed itself into the National Fascist Party (*Partito Nazionale Fascista* or PNF) and adopted a new programme. Grandi and Mussolini put on a public display of reconciliation and unity, and the Pact of Pacification was officially buried shortly after.

The extent to which Mussolini was 'the leader who follows' was indicated in the first party statute of December 1921, a compromise between Mussolini's desire for centralisation and entrenched local Fascist positions. The executive organs of the new party were the Central and Management Committees, both elected by a national congress. These central agencies laid down the political and administrative policies which the provincial federations, *fasci* and squads were expected to follow. But the choice of squad commanders and provincial party leaders was a matter for local initiative and congresses.

The compromise between centre and periphery extended even further than this, because the Fascist Party retained important aspects of the anti-party movement it had apparently replaced. These made the PNF different from other parties and its co-option into a parliamentary framework unlikely. The PNF was certainly a political organisation which had a large following and a programme to match it. The snapshot of the social composition of the party provided by its own sample of about half the total membership in November 1921 can give a false impression. Nearly 50 per cent of members were agricultural labourers and industrial workers, certainly in the countryside, largely the product of squadrist coercion. The party's unforced membership was a hetero-geneous coalition of men drawn from the 'old' and 'new' middle classes, mainly living in the north and the centre of the country. They were both the survivors and victims, and the beneficiaries and products of Italy's capitalist development from the late nineteenth century. Members included commercial farmers and industrialists; managers and techni-cians in agriculture and industry; state and private-sector white-collar employees and professionals like clerks, lawyers, soldiers, school and university teachers and their students; as well as artisans, shopkeepers and small farmers, whether peasant proprietors, sharecroppers or tenants. There is some evidence to suggest that Fascism was drawing into politics middle-class people who were new to or previously absent from political activity. Certainly, over 90 per cent of the party's national and provincial leaders were middle class, including not only men with a political past but also men who were entering politics as Fascists.

There was and is nothing unusual about political and party leaders being middle class in occupation and background. But the leadership of the PNF was distinguished by its relative youthfulness and, connected to this, its war service. There was some justification in the age profile of Fascism for the almost anthropomorphical vocabulary of the Fascist claim to represent new youthful national energies hardened in the war, which would sweep away the old corrupt political class and a discred-ited and redundant political system. The presence of so many young educated ex-junior rank army officers among the leaders of the party's military and political formations was presumably one of the reference points for the contention of Mussolini's biographer, De Felice, that the Fascism of the 1920s was a movement of 'rising' or 'emerging' mid-dle classes mobilised into political action by the war experience and the immediate post-war crisis to become political 'actors' in their own right as a middle-class party. The use of 'presumably' reflects De Felice's own vagueness in defining exactly whom he thinks constituted Fascism's social base.

De Felice's argument, or intuition, can be filled out. The longer-term sociological trends in Italy, and elsewhere, appear to indicate that the 'rising' middle classes were the 'new' middle classes connected to modern economic development, especially the growth in the tertiary sector of service and white-collar private and public employment. Certainly, these groups were well represented in the PNF's 1921 membership, as were the other fastest growing social sectors of the war and immediate post-war period, small farmers who benefited from the wartime inflationary spiral to extend their holdings or buy the farms they rented. The youth of the movement's leaders was matched by that of its members. The new party recruited over one in ten of the country's secondary school and university students, most of whom were from middle-class backgrounds, upwardly mobile in terms of expectations and prospects but facing high post-war graduate unemployment.

De Felice's intention in drawing attention to Fascism's 'rising' middle classes was to show that the movement had, and retained, an 'innovating' strand, denoting the middle classes' long-term political aspirations, and was not simply agrarian 'reaction', pulling in lower middle-class people to protect their threatened socio-economic status. For De Felice, this 'Fascism-movement' persisted in its various versions into the life of the Fascist regime of the late 1920s and 1930s, never entirely sidelined in a Fascist dictatorship which apparently stabilised itself as the defence of conservative, established interests. What the new Fascist Party was and what it represented, at this stage of its growth in the early 1920s, can now be examined.

This middle-class membership had, of course, come to Fascism in numbers only from late 1920. The motivation was the actual and perceived threat to their social and economic position posed not only by the wartime and immediate post-war conditions of inflation and high white-collar and intellectual unemployment, but also and primarily by the experience of the *biennio rosso*. The conjuncture of events of late 1920 and early 1921, and the social heterogeneity of the middle-class alliance brought together by Fascism in a common struggle against socialist revolution and the advance of proletarian organisations, might suggest that the movement was incapable of achieving a coherent and collective purpose and direction other than anti-socialism. Was this basically all that Fascism amounted to?

Fascism's anti-socialist offensive certainly grouped together men of different political outlooks. What linked them was the belief that Fascism at a time of crisis would best defend the class interests apparently threatened by a combination of proletarian militancy and government passivity in face of that militancy. While the priority remained the defeat of socialism, it was possible for right-wing liberals and *Popolari*, nationalists, syndicalists, republicans and monarchists to find a place in Fascism and to see it as a short- or long-term vehicle for their class and political aspirations. In this sense the rapid coalescing of middle-class people in

Fascism justified and embodied the original conception of the *fasci*: a movement rather than a party, unashamedly eclectic, plagiarising men and ideas, whose unity came in action and from the pressure of extraordinary circumstances. Significantly the creation of the PNF and the hardening-up of the Fascist programme followed rather than preceded the great surge in the numerical and territorial expansion of the movement, inverting the usual progression from thought to action in a political organisation. This was a tribute to the movement's opportunism, or as the Fascists themselves saw it, to the way that action was shaping a new reality. However, the new party's programme, and especially its organisation and conduct, indicated that Fascism was rather more than an anti-socialist reflex.

The PNF's programme gave a productivist sheen to the defence and promotion of middle-class interests. A general commitment to private property and any policy likely to favour economic efficiency and maximise production was translated into specific proposals for the privatisation of public utilities, cutbacks in and tight control over government spending, and tax and fiscal reform to stimulate private enterprise. This was a rolling back of the state, in other words, in the interests of taxpayers and entrepreneurs. A productivist rationale was also given to the corporative and class collaborative aspects of the programme, which envisaged the legal recognition of professional and economic corporations and their inclusion in a system of joint parliamentary and corporative representation to cater for the individual as citizen and producer respectively. This partial diminution of parliamentary powers and functions in a corporative direction was admittedly a very insipid version of the national syndicalism enthusing some provincial Fascist leaders and labour organisers in the Po Valley. The *laissez faire* economic perspective sat rather uneasily within the anti-liberal and statist framework given to the programme as a whole. The nation, the 'supreme synthesis of the material and immaterial values of the race', was the ultimate reference point for Fascism. The state as 'the legal incarnation of the nation' was therefore 'sovereign' and subordinated all other individual and collective rights and values. It was this primacy of the state over the individual as the custodian and promoter of the national will which justified the proposals for the greater nationalistic and militaristic content and tone to be given to elementary education. Such reforms would enable the school system together with military service and sport, to 'develop in the bodies and minds of citizens, from childhood on, an aptitude and habit for combat and sacrifice on behalf of the fatherland'.

Complementing the productivism of the party programme was the intention expressed in the party statutes to form *gruppi di competenza*, or technical study and consultancy groups, in each *fascio* if possible. These would be a pool of technical and professional expertise for the party to draw on for the reform and efficient management of the state administration, public services and the economy. The groups, which in practice did not get off the ground until late 1922 and early 1923, were meant to be a way of recruiting or co-opting into Fascism men of talent and ability, an embryonic new technocratic and managerial élite at the party's disposal. If nothing else, the *gruppi* indicated the party's intention to equip itself for the task of running the state after taking it over.

But as well as being a political organisation with a programme and apparatus geared to middle-class constituencies and aiming at the transformation of the liberal parliamentary system, the PNF remained very much a 'combat' organisation. Indeed, the political and military organisations and roles of the PNF were indistinguishable. This was becoming the case in organisational terms anyway. Increasingly in 1921 and 1922, the commanders of the squads were also the heads of the provincial party federations. The local Fascist bosses, who were called *ras* after the name for Ethiopian chieftains, combined in their own persons both military and political authority. The party's declaration in mid-December 1921 that all party members were to regard themselves as squadrists might well have been a tactic to pre-empt any government action to dissolve paramilitary organisations. No government would easily embark on the dismantling of a party of a quarter of a million members. But this position really only confirmed the formal shape that the party had assumed at the point of its creation: an armed militia claiming to represent and personify the nation and set on conquering the country and the state. As the November programme stated, concerning 'organisation for combat the PNF forms a single entity with its own squads, and these constitute a voluntary militia in the service of the nation-state, a living force embodying and defending the Fascist idea'.[14] Squadrism, in other words, was not to be sacrificed to the political tasks of the movement now that the squads were apparently winning the battle against socialism. Squadrism was essential to Fascism and helped to define it, shaping the ethos and practice of the movement and influencing both the route it took to power and its method of governing thereafter.

The squads were gangs of mainly middle-class young men, many of whom had served as lower-rank officers during the war. They were university and secondary school students, sons of the professional people, local traders, officials, businessmen and farmers who supported or sympathised with Fascism's drive against socialism. In some areas, like Florence, the squads had a plebeian element, drawing in the drifters and petty criminals of urban lowlife whose opportunism and lack of scruples were covered by their participation in a patriotic cause and the exceptional conditions of 1921–22. The squadrists' activities set them apart from the 'respectable' and propertied men who financed and backed them. As men of action and violence, they despised the 'bourgeois' attitude and mentality of their supporters who in their view were complacent, materialistic, playing safe. Adopting and acting out the daredevil slogans of the Fiume legionaries, 'I don't give a damn' and 'living dangerously', they self-consciously evoked the spirit of activism and dynamism of the generation who had fought in the war.

Action placed the squadrist above law, convention and morality because its demonstrable success was its own justification. They were achieving by doing, creating a new reality through action, removing apparently insurmountable obstacles by sheer acts of will. In a remarkable sublimation of the squadrists' actual links to employers and of the connivance of prefect and police which facilitated the success of their operations, violence acquired a kind of purity as action in its simplest, most straightforward form. It resolved complicated and intractable situations immediately and definitively, literally at a stroke. The cult of violence and action gave squadrists a special sense of being an heroic élite and vanguard, a cut above all politicians, including those in the Fascist movement itself, who talked rather than acted. Violence became a way of life for squadrists, at the same time the source and expression of a squadrist mentality and values.

Importantly then, violence was both means and end, and this was also in the logic of the initial use of force to settle class conflict. The squads from the city *fasci* who spread out into the surrounding countryside wanted to contest and then destroy the apparently impregnable economic and political strength of Socialist organisations. They saw themselves as an army operating in the enemy's own territory and behaved like an occupation force which had to dominate and subjugate a hostile population. In this kind of context, violence could not be applied just once. It had to be applied continuously, or at least the threat of reprisal had to be always there, if opposition was not to revive. The squads effectively created a climate of terror, deterring resistance and dissent in both the present and the future. Imperceptibly, coercion and the retention of an apparatus of coercion justified itself not only as an instrument of conquest but also as a means of control. In this way, squadrism was beginning to outstrip the defence of the class interests of the farmers and businessmen who sponsored and benefited from the use of force against their workers.

The recourse to violence also marked the end to dialogue. Socialists were not to be negotiated with; they were enemies of the nation who had to be crushed, and permanently so, which was why the Fascists took over the role of organising the workers in 'national' syndicates. This was another good reason for the maintenance of coercive controls, since a proletariat barely 'liberated' from Socialism would have to be 'forced to be free'. The habitual use or threat of violence, 'legitimate' because exercised by a militia that claimed to personify the nation against those it identified as dividing the nation, demonstrated that the Fascists aspired to dominate affairs in an exclusive way, allowing no alternatives to exist. This in practice was how the rule of the *ras* operated in some northern and central provinces by the summer of 1922. Squadrism was creating the model of a single party system of rule, a kind of permanent terror, destroying its rivals by force and imposing an absolute control justified by its credentials as the national movement.

So the PNF was a political party which was unconventionally also a military organisation employing military methods of control. Its mode of action was incompatible with and subversive of the principles and conduct of democratic parliamentary politics. The belief of Giolitti and other liberals that the PNF could be successfully co-opted within the parliamentary system was illusory. They did not realise that violence was central to squadrist Fascism, rather than only a method of political struggle adopted temporarily and extraordinarily to defeat a perceived threat of proletarian revolution. The attempt by some provincial party organisations to make permanent squadrist methods of control, the intention to group in the party the managerial and administrative cadres for efficient government, and syndicalist–corporatist aspirations to create a new state, showed that Fascism was not reducible to a temporary anti-socialist crusade. As we shall see, however, the tactics that Mussolini and Fascism adopted to win power entailed a compromise rather than a complete break with Italy's political and economic establishment and parliamentary system. This perpetuated the confusion and illusions about Fascism's nature and function.

9. THE MARCH ON ROME

Giolitti's successor as Prime Minister, Bonomi, seemed to have some sense of the subversiveness of a political movement which imposed a single view through violence. His methods of handling Fascism were, however, basically no different from nor any more successful than those of Giolitti, at least up to his resignation in February 1922. The attempt to 'normalise' Fascism by negotiating an agreement to end violence through the Pact of Pacification had failed. Government directives like Bonomi's circular to the prefects in December 1921 telling them to disband all armed organisations highlighted but did not confront the same problems of enforcement that had blighted Giolitti's orders to repress and punish illegality. This was the circular which the PNF had anticipated by proclaiming all PNF members squadrists. Mussolini correctly judged that the challenge would be evaded by the government, because it would involve dissolving a mass movement and recognising that violence was an endemic and not incidental ingredient of Fascism which required special countermeasures. But as usual, the directive was not focused specifically on Fascist violence, and its implementation was left to the discretion and initiative of individual prefects. The result was that the prefects proceeded energetically against the *Arditi del Popolo*, left-wing anti-Fascist paramilitary groups set up in 1921 to combat squadrist violence. But they did or could do little to restrain Fascist coercion, reflecting the provincial party's dominance in local affairs, buttressed by the squads and the collusion of state authorities and the influential men of provincial society in Fascist violence. The prefects and police were being expected to exercise powers which effectively they no longer had.

During the spring, the summer and the autumn of 1922 organised Fascist violence took the form of province-wide and regional mobilisations of squads, a kind of creeping insurrection. These offensives aimed to extend Fascist control into areas where Fascism was weak or having difficulties and its political opponents were still strong. Their target and victim was also the authority of the state. In May 1922 Balbo called out the squads of the province to organise and marshal the occupation of Ferrara by thousands of landless labourers in the syndicates in order to pressurise both the prefect and central government to concede public works. Relieving unemployment with public funds kept workers in the syndicates without rupturing relations between the party and the syndicates and their patrons among the agricultural employers. Farinacci, the

Fascist boss of Cremona, would even argue that taking national power and thereby gaining access to ministries which dispersed public monies was vital to achieve by the start of the next winter if the party was to retain its mass following.

The holding of provincial power almost inevitably required Fascists to assume extra-provincial perspectives, though this basic political lesson was lost on the Socialists during the *biennio rosso*. Balbo realised that 'the local situations do not count if the life of the whole nation does not change... we must conquer the nation.'[15] His Ferrara squads then joined a general mobilisation and concentration of Emilian squadrists in Bologna in late May and early June to force the transfer of the prefect, Cesare Mori, who was trying to enforce the law against Fascist illegality. Even more sensationally in September, the squads of Venetia occupied Trento and Bolzano, the main towns of the largely German-speaking South Tyrol, the annexation of which in 1919, brought Italy's frontiers to their natural geographical limit of the Alps. The government-appointed civil commissioner was made to resign, because the Fascists objected to what they saw as the administration's lack of zeal in 'italianising' the region. Nowhere was it clearer that Fascism claimed to substitute itself for the state whenever the latter was seen to default in the defence of national interests.

But the turning point in the creeping insurrection came in the aftermath of incidents in Cremona in July, when Farinacci mobilised the provincial squads against the Socialist city council. In a general rampage Fascists entered and damaged the home of the PPI deputy and labour organiser, Miglioli. Mussolini had always feared that the uncontrolled extension of Fascist violence would eventually isolate the PNF politically and bring about an anti-Fascist government. This was one of the reasons why he preferred to work towards power through a parliamentary combination rather than risk everything on a putsch. Now these events finally provoked a parliamentary response to the Fascists' spring and summer offensives against their opponents, which was undermining the authority of the state. A vote of no confidence carried against the government led by the Giolittian deputy, Luigi Facta, who had succeeded Bonomi in February 1922 only because the PPI refused to support Giolitti's return as Prime Minister, specifically cited the government's failure to repress Fascist disorder. A government crisis had been directly precipitated by the problem of Fascism, and in political and parliamentary logic it should have been resolved by the formation of an anti-Fascist coalition.

The breaking of the government crisis cut across discussions taking place since June between the PPI leadership and the reformists in the PSI, which were finally broaching the question of the reformist deputies participating in the formation of a government. Bonomi, one of several politicians invited by the king to try to form a government, attempted to cobble together an anti-Fascist centre-left coalition including the PPI, reformist Socialists and left liberals. Bonomi's soundings were torpedoed from all directions. The maximalist PSI leadership repudiated the possibility of Socialist collaboration with or in any government, keeping to the by now self-destructive line that worse was better and that the party should act to deepen rather than resolve the political crisis of the bourgeois state.

So as always since the 1919 elections, a parliamentary majority depended on an agreement between the PPI and the liberal groupings. Giolitti publicly ridiculed the idea of a coalition bringing together Socialists and Catholics, which made it clear that he and his group would not support the formation of any government against Fascism. If Fascism was the problem, then the answer was not an anti-Fascist government, which would risk civil war, but a government including Fascists. This familiar stance of Giolitti, that Fascism could be tamed by power, was in fact a capitulation to force and illegality. Fascism was a problem only because of its illegality. If Fascism was a normal political party, then with a parliamentary representation of only thirty-six seats there would be no question of it having to be in government. This was a necessity because of the illegal threat that Fascism posed. The right-wing Salandra liberals were at least less equivocal. They saw Fascism as a necessary and legitimate reaction against Socialist subversion, justified by the incapacity of government to resist revolution, and anticipated Fascists entering a strong anti-socialist ministry headed by Salandra.

The conservative Catholics in the PPI were also more anti-Socialist than anti-Fascist. Their opposition to a PPI–PSI agreement, which Miglioli had attempted to forge at a local level in Cremona in March 1922 to resist Farinacci's offensive against both Catholic and Socialist unions in the province, induced the PPI leaders to put party unity before the opening to the reformists. Some liberal and Catholic deputies were willing to accept Fascism in government, or at least were unwilling to accept the formation of an anti-Fascist government as the logical outcome of the July crisis. Their stance showed the extent to which the collusion of conservative circles with Fascism in the provinces was now bearing on parliamentary alignments at the centre.

The final tragic twist in the July 1922 political crisis came with the call of the so-called Alliance of Labour – an anti-Fascist grouping of some unions formed in February which had the support of Socialist, Communist and Republican parties and the Anarchists – for a 'legalitarian' general strike to restore political and union liberties. If this was a desperate attempt to influence the resolution of the parliamentary crisis and bring pressure to bear for the formation of an anti-Fascist ministry, then it was entirely counterproductive. The strike call created the situation it was meant to prevent. Not only did the strike compromise the outcome of the consultations for the formation of a new ministry, which had eventually once again been entrusted to Facta. It also provided Fascism with the pretext to stage massive mobilisations of the squads. Ostensibly to break the strike, which was anyway poorly organised and supported, the real aim was to extend Fascist control into other areas, including some of the major industrial cities where Fascism was struggling to make an impact. The removal of the Socialist city council in Milan and the breaking of the Socialist dockers' co-operatives in the port of Genoa were significant gains of the August mobilisations, which also took place in Leghorn, Ancona and Bari. The Fascists had effectively pre-empted a government response to the strike, acting as if they alone were entitled to defend the nation's 'right to work'. They had again both usurped and demonstrated the impotence of state authority; the prefects and police were unable to prevent the concentrations of the squads or the violence which followed.

The events of July and August were important in two ways. First of all, they gave a measure of the extent to which Fascism had by the summer of 1922 already become the new state. The movement had taken off in late 1920 as a product of perceived government weakness in the face of Socialism; during 1921 and 1922 Fascism became the cause of government weakness. It was not simply that central government was unable to contain Fascist violence in large parts of the north and the centre of Italy and in Apulia. Organised violence had become a system of control as well as conquest. As a consequence, *de facto* power had passed from constituted state authorities to the PNF, or rather to the provincial Fascist bosses, the *ras*, who presided over a kind of military occupation of some of the countries. The provincial party executed law and order functions according to its own lights. It exercised an arbitrary terror against its opponents and created a climate that made it difficult for prefect, police and judiciary to act independently and uphold the laws and dispense justice in an impartial way, even if they had wished to. Local government had been taken out of the hands of elected councillors and given to nominated prefectural commissioners, who were usually Fascist followers or sympathisers or officials of the prefecture running 'technical' and non-political administrations. The party men arbitrated in labour disputes, and through the syndicates controlled the labour market.

Secondly, the July crisis, which was caused by Fascism, had not led to the formation of a government capable of resisting Fascism. It was increasingly unlikely that parliament would produce an anti-Fascist majority; in fact, quite the reverse. It was true that the reformist Socialists in parliament were by the summer of 1922 ready to enter or support an anti-Fascist government. But the PSI leadership's reiteration of its intransigent post-war position meant that the reformists could not carry the rest of the party's parliamentary group with it. They were later, in early October, formally expelled from the party for their willingness to collaborate with a bourgeois government. By the time some Socialist deputies were available for an anti-Fascist coalition, many liberals and right-wing Catholics were now themselves unavailable for such a solution, given the collusion with Fascism's anti-socialist offensive at the local level.

A mutually reinforcing cycle connected political developments at the centre and the periphery from late 1920 to late 1922, linking the weakness of parliamentary government and the growing extra-parliamentary strength of Fascism. What was seen as the failure of central government to resist Socialism in the provinces provoked the Fascist reaction as a kind of middle-class self-help. As a result, state authority drained away in the provinces where the Socialist threat appeared greatest, with the Fascists substituting themselves for a defaulting state and in particular breaking the state's monopoly of force. Parliamentary attempts to respond to the growing Fascist usurpation of provincial authority and co-opt Fascism into the Giolittian National Bloc succeeded only in accelerating the process of disintegrating authority in the provinces by orienting local élites and state officials towards Fascism. This, in turn, heightened parliament's impotence at the centre. In 1922 it was impossible to form a coalition which would take a stand against Fascist violence, because many liberal and Catholic deputies were convinced that Fascism's action against Socialism was legitimate, and that the best way to contain Fascism was to give it a share in power.

If from the summer of 1922 it was difficult to see how Fascism would not soon enter government, what remained less clear was the way in which this would happen and the weight Fascists would have in a coalition government including them. As Mussolini put it in his speech to the PNF congress in Naples on 24 October, days before coming to power: 'legality or illegality? Victory by means of parliament, or through insurrection? Through what paths will Fascism become the State? For we mean to become the State!'[16] The question was rhetorical, and posing the problem in such an antithetical way was an intrinsic part of the strategy adopted by Mussolini and the central party leadership in the autumn of 1922. A meeting of Mussolini and PNF and militia leaders decided on 16 October to prepare for an insurrection, a 'March on Rome'. This was undoubtedly what the bulk of provincial squadrists and *ras* and some of the central leadership including the PNF Secretary, Bianchi, wanted and expected, since a violent taking of power would allow a decisive break with the parliamentary system. The squadrist mobilisations of the time and the efforts spearheaded by Balbo to make the squads into a national military organisation took on an even more sinister aspect as dry runs and preparation for an armed coup.

But preparing for a revolt was not incompatible with seeking power using a parliamentary and political route. As it turned out, the two paths to power were mutually reinforcing. Mussolini realised that the squads could not seize power for Fascism if the government ordered the army to resist. It was this fear of a coup failing which made Mussolini more hesitant than Bianchi or Balbo and more concerned to keep other political options open. By playing down the movement's republican tendencies and praising the armed forces to the skies as the great national institution, Mussolini aimed to neutralise any opposition to a Fascist takeover in military circles and from the king, commander-in-chief of the armed forces. In a speech at Udine in September Mussolini declared that 'the regime can be profoundly altered without touching the monarchy', though the statement was followed by the threat that if the king should oppose the 'Revolution', the monarchy would itself become a target.[17] Conciliation and threat operated in tandem: the existence of a private party army gave Mussolini enormous political leverage, because it allowed him to negotiate from a position of strength. The possibility of a squadrist rising was used as political blackmail, for if Fascism was not given power in a legal and constitutional way then it could threaten a coup. It was not incongruous then, for Mussolini and other PNF leaders to be negotiating with the most important liberal politicians for a stake in government and simultaneously planning and staging a coup. The latter was a way of bringing pressure to bear, to achieve the former on the most advantageous terms for Fascism.

This reading of Mussolini's twin-track strategy can be confirmed by the 'March on Rome', which as Adrian Lyttelton argues, was an exercise in successful 'psychological warfare'.[18] The first stage of the 'March' was to draw on Fascism's provincial strength, and required the seizure of government buildings in the provincial capitals in north and central Italy, before the convergence of three small squadrist armies on Rome itself. This first instalment was carried out successfully enough on the night of 27 and 28 October to induce a failure of will at the centre. As news of occupations of prefectures filtered in to the Ministry of the Interior overnight, it must have appeared as if the coup was succeeding and that state authority was collapsing. Certainly, applying the martial law decree decided on by Facta's government, which crucially was reactive and not pre-emptive, would now involve rolling back these initial Fascist seizures. Doubts as to whether army garrisons, which had already shown tolerance or sympathy for Fascism in 1921–22, would be prepared to take sides in a civil war might well have influenced the king to rescind the martial law decree on October 28. It must have also struck the king as absurd to risk bloody civil conflict over Fascism and to take responsibility for it, when all the liberal leaders he had consulted were recommending or resigned to Mussolini's entry into government. The revocation of the emergency decree obviously meant that the army would not be employed against Fascism. That put Mussolini in a correspondingly strong position from which he could hold out for nomination as Prime Minister not simply as a member of a Salandra-led government, which was apparently the king's preferred solution. This duly happened on 30 October once Mussolini had arrived from Milan by train and not at the head of his stranded squadrist armies who were permitted a triumphal march through Rome on the day after.

Was Mussolini's coming to power in these extraordinary circumstances to be regarded as the outcome of insurrection or as normal constitutional practice? The ambiguity lay in the fact that it was both and neither at the same time. The constitutional forms were respected; the king as head of state had officially invited Mussolini to form a government before the squads could get within firing distance of Rome. However, this was not a normal political crisis sparked by a no-confidence vote in parliament, nor was it resolved in a parliamentary way. The king acted under duress; the outcome was determined by the extra-parliamentary pressure and force exerted by a party militia. Paradoxically the 'March on Rome' could be taken by liberals as an indication of Fascism's accommodation in a parliamentary framework and by Fascists as the start of their anti-parliamentary revolution. The ambiguity over the parliamentary or revolutionary legitimacy of Mussolini's appointment as Prime Minister was to condition and cloud the early years of Fascist government.

2 Between 'Normalisation' and 'Revolution', 1922–25

1. THE VARIOUS FASCISMS

In retrospect, the period from October 1922 to January 1925 marked the transition from the liberal parliamentary system to the Fascist state. Like many political transitions it was an untidy and complicated process, a hybrid of elements of the old and new political order as one overlapped with and superseded the other. It seems difficult to establish precisely what were the intentions of Mussolini and the PNF. Were they intending all along to set up a single-party totalitarian dictatorship? Or were they aiming at something rather less drastic, a strong government certainly, but still one compatible with the existing parliamentary and constitutional framework until driven off course by the fallout from an unpredictable event, the murder of the Socialist deputy, Giacomo Matteotti, in June 1924, which precipitated the definitive rupture with the parliamentary system?

One of the reasons for the confusion, illusion and uncertainty surrounding the direction that Fascism intended to take was that Mussolini's coming to power was as much parliamentary as insurrectionary and did not represent a clean and decisive break with the existing political system and its practitioners. Fascism's drive to power had subverted parliament but not eliminated it. If Mussolini's nomination as Prime Minister was the outcome of many liberals and the king capitulating to force or the threat of force, it was still the case that they had agreed to it happening within rather than outside and against parliament. A Mussolini government still needed to be endorsed by a parliamentary vote of confidence, and since the PNF had only thirty-odd seats in the Chamber of Deputies, a coalition was unavoidable. The question was how far and for how long Fascism would be conditioned by this compromise with the liberal political establishment and its parliamentary institutions. If Fascism intended to change things, then it would of necessity be a gradual and progressive matter, a process in other words.

The other main reason for the lack of clarity about Fascism's eventual shape and orientation once in power was that it was a catch-all movement whose unifying myth was the nation and the national interest. It offered not one coherent vision of the future and a strategy of how to use power to realise such a vision, but several blueprints and strategies of varying degrees of coherence. Fascism was a disparate alliance and was internally divided over both ends and means. Very broadly, the basic tension was between the various forms of 'normalisation' desired by conservatives and moderates both within and outside the PNF, and the 'radicalisation' demanded by the squadrist and national syndicalist groups. Mussolini increasingly came to straddle these tensions and to some extent mediated between them, alternately and sometimes even simultaneously taking up conciliatory and intransigent positions. These tensions in part lay behind the dissidence and internal conflicts afflicting the PNF in 1923 and early 1924, though they also overlaid a jostling and competition for power among provincial party factions which otherwise were often agreed on objectives and methods.

The Fascist syndicalists had a reasonably articulated view of how the syndicates would be the building blocks of a new political order and system of popular representation. Their immediate concern after the 'March on Rome' was to extend the range of control of the syndicates over employers as well as workers, especially in industry where they had penetrated least. In the desire to widen Fascist control over economic and social groups and interests, they often had natural allies in the provincial *ras* and squadrists. Their conception of the 'revolution' came down to a crude 'fascistisation' of the personnel and practices of all organisations and institutions, putting Fascists at their head. Their ideal was to perfect and perpetuate the decentralised one-party tyrannies which had emerged from the squadrist offensives of 1921–22, with the PNF through the *ras* and a permanent squadrist terror exercising an absolute power and influence over all areas of life of the provincial community. Farinacci, the Fascist boss of Cremona and the spokesman and epitome of provincial 'intransigence', urged 'legalizing Fascist illegality',[1] which was perhaps not as self-defeating as it appeared. Getting the government to frame and enforce laws abolishing other parties, and political and civil freedoms might well mean passing to state organs powers and functions at present arbitrarily wielded by the Party. But as with the 'intransigent' demand that the newly constituted Fascist Militia should be the Fascist state's political police, it could also mean the PNF becoming the state, assuming in this case the repressive function of government.

It was precisely this confusion or dualism of party and state authority and function characterising *ras* rule and the early practice of the Fascists in central government which offended the so-called 'revisionists' in the PNF. They were a small group centred on Massimo Rocca and Giuseppe Bottai relying on Mussolini's intermittent sympathy to compensate for their lack of a strong party base. These were the 'normalisers' within Fascism who argued that reform of the 'intransigent' party should precede and make possible an orderly reform of the state. The violent, undisciplined, decentralised party of 1921–22 might have proved an agile combat organisation. But now that Fascism was in power, its style, methods and leadership were inappropriate for the political tasks of government and running and reforming the state. The party should become the organisation in which new Fascist managerial and technocratic élites circulated and were formed.

'Revisionist' hopes for a meritocratic Fascism focused on the *gruppi di competenza* or technical study groups, whose development had been the job given to Rocca in September 1922. National *gruppi* started up in 1923 to consider and propose reform in education and the state administration, and another was approved to deal with constitutional reform. They were envisaged not only as 'think-tanks', but also as the embodiment and vanguard of constitutional change, embryonic corporative bodies or National Technical Councils, the leading wedge of functional and economic representation in a modified, but not transformed, mixed corporative and traditional parliamentary system. This very much followed the lines of the 1921 PNF programme. Portraying the party as a prospective élite of competence who would efficiently manage a stronger executive opened up the PNF to the collaboration of all experts, specialists and professionals. It was in this mood that the 'revisionists' could welcome the merger in 1923 of the PNF and the Nationalist Association with its membership and connections among the state's ministerial and judicial bureaucracy, as an injection of talent and expertise into Fascism's task of 'national' reconstruction. The 'intransigents' were against any such openness to non-Fascists in a spirit of national pacification and reconciliation. The 'rights of revolution', their participation in the combative and insurrectionary movement, gave them exclusive claim to be the new Fascist governing class. As a result the *gruppi* were obstructed and opposed by many in the party as a rival and unsound training ground of the Fascist élite.

Fascism's conservative 'fellow travellers' among right-wing liberals and Catholics certainly expected Fascism to provide at least a period of strong government after the turbulence of the *biennio rosso*. To this end they voted in parliament to give Mussolini emergency decree powers in economic, fiscal and administrative matters for a year from December 1922. Some, like Salandra, echoing the coup against parliament in 1915, wanted to go beyond this temporary suspension of parliamentary control of the executive and strengthen the power of the king and government at the expense of the legislature. If the Fascist government did this, it would still be acting within the bounds of constitutional 'normality', as long as it also put an end to continuing party and squadrist illegality and revamped the authority of state organs by freeing them from party interference. Some 'normalisers' even anticipated the PNF's dissolution, now its anti-Socialist crusade was completed and Fascism was in power, and Fascism's merging into a broad political alliance of the conservative right.

Such views on party–state relations were shared by conservative 'normalising' dissidents in the PNF, like Alfredo Misuri in Perugia, Dino Perrone-Compagni in Florence, and Ottavio Corgini in Reggio Emilia. These were men who significantly were linked to agrarian associations now resisting the corporatist controls being pushed by party and syndicates in agriculture. The Nationalists were close enough to Fascism politically to be both rivals and allies, and after the merger became the 'official' Fascist right-wing. They had a relatively coherent view of an authoritarian corporatist political and social order which was to shape much of the Fascist state created after 1925. They were less bothered than Salandra and other liberals about preserving a parliamentary system in some form. But they were monarchist, and as believers in state authority and orderly institutional change were another of the 'normalising' pressures on the Fascist coalition government to end party violence and its chaotic and improvised domination of provincial affairs.

Many of Fascism's non-Fascist political supporters, and interest group organisations, including *Confindustria*, looked to Mussolini rather than Fascism for the limited political reform and strong, stable government which they thought necessary. Mussolini was willing enough to be taken as a 'normaliser' like them, and the only one who as leader of Fascism and head of government could restrain and control the Fascist movement. Mussolini used the pose of mediator between the Fascist movement and its so-called 'flankers' as a means of extending their political support for his government: whatever he did was a lesser evil compared to the greater evil of an unchecked, party-led revolution.

2.   DICTATORSHIP BY STEALTH

After October 1922, then, a confused and confusing political situation was created by Fascism's coming to power through compromise with the country's existing political institutions and liberal political class, and by apparently unresolved arguments within and outside the PNF over Fascism's objectives and methods. It is, however, still possible to say that the hopes and expectations of 'normalisation' were misplaced in the period 1922–24. Fascism was perceptibly moving towards a one-party state or a progressive monopolisation of power in a process of creeping dictatorship, or to paraphrase Mussolini, 'plucking the chicken one feather at a time'.[2]

This process was evident in Mussolini's speeches and actions and in those of the Fascist government and party, and started as soon as the government had been formed. In the first place, new party organs were created and the government embarked on drastic constitutional reform. The Fascist Grand Council, which met first in December 1922, was an assembly initially of Fascist leaders in the top party, syndicate and state positions. It gathered frequently in the early years of the Fascist government to discuss and formulate the main lines of Fascist policy. It was Mussolini's creature, in the sense that he called for and presided at the meetings, set the agenda and could co-opt people as members. The Council spent much time dealing with the PNF's internal crises and organisation, and in October 1923 formally put itself in charge of the party, becoming an important mechanism of centralised control of the movement under Mussolini's leadership.

Mussolini portrayed the Grand Council as a consultative body co-ordinating the action of the PNF and the government. This was hardly reassuring to 'normalisers' wishing to end party interference in government and the state. The Council, an exclusively Fascist organ which only Fascist ministers in the coalition government attended, met to align government policy to that of Fascism and hence extend Fascist power. The Council had no legal or quasi-constitutional status until 1928 and was basically an alternative Fascist cabinet existing alongside and pre-empting the actual cabinet or Council of Ministers. The Grand Council's position as a *de facto* party organ parallel to and superseding its government equivalent matched at the centre the party–state dualism between provincial PNF secretaries and prefects in the localities. It indicated the way that the balance was swinging towards the party. The Council took unconstitutional decisions in its first meeting, passing to Mussolini the king's prerogative to choose the date of elections. It also made coalition government meaningless by diminishing the standing of the Council of Ministers, which was sometimes asked to endorse measures decided beforehand by the party assembly. The route followed to enact one of the government's early major innovations was instructive. The decision to create the Fascist Militia, or MVSN, was taken at the first improvised meeting of the Grand Council in December 1922, then approved by the Council of Ministers and embodied in a decree law of January 1923.

The foundation of the Militia was seen in some quarters as an important act of 'normalisation' in that it regularised the position of the Fascist squads by incorporating them into a national paramilitary organisation which would presumably ensure they acted in a more disciplined way. Certainly, one of the aims of the reform was to improve Mussolini's hold over the party and bring it under greater centralised control by breaking the local links between the *ras* and the squads. Many squadrists were reluctant to join the MVSN in 1923, a diffidence encouraged by the party bosses precisely because of the threat to local control of the squads on which their provincial tyrannies rested.

However, the formation of the Militia was an obstacle to 'normalisation'. Its job was to maintain internal public order – in other words, to defend Fascism against its political opponents – and to impart the warlike spirit of the combatants and squadrists to the nation's youth in premilitary training. Its political function was clear: at the orders of Mussolini not the king, the MVSN was a now legal private army to keep Fascism in power at public expense; no other political party could legally give itself a paramilitary arm. Until the Matteotti crisis Mussolini always resisted calls for the suppression of the Militia or its transformation into a military force integrated into the army's command structures. This attachment to the Militia as the armed bodyguard of Fascism showed that Mussolini had ultimately staked his retention of power on the extra-parliamentary coercion of a party army. It was the clearest possible indication that Fascism repudiated free and equal political competition between parties, because nothing short of force would make Fascism give up power.

One of the very first issues discussed by the Grand Council was electoral reform. It was the only matter of political significance put to parliament during the period of the government's temporary emergency decree powers, and in approving it parliament effectively destroyed the principle of parliamentary government.

The so-called Acerbo law was a hybrid of majority and proportional representation electoral systems. The electoral list which gained the largest number of votes, provided this exceeded a quarter of the total votes cast, received two-thirds of the seats in the Chamber of Deputies; the remaining one-third of the seats would be allocated proportionally among the other lists. The measure, transparently designed to give Fascism the opportunity of securing an unassailable majority in parliament, was so drastic as to be 'constitutional reform'.[3] A party winning barely 25 per cent of the popular vote would find a Chamber packed with its own supporters and could form a government that would enjoy such an automatic and unbeatable parliamentary support as to make recourse to parliament superfluous. The Acerbo law undermined the principles of one man's vote being equal to another, of governments being ultimately accountable to the choice of the electorate and responsible to an elected parliament. The effect of the law was to transfer choice and decision from the electorate to the selection and composition of the governmental electoral list. This was to be a very important lever in the government's erosion of political pluralism.

It appears staggering at the time and in retrospect that this bill should have passed through parliament on the votes of liberal deputies, even though most of them certainly hated the post-war proportional system which had destroyed the axiomatic pre-war liberal parliamentary majorities. Their acceptance of the Acerbo bill must presumably be related to the continuing misperception that Fascism could be 'normalised'. Salandra argued that electoral reform would constitutionalise and legalise Fascism. He seemed to be assuming that with a secure parliamentary majority Mussolini would accept that his mandate to govern came from parliament, removing the dependence on a violent and revolutionary Fascist movement.

But party violence was an essential component of the 'double-track' tactics which Mussolini and Fascism had applied in 1922 before and during the 'March on Rome' and which they continued to use up to the general election of April 1924. Blending conciliation and the threat and actual use of violence, Fascism unravelled the democratic parliamentary system within which the government appeared to be working. Squadrist intimidation continued after October 1922 not only to preserve entrenched party positions in that self-justifying cycle of coercion, but also to take in 'unfascistised' areas of political and economic activity. The attacks on the working-class neighbourhoods of Turin and Parma, and the *ras* Turati's mobilization of the provincial squads against the PPI and Catholic organisations and town councils in Brescia, all in late 1922, were typical incursions into enemy territory. Responsibility for organised political violence lay also now with the state and the government, following the formation of the Militia as a state organ and of a unit in Mussolini's press office to harass and intimidate prominent opponents of Fascism as well as PNF dissidents.

Party pressure on political opponents and non-Fascist organisations worked in tandem with the actions of state authorities. Not only were the prefects generally tolerant of the coercive methods of the governing party; they also applied administrative measures of their own, using the wide discretionary powers they had under existing legislation in order to dissolve local elected councils and disband unions, co-operatives and Chambers of Labour for alleged irregularities, their assets passing to the Fascist syndicates.

The combined and cumulative action of party and state authority was never so effective or necessary as in the syndical sphere. Edmondo Rossoni, the head of the national confederation of Fascist syndicates, was pushing the idea of 'integral syndicalism' both before and after the 'March on Rome'. This meant the formation of 'mixed syndicates' or corporations, with employers and workers in the same legally recognised organisation with exclusive rights of representation. 'Integral syndicalism' clearly embodied Fascism's class collaborative and productivist objectives. But it also resolved a practical dilemma facing Fascist syndicalism. In agriculture, the syndicates struggled to reconcile their links with squadrism and the big farmers, without which they would barely have existed at all, and the need to keep together their initially coerced worker members by getting farmers to respect labour agreements guaranteeing employment. This lay behind the repetition in the summer of 1923 of the conflict between syndicates and agrarian associations in many of the Po Valley provinces, which intertwined with factional rivalry within the local PNF.

The dilemma was similar in much of industry, though here the syndicates had to do something to improve their relatively low membership among industrial workers. Taking action on behalf of workers against employers was obviously one option, but this as obviously alienated employers when the control of labour was what recommended Fascism to them. 'Integral syndicalism' was a way out of the impasse, because the 'mixed syndicate' would incorporate employers and allow them to be disciplined and controlled as well as workers in an embryonic 'community of producers'.

Rossoni's concept could be realised only with party and government support, not only on the ground but also from the centre. The Grand Council endorsed 'integral syndicalism' in March 1923, and in November recognised as the sole 'official' organ of farmers, FISA, the Fascist farmers' union set up a year before in competition with the existing national organisation, CONFAG. 'Integral syndicalism' and the loss of organisational autonomy it apparently entailed met strong resistance from *Confindustria*. As a result, the Palazzo Chigi agreement brokered by Mussolini in December 1923 acknowledged that industrial employers and workers should organise separately, but that each side – *Confindustria* and the Fascist syndicates – should co-operate to the implicit exclusion of other organisations. This was a step towards the union monopoly of the industrial syndicates, which was definitely negotiated in the Palazzo Vidoni pact in October 1925 and built into the regime's labour and corporative legislation of 1926. 'Integral syndicalism' prevailed in agriculture after the imposed merger of FISA with CONFAG in 1924. This guaranteed a voice for the southern landowners strongly represented in the latter without undermining the hold in the old and enlarged FISA of the commercial and 'productivist' entrepreneurial farmers of the Po Valley.

It should be clear that between 1922 and 1924 organised economic interest groups were being brought into the Fascist orbit. This was happening more rapidly and comprehensively in agriculture than in industry, cutting out the liberal politicians and lobbyists who had traditionally mediated between these groups and government. The aim of the Fascist bodies involved in this process and of the Fascist syndicates was to gain the exclusive right to organise in the economic and union arena. The means used to achieve this combined simultaneous party and state action at the centre and the periphery, ranging from squadrist violence and biased prefectural intervention against non-Fascist organisations to national agreements. As was evident in the self-perpetuating cycle of violence and intolerance of squadrist Fascism, a monopoly of organisation and representation was ultimately the only way the Fascist syndicates could survive. In a competitive situation workers would and could join other organisations. This was demonstrably still the case in industry, and was the perpetual fear in agriculture if control of the labour force loosened. Complete and permanent control was the answer; the only safeguard of the syndicates' existence was to prevent their rivals from existing. In the economic and labour as in the political sphere, the Fascist Party and government were working to erode the bases of a pluralist society.

Practically all of Mussolini's speeches in 1923, to party or non-party audiences alike, were alternately menacing and conciliatory and could plausibly be read either way. His first and notorious speech to the Chamber of Deputies as Prime Minister in November 1922 set the tone for the approach he would follow towards other politicians and parties over the next eighteen months. 'I could have transformed this drab, silent hall into a bivouac for my squads ... I could have barred the doors of parliament and formed a government exclusively of fascists', he declared, adding, 'but I chose not to, at least for the present'. He had formed a coalition government not in order to secure a parliamentary majority, 'which I can now get along very well without', but to rally 'all those who, regardless of nuances of party, wish to save this nation'.[4] The speech explicitly rejected the notion that his government was legitimate because it was accountable to parliament, but simultaneously held out the poisoned chalice of co-operation with Fascism.

It soon became clear that collaboration was possible only on Fascism's terms, and that co-operation could not be genuine and mutual as between equals, but more like the relationship of a blackmailer with his victims. The government's conservative 'flankers' were constantly confronted with the threat of a Fascist 'second wave' unleashed by the party and Militia unless they backed its policies. Nowhere was this more evident than during the parliamentary debate on the Acerbo bill in July 1923. In a Chamber ringed with armed squadrists and Militiamen, which gave a tangible feeling of physical intimidation to the Deputies, Mussolini rephrased once again the message of the 'bivouac' speech, saying effectively that if the Deputies did not vote for a gerrymandered parliament, there would be no parliament.

The collaboration which was no collaboration at all was offered across the spectrum of organisations and parties. Mussolini made two overtures to the leaders of the main union confederation, the CGL, in November 1922 and July 1923, offering them a post in government and suggesting a merger of the syndicates and non-Fascist unions. Here was

an attempt to remedy the weakness of the Fascist industrial syndicates and
tie workers' organisations to the government while detaching them from
the Socialist Party. Significantly, the initiative came to nothing, and not
only because of PNF and syndicate opposition to the deal. The CGL
put an unacceptable condition on the possibility of co-operation, union
freedom of organisation, which would require the government, PNF
and syndicates to lift their pressure on non-Fascist unions and live by
the give and take of a free and pluralist society.

It was significant that the apparently conciliatory call for patriotic
co-operation in the 'bivouac' speech was directed not at parties but at
men 'regardless of the nuances of party'. As was evident in the approach
to the CGL, Mussolini's real target was the PSI and its reformist working-
class base. He wanted to divide, fragment and disintegrate the anti-Fascist
and non-Fascist movements and parties, again employing the characteristic
blend of force and concession. This tactic was applied to the PPI,
Fascism's main political and democratic rival after October 1922.

The PPI was itself internally divided in its attitude to Mussolini's
government. The PPI parliamentary group had decided to vote confidence
to the new government and *Popolari* were ministers in the coalition, in
the hope that their presence would keep the government to a constitutional and legal path and deflect Fascist attacks on Catholic organisations.
The party's conservative grouping were willing to enter a formal 'clerico-
moderate' parliamentary alliance with Fascism and right liberals, but
much of the rest of the party were moving towards an anti-Fascist
stance. Sturzo was able to prevent the PPI from splitting into pro-Fascist
and anti-Fascist wings at the party's congress in April 1923, which
decided that they would continue to support the government on condition
that it kept within the bounds of constitutional and legal 'normality'. Significantly, Mussolini was not prepared to accept conditional support of this
kind, and he dismissed the PPI ministers from the government.

Mussolini skilfully involved the Vatican in his attempts to destabilise
the PPI. Fascism's anti-Bolshevism, even its anti-liberalism, were certainly
congenial to the Vatican. But the government made important concessions
to the Catholic religion in its 1923 educational measures, and held out
the prospect of further gains in a more general settlement of church–state
relations. All of this was to demonstrate that the Vatican could deal
directly with government, and that the PPI was redundant as the party
ostensibly defending the church's interests. Such a view suggested
a limited perception of the role of the PPI. But it would have struck
a chord with Pope Pius XI, who believed that Concordats, formal

bilateral agreements between the Vatican and national governments, and a Catholic laity organised in bodies directly dependent on the ecclesiastical hierarchy, were a surer way of preserving and extending the church's influence in society.

Mussolini's overtures had made the PPI one of the obstacles to a possible church–state understanding. Continuing squadrist violence against the PPI also served to make the PPI rather than Fascism a problem for the Vatican. There were signs that Fascist violence was turning on the clergy and church organisations as well as the party. The threat of the church being drawn into a generalised anti-clerical campaign because of the PPI's anti-Fascism was precisely the reason given for Sturzo's resignation as party leader in June 1923. Fascism's unsubtle blackmailing of the Vatican, which aimed at weakening the PPI, came deliberately at the point of parliament's consideration of the Acerbo bill. The passing of the bill depended on the PPI's support or abstention, but it was also the lever to break up the party. In order to cover their divisions the PPI parliamentary group decided to abstain, only for some right-wing Catholic deputies to vote for the bill at the last moment. The party lost about one in five of its deputies and practically all of its senators in the expulsions and departures which followed the vote. Some of these pro-Fascist Catholics were included as candidates in the governmental *listone* or 'big list' which stood in the 1924 elections. Once it was clear that the PPI would not give unconditional support to the government, Mussolini had successfully prevented the party from defending parliamentary democracy by widening its internal divisions. The PPI's conservative wing had been detached and brought into the Fascist orbit. The centre and left had been neutralised both by the need to preserve a precarious party unity and by the Vatican's distancing from the PPI under the pressure of Fascist violence and blandishment.

3. THE CONQUEST OF THE SOUTH AND THE 1924 ELECTION

The merger of the Nationalist Association with the PNF in March 1923 was part of Fascism's absorption of pro-Fascist groups which were initially either independent organisations or belonged to other political parties and groupings. This process of co-option culminated in the formation of the *listone* for the 1924 elections. The recruitment of the Nationalists helped Fascism to extend its political control to the south and the islands. The price it had to pay was the sacrifice of the PNF's radical pretensions in the area to the 'transformistic' and clientelistic politics of the south.

The rider to the fusion with the Nationalists was the dismissal in May 1923 of Aurelio Padovani, the PNF leader in Naples and zonal MVSN commander, whose 'intransigent' republican and anti-clientelistic Fascism was the model for a string of young party bosses throughout Campania. This kind of southern Fascism resembled that of the northern *fasci* of 1919, both in its ex-junior army officer and university student base, and its lack of political weight. Padovani and some of his acolytes in Campania had built up a relatively combative party and union organisation. But in most southern *fasci*, where they existed at all before October 1922, the few young men who saw Fascism as the new ex-combatant élite regenerating a corrupt politics and society had locked the PNF into self-perpetuating political isolation.

Southern politics revolved around personality and municipality: control of the local council was the source of favours which kept the electors sweet; who you were and what your connections were mattered above all in the murky exchange of patronage for votes which passed as political activity. The youthful parvenus running the *fasci* were nobodies who promised nothing. They remained so, while they continued in their well-meaning but naïve crusade against the old men and the old ways to exclude from the PNF the local worthies and their factional followings. So in Campania, as a reaction to and refuge from Padovanian 'intransigence' in the PNF, the dominant local clienteles drew closer to the Nationalists. They expanded in many other parts of the south following the 'March on Rome', as the usual factional infighting over municipal power took on the appropriate political labels of the time. An Interior Ministry report on the Basilicata in early 1923 spoke volumes for the shallow and opportunistic roots of Fascism in many Southern regions: 'Where there is a mayor, a communal administration supported by the old clienteles, camouflaged as Nationalists, there arises Fascism, or better, the other opposition clienteles dress themselves as Fascists and the Fascist section is created.'[5]

The *en bloc* entry of the Nationalists into the PNF made a partner out of a rival in the south and inserted their clienteles within the party. Fascism co-opted the southern liberal politicians and their local and regional followings in the same way, using the fact that it was now the party of central government to overcome the PNF's absence or weakness on the ground before October 1922. Liberals in the south were government supporters before they were liberals, because what interested them was access to the patronage and resources of the state. It was no wonder that Mussolini in his coalition government continued the liberal government tradition of appointing prominent southern politicians to head the Ministries of Posts and Telegraphs, and Public Works, which payrolled thousands of real and phantom jobs in the south.

All that was needed was to convince the local notables who delivered the votes that the PNF now represented the best line of connection to central government. The prefects of the southern provinces worked hard to make Fascism known and accepted locally. They made use of the time-honoured levers of prefectural interference in provincial affairs on behalf of the central government, control over public spending and public sector employment and the power to dissolve municipal councils, to cajole and co-opt the local men of substance into the party. In places like Avellino and Benevento, the prefect was the architect and arbiter of the provincial PNF. The 'ministerialism' of southern politics also worked against those few prominent liberal leaders – Nitti in the Basilicata and Giovanni Amendola in Salerno – who resisted co-option by Fascism and became a kind of 'constitutional opposition' before, during and after the 1924 elections. As the 'outs' of local and national politics, they had no channel to the government favours and funds previously sustaining their own clientelistic followings, which were steadily 'transformed' into backers of the government party.

The formation of the *listone* was the other way of making the PNF the indispensable conduit of political influence in the south. In line with the kind of co-operation first offered in the 'bivouac' speech and reiterated in Mussolini's speech of January 1924 after the dissolution of parliament for the forthcoming elections, the *listone* was put together on the basis of 'men, not parties'. Since the Acerbo law weighted the allocation of seats so much, the sure way of being elected was to be included in the government list of candidates. This inducement was enough for southern politicians and outgoing deputies to join the PNF. Once the major personalities of the southern liberal parliamentary grouping were on the *listone*, their followers and factions came too.

The *listone* then marked the absorption into Fascism of its 'flankers' among rightist and southern liberals, Nationalists, conservative *Popolari* and others. The process had gone furthest in the south: whereas about a quarter of candidates on the *listone* in Venetia, Emilia and Tuscany were 'flankers', 60 per cent of government candidates in Sicily were liberals. The election results reflected the vote-gathering rewards of southern *trasformismo*. The *listone* nationally won nearly 65 per cent of the vote and 374 seats, but did not have a majority over the other electoral lists in Piedmont, Liguria, Lombardy and Venetia. It gained majorities in the heartlands of squadrist Fascism, Emilia and Tuscany, where particularly in rural districts the squads had ensured the vote – 100 per cent for the *listone* in some areas of Ferrara; and in the south and the islands, 68 per cent of votes cast in Sicily going to the *listone*, including blocs of votes delivered by liberals whom the 'intransigent' party leader in Palermo, Alfredo Cucco, had previously excluded from the PNF as *mafiosi*. Of the 374 elected, about 60 per cent were Fascists; the rest were the 'fellow travellers' now adopting the Fascist label.

This pattern of results would not have been out of place in pre-war Giolittian Italy, where the bank of government supporters in parliament were southern liberals. The 1924 elections could be seen as the culmination of a vast exercise in *trasformismo*, with Mussolini as 'super-transformer'. It might appear that Fascism was the victim as much as the beneficiary of *trasformismo*. This was especially so in Sicily where the PNF was sucked into the world of clientelism in 1924 and never re-emerged. The central party leadership was alternately bemused and exasperated by their inability to make sense of and affect the island's personalised and parish-pump politics. More generally, Mussolini's government had given southern Fascism a conservative cast as a result of its basic decision to ditch Padovani and his anti-clientelistic party and syndicates. By accepting rather than challenging the usual southern mode of politics and co-opting its practitioners, Fascism had preserved the traditional land-holding system behind clientelism. Fascism's conquest of the south appeared to mean the south's conquest of Fascism, with Mussolini basically renewing the Giolittian deal whereby the south's political representatives supported the government in return for government's non-interference in the region's socio-economic structures.

But Mussolini's *trasformismo* was different because it was permanent. Co-operation on the basis of 'men, not parties' aimed at the disaggregation or disintegration of existing non-Fascist parties; the Fascist 'normality' was for there to be no other parties, no position independent of Fascism. In the 1924 elections the parties remaining as independent political formations were the two Socialist parties, the Communists, the Republicans, the PPI and the southern liberal opposition of Amendola and Nitti. They had to stand outside the *listone* and accept inevitable political defeat, competing only for a third of parliamentary seats. Even the non-oppositional 'flanker' lists, like the Giolittian liberals in Piedmont, were in the same position as Fascism's declared political opponents because they insisted on standing separately and did not join their fellow liberals in the *listone*. The 'flankers' in the *listone* had lost their political independence; they ran as Fascists and not as liberal allies of Fascism. They were not members of an electoral coalition, like the one the Fascists had themselves joined in 1921, but incorporated into a one-party bloc.

In this light, the practice of the Fascist Party and government, the creation of Fascist institutions which operated alongside and against the existing framework of parliamentary democracy, and electoral reform, indicated that what Mussolini and Fascism were aiming at between 1922 and 1924 was a gradual change to a more authoritarian political order, where the PNF would effectively monopolise political power. It was not yet formally a one-party state or dictatorship, at least in a legal and institutional sense. But the situation was approaching that in fact, and it was certainly not 'normalisation'.

4. THE MATTEOTTI CRISIS

If this is a correct reading of the actions and intentions of Mussolini's government, then the political crisis caused by the abduction and murder of the reformist Socialist Deputy, Matteotti, in June 1924, was not such a clear watershed between the periods of liberal parliamentary and Fascist systems of government. However, it did in the end mark the final and definitive point of rupture with the old system and fatally expose the illusions of 'normalising' Fascism. Matteotti's speech to the new Chamber of Deputies on 30 May catalogued the violence and coercion of the Fascist election campaign, and denied that a government whose parliamentary majority was contrived by fraud and intimidation had the right to govern. The speech was itself a serious blow to the 'normalisers'. The anti-Fascist opposition was refusing to accept the validity of its political defeat, at the very point that both 'flankers' like Salandra and 'revisionist' Fascists like Rocca were saying that Fascist power was legitimised by its electoral victory and hence PNF violence should end and national pacification begin.

The revenge promised and meted out to Matteotti, who was kidnapped and beaten to death by a group of Fascists on 10 June, was nothing less than might have been expected of a movement and government which was intolerant of opposition. The body was discovered in mid-August. Fascinating recent research indicates that Matteotti's killing had as much to do with the risk of revelation of the corrupt dealings of Fascist leaders with US oil and business interests as with the exposure of electoral corruption.[6] Its claim that the gang who murdered Matteotti was an embryonic Fascist secret political police engaged, as Nazi German SS policing later would be, in ideological warfare or terror against 'the enemy within', is rather more convincing when viewed in the short term than in the long term. The gang's activities anticipated the PNF's violent offensive against Fascism's perceived enemies in 1925–26, following the resolution of the crisis created by Matteotti's murder. But Fascist policing in the 'totalitarian' regime proper from the late 1920s did not really follow the 'ideological' German Nazi route.

Matteotti's disappearance was immediately critical because even though Mussolini's direct responsibility could not be proven, the gang making the attack were assumed to be linked to his press office and acting on orders from his closest entourage. The assault could not be passed off as the regrettable unauthorised action of provincial squadrism; it originated in government circles.

About 150 PPI, Socialist, Communist, Republican and Amendolian liberal deputies withdrew from parliament in protest at the end of June. Adopting their name from a famous political protest against tyranny during the Ancient Roman Republic, the so-called 'Aventine Secession' was as much a response to the elections as to Matteotti's seizure: they declared that they alone represented the nation and were determined to overthrow the Fascist government. Their anti-Fascism kept to the high moral, legal and constitutional ground; only the Communists contemplated some form of popular protest to topple the government. The Aventine clearly expected the king to withdraw his confidence from a Prime Minister implicated in criminal activity and sanction the formation of a government that would repress PNF illegality and violence. In retrospect, abandoning parliament was probably a mistake, because the king's inaction could be justified on the constitutional ground apparently occupied by the Aventine. Since neither the parliament nor the Council of Ministers moved against Mussolini, the king could pretend that there was no government crisis which demanded his intervention.

In fact, the Matteotti crisis, by raising the possibility of an anti-Fascist government, seemed to clarify for the king and other important institutions and interest groups why Mussolini's government was preferable, if only as a lesser evil. The king might well have been struck by the return of the dilemma confronting him at the time of the 'March on Rome', and which Mussolini constantly raised in his two years of power in order to bend Fascism's conservative 'flankers' to his political will. If the Fascist government fell, even on a parliamentary vote of no confidence, the fear was that the Fascist movement would resist by force. Six Militia legions were mobilised in June and given arms on request by the army. The MVSN was carrying out precisely the role for which it had been created: a private party army at Mussolini's orders to defend the 'Revolution'.

Similar fears of a civil war arising from Fascism's likely refusal to go peacefully emerged from the Pope's public intervention in September 1924 to scotch talks within the Aventine on the possibility of PPI and Socialist participation in an anti-Fascist coalition to succeed Mussolini. Shades of July 1922: co-operation between Catholics and Socialists, even reformist Socialists, was clearly unthinkable, especially when it involved bringing down Fascism which had saved the country from Bolshevism.

Confindustria did not take a public stance as an organisation on the crisis, but its leaders confirmed the Mussolinian, if not Fascist, position of the previous two years in a private communication to Mussolini in September. 'We are government supporters by definition', the head of FIAT, Agnelli, had declared after the 'March on Rome'.[7] This particular government had been the businessmen's friend. It had ended the rampant union power of the *biennio rosso*, removed high tax Socialist local councils and repealed post-war social legislation. It had generally combined implementation of the PNF's *laissez faire*, privatising and productivist programme of 1921 with a not so hands-off state salvage of banks and firms hit by the 1921–22 recession. Now in 1924, the criminal acts of Fascism seemed to be the cause of instability. But the secret memorandum's answer was not the fall of the government, which would be Socialism's opportunity, but a 'normalising' Mussolini-led government.

It is difficult to suppress the feeling that one has been this way before. The common and consistent elements in these conservative responses to what appeared to be the crisis of Fascism were the fear of the alternatives to Fascism and the corrosive effect of Fascism's essentially violent and coercive character. If the overturning of the government would provoke violent Fascist resistance, then it would be better not to try; if Fascism had brought about its own crisis, then the crisis, by opening up alternatives, only made its continuation appear all the more necessary.

In this light, Mussolini showed a sure political touch when he attempted to recast his government, apparently shorn of its illegality, in June and July. The men suspected or accused of involvement in the attack, Aldo Finzi, Giovanni Marinelli, Rossi and Emilio De Bono, were dismissed from their party and government posts. In the most significant and symbolic change, Mussolini gave up the titular headship of the Interior Ministry to the ex-Nationalist, Luigi Federzoni. In an even more indicative move, a government decree law in August threatened to take away the Militia as Fascism's exclusive armed guard. The MVSN was to be integrated into the armed forces: it would swear an oath of loyalty to the king, and be officered by retired army men rather than by ex-squadrist commanders, making it a national and not a party formation.

The Matteotti crisis was an opportunity to 'normalise'. But it was equally an opportunity to carry forward the 'intransigent' Fascist revolution by finally destroying and replacing the liberal state and ending the 'transformistic' compromises with the old men and the old order which blocked the path to power of the exponents of provincial Fascism. In the 'intransigent' view, only the continued existence of the vestiges of parliamentary government and of conditions of freedom made the Matteotti case into a political crisis of Fascism. Fascism had always ultimately rejected the legitimacy of parliament, and the Militia was on hand to show that Fascism could only be ejected by force. The party 'intransigents' argued with some logic that it was absurd for the government to go on behaving as if its survival depended on the king and a parliamentary majority. Liberty would have to disappear once it meant the right to criticise and overturn the Fascist government. The argument seemed to have been won when a meeting in August of the PNF National Council, a body composed of Grand Council members and all the provincial party leaders, decided to review the constitution and bring into being a Fascist state, setting up a special commission for the purpose.

The new Militia regulations came hard on the heels of the PNF's crucial decision and appeared to contradict it. The problem for Mussolini was that he was finding it increasingly difficult to straddle 'normalisation' and 'revolution' in this way. In December a definitive choice had to be made after the publication in Amendola's newspaper of Rossi's deposition implicating Mussolini in Matteotti's murder. Giolitti had earlier gone into opposition in parliament. With these new revelations it appeared that even the *listone* majority was crumbling at the edges as two Salandran liberals looked likely to resign from the government. On the other hand, a MVSN conspiracy which had been brewing in the 'intransigent' party strongholds of Emilia and Tuscany literally erupted on Mussolini's doorstep on 31 December. Angry and exasperated Militia consuls, whose immediate concern was the effect of the MVSN reforms on their own positions of command, threatened to Mussolini's face that they would take action against Fascism's opponents, with or without him. The situation clarified, in his famous speech to parliament on 3 January 1925 Mussolini assumed responsibility for all that had happened since taking office and promised decisive action within two days, which would, in fact, inaugurate the dictatorship.

3 The Construction of the 'Totalitarian' State, 1925–29

1. 'TOTALITARIANISM'

Mussolini first used the term 'totalitarian' publicly in his speech to the PNF's national congress in June 1925. He spoke of Fascism applying its 'ferocious totalitarian will' to the remnants of opposition and to the 'fascistisation' of the nation so that 'tomorrow Italian and Fascist, rather like Italian and catholic, mean the same thing'.[1] This usage corresponded to the earlier coining of the term by anti-Fascists lamenting Fascism's desire not only to defeat but to destroy its opponents and monopolise power. It hence referred also to the explicitly 'totalitarian' drift of provincial squadrism and syndicates from 1921 to 1922 to eliminate all political opposition and ensure party control of all aspects of life. The operation of party rule under the *ras* was 'totalitarian' even before the term was officially formulated. As we shall see, the provincial party extremists revived all the themes of 1923 'intransigence' during 1925, when they attempted to generalise and formalise their experience as the basis of the new Fascist system.

The official concept of Fascist 'totalitarianism' was not only derived from the actual practice and tendency of early 1920s squadrism. It also synthesised some of the pre-war 'counter-cultural' nationalist thinking on the shape of a new non-democratic and post-liberal state, with the 'total war' experimentation in unaccountable government during the First World War. Mussolini's connection of 'totalitarian' to a process of 'fascistisation' echoed the description of Fascism as a 'total conception of life'[2] in March 1925 by Giovanni Gentile, the Hegelian philosopher and pedagogue who was Minister of Education from October 1922 until July 1924. His speeches and writings provided, at least until the 1930s, one of the most important and publicised ideological rationalisations of the Fascist phenomenon. Gentile's use of the term 'total' conveyed Fascism's claim to ubiquity and a comprehensive, all-encompassing outlook on life,

96

like a religious faith inspiring all facets of existence. Individuals only found full self-realisation through unity and identification with the state, which was not a neutral umpire of society but an 'ethical' authority embodying moral values and inculcating them in society. Such a vision subordinated individuals to the state and imposed no limits on the activity of the state, which educated and moralised them in conformity with its values and purposes so as to achieve the unity of the two.

The definition of 'totalitarian' given the widest currency was Mussolini's formulation of October 1925: 'everything within the state, nothing outside the state, nothing against the state'.[3] This rationalisation owed most to Alfredo Rocco, the ex-Nationalist jurist and ideologue. He was one of the most enthusiastic advocates of the merger with the PNF in 1923, precisely because he believed that Fascism in power was the vehicle for the realisation of already well-developed plans for the reorganisation of the state. Obviously impressed by the bleak rationality and coherence of Rocco's blueprint, Mussolini appointed him Minister of Justice in January 1925, and he was responsible for drafting the major legislation which transformed the state between 1925 and 1928.

Rocco drew on an idealised model of the government's wartime mobilisation to project a view of a sovereign and all-powerful state which regulated and co-ordinated all the organised groups in modern society, from the industrial cartel to the trades union. Once again, as for Gentile, all the boundaries between society and state disappeared. Social and economic organisations, in liberal Italy operating as competitive private and sectional interest groups and hence always at cross purposes with the national good, were to be absorbed into the state. They would become legally recognised organs of state exercising control over their members in the national interest as defined by and embodied in the state. The Nationalist outlook characteristically blended the nation-state's internal and foreign policies. Such a concentration and disciplining of national energies and resources through the state would alone empower the Italian nation to engage successfully in the only struggle which counted, the inevitable imperialistic conflict for power and primacy between competing states.

Mussolini's adoption of a statist idea of 'totalitarian' was significant. It differed subtly from the 'intransigent' party's view of the Fascist movement progressively encroaching on and controlling the functions and activities of all organisations and institutions. It would justify the subordinate incorporation of every body, including the PNF, under the indivisible authority of the state.

Mussolini's public statement of the 'totalitarian' nature of Fascism in 1925 was the first time the term had been used to define a political regime in the making. It was deliberately meant to mark the point of rupture with the previous system heralded by the 3rd of January speech. Although the Fascist 'revolution' was usually later backdated to 28 October 1922, 'totalitarianism' was both the definition and justification of the new Fascist state.

The construction of this state was real enough, and it did represent a fundamental change. But all along, the measures taken to create the new system of government reflected a symbiotic balance and a series of compromises between institutions, and political and economic forces which had been revealed during the Matteotti crisis and its resolution in Mussolini's 3rd of January speech. That speech was precipitated by an ultimatum from the Fascist Party and the Militia, the hard core of the government's support throughout the crisis, that if Mussolini did not launch the 'second wave' of the Fascist revolution, then they would do so without him. The other reason for Mussolini's survival was that the ex-Nationalist and military ministers did not resign from the government, even during the dramatic coda to the crisis in November–December 1924. Their stance confirmed the king's decision not to dismiss him. Mussolini had to respect this balance in paying off his political debts after January. The presence of ex-Nationalists in the government was strengthened. Rocco was appointed to the Justice ministry, while in February, Farinacci, the *ras* of Cremona and the epitome and spokesman of provincial 'intransigence', was made national head of the PNF. The outcome of the Matteotti crisis was the decision to destroy the liberal state, but still in play was the form the new Fascist state would take. In particular, the way the issues of party–state relations and worker–employer relations were resolved was to have a crucial bearing on the orientation of the Fascist regime.

2. THE PARTY AND THE STATE

As national PNF Secretary, Farinacci started to reorganise and unify the party around the methods and goals of provincial 'intransigence'. By his appointments and exhortation, he extended the practices of *ras* rule from its Emilian and Tuscan strongholds to Liguria, Venezia Giulia and the big cities of the south and Sicily. He intended to realise full power to Fascism by unleashing a fresh wave of violence, coercion and pressure, where party control was once again linked to the action of the squads in a crude and unchecked 'fascistisation' of state and society. In the spring and in the summer of 1925, encouraged and directed from the centre, the provincial party instituted a kind of terror. Its physical and verbal offensive took in the remaining known opponents of Fascism, the leaders and members of Catholic organisations, bankers and industrialists, and as a particular target, the civil service, including the least 'fascistised' personnel of the ministerial bureaucracies in Rome. The campaign involved not only anti-Fascists but also the non-Fascists, the uncommitted, the 'enemies within', including those 'opportunistic' members who had joined the winning side after October 1922. Farinacci decided to close the party to new members in November 1925. Although reversed by the Grand Council a few months later, it was clearly the signal for a purge of membership and a sign of his commitment to a 'revolutionary' vanguard party restricted to the political élite who had participated in the movement's squadrist and insurrectionary origins.

The campaign ignored Federzoni's insistence from the Interior Ministry that law and order should be enforced by state organs, the police and prefects, who would soon be equipped with new and wider repressive powers in government bills now going through parliament. It could do so with impunity, because the party boss backed by the squads could still rely on that subordination and connivance of provincial state authorities which had facilitated the original squadrist offensives of 1921–22. Indeed, the party was stimulated and not restrained by the impending legislative action of the government. The bill to limit the right of association was to include a retroactive ban on state military and civilian employees belonging to secret societies, wide enough to outlaw any association but probably aimed at Masonry. It was introduced in January and became law in November, and its parliamentary passage was accompanied by the party's attempt to implement the measure *de facto*. Many civil servants were Freemasons, and the campaign against Masonry was a wedge for the party's intended 'fascistisation' of the state bureaucracy, the professions and business.

From this sprawling party attack emerged a sense of the PNF's understanding of its 'totalitarian' status and role. It was aiming at what Farinacci later called 'the strictest dictatorship of the Party in the Nation'.[4] It saw itself as the élite guardian of the Revolution, standing outside the government and state, the better to 'fascistise' them. It was the carrier of 'permanent revolution' or at least permanent terror, since only the party's control exercised indefinitely and without restriction could ensure that society and institutions became and remained Fascist. There was a clear contrast between this version of 'totalitarianism', which saw the party as independent of and superior to the state, and the vision behind Rocco's drafting of the legislation of 1925–26. That made the state the source of all power and authority, emanating through the enactment and application of laws by the permanent organs of the state, the executive and the judiciary.

Between November 1925 and April 1926 and during November 1926, in two swathes of lawmaking whose timing found a pretext in the first and the last of four attempts on Mussolini's life, Fascism legislated itself into permanent existence. Some of these laws and decrees formally eliminated all existing opposition and made illegal any possible anti-Fascist activity, creating a vast machinery of legal repression and effectively installing a one-party and police state.

It is certainly possible to connect these measures to some of the illiberal practices of liberal governments preceding Fascism. In the liberal state, the independence of the judiciary from the executive branch of government was often honoured more in principle than in reality, and the prefects and police had and used discretionary legal powers to restrict individual and collective freedoms. But this scarcely justifies the conclusion that there was no break in continuity between the liberal and the Fascist state system, as if Fascism was more of the same, only worse. The context of repression was qualitatively different, because these so-called 'exceptional laws' changed the relationship of state to individual. The latter was deprived in both principle and practice of any rights, even the right of redress, against the state and its agents whose actions were therefore unaccountable. This emerged most clearly in the decree of Public Security of November 1926, where a provincial commission run by the prefect could put under police sanction and surveillance 'whoever are singled out by public rumour as being dangerous to the national order of the state'.[5] The Special Tribunal set up by the law for the Defence of the State, also of November 1926, quite literally applied the summary justice of the court martial to the judgement of civilians charged with political crimes. In both cases, the state administered its own justice without recourse to the normal courts of law. The prefects and police had an almost unlimited remit to penalise and restrain individuals whom they only had to suspect of being 'dangerous'. The definition of 'public order' was widened to include the defence of institutions and policies of the Fascist state, extending the areas of life in which the police could intervene.

Mussolini's patience with the party's 'revolution from below' finally broke in October 1925 when Fascists in Florence went on a public rampage against Freemasons. He vigorously denounced illegal party methods in the Grand Council, which decided to dissolve the squads and purge the Florentine *fascio*, one of the most 'intransigent' in Italy. The party had itself demanded the framing of the repressive measures to defend the Revolution and 'legalise Fascist illegality'. But the imminent passing of these into law gave the prefects and police the means to maintain Fascist rule and devalued the functions of political and social control exercised informally and arbitrarily by the party. Once order could be ensured through state organs applying Fascist laws, coercion by the party, which alienated public sympathies and destabilised the state administration, became increasingly redundant.

It was with this realisation and from this perspective that Mussolini replaced Farinacci as Party Secretary in March 1926. His successor, the Fascist boss of Brescia, Turati, restructured the provincial extremist party which had brought Mussolini to power. He integrated the PNF into the Fascist state in a way which conformed with the statist conception of 'totalitarianism' adopted by Mussolini. This view was reiterated in Mussolini's famous circular to the prefects in January 1927, which insisted that the party, 'simply the instrument of the state's will', must 'collaborate in a subordinate fashion' with the prefect, 'the highest authority of the state in the province'.[6] Here was an unequivocal repudiation of party control in the provinces, where it had overlapped with and superseded governmental authority.

The revamping of state authority would remain a statement of principle as long as the provincial party was not reconstructed. The new Party Statute of October 1926 abolished the election of all party posts, ending the acclamatory legitimation of the provincial party leader in local assemblies which was what internal party democracy amounted to in most areas. The hierarchical nomination of party posts from above anticipated Turati's concerted campaign between 1926 and 1929 to dismantle the substance and style of the 'intransigent' party. On an organisational level, Turati demanded that provincial party federations conform to centrally defined bureaucratic and financial procedures. This broke with the cavalier and unaccountable administrative practices which masked the arbitrary, personalised and often corrupt the way in which the local *ras* ran his province.

Turati's more direct challenge to the 'intransigent' party struck at the source of its power to arbitrate provincial affairs, which lay in the squads.

In a purge continuing into 1928–29, probably about 60 000 ex-squadrists and early Fascists were expelled or defected from the party. Pro-Farinacci 'intransigent' provincial leaders were replaced or domesticated. Other party bosses were removed, sometimes spectacularly, as in the case of the disgrace of Mario Giampaoli in Milan in 1929, whose dismissal unravelled a seedy network of squadrist protection rackets in suburban food markets. Hand in hand with the expulsion of squadrists went the recruitment of more passive members to the party in 1926. These lay among white-collar public employees of an 'unfascistised' state administration and various fellow-travelling groups – the very opportunistic latecomers whom Farinacci felt had no place in the party. That the purge and recruitment policies were complementary could be gauged from what happened in some parts of the south, where the increase in number of public officials joining the party was most marked. In Sicily, the removal of the young parvenu provincial party leaders patronised by Farinacci, like Cucco in Palermo and Damiano Lipani in Caltanissetta, allowed in the old liberal politicians whom the 'intransigents' had kept out as men of clientelism and the mafia.

Having lost the battle for party supremacy over the state, Farinacci imaginatively proposed the merger of party and state positions in a kind of supercharged 'political prefect'. Given its source, the idea never got off the ground, but a real point had been made. The PNF's subordination to the state would not necessarily have liquidated its political role and influence if party leaders had occupied state positions. The fusion of both state and party authority, combining party and state office in the same person, in fact only occurred at the top and the bottom. Mussolini was Head of Government and *Duce* of Fascism. Sometimes, the Political Secretary of the *fascio* was also the *Podestà*, the term given to the municipal state office which replaced the previously elected mayor and council in the laws of February and September 1926 reforming local government. But this was hardly the preferred situation, and prefects probably resorted to it as an expedient to compensate for the shortage of leadership material in small communes.

Fascists certainly became prefects, and PNF pressure on the service grew once prefectural powers were restored and extended in the Fascist state from 1926. But the influx of party men into the Interior Ministry was controlled. 'Fascist prefects', meaning those with a genuine Party background and pedigree who came from outside the career administration, rather than state officials who had taken out PNF membership, counted for about one-fifth of all prefects in office in 1928, one-quarter in 1934 and a third in 1937. The government thus continued to rely on the career service for about two-thirds of its prefects, confirmed by a 1937 decree which stipulated that at least 60 per cent of prefects should be drawn from the Interior's own ranks. As far as one can gauge this, whether an official had a philofascist, anti-Fascist or non-Fascist record of service made no difference to his being appointed as prefect and remaining in the service. These conditions reflected the inability of the PNF to throw up cadres of sufficient quality for such a key position in the state apparatus. They also showed the Fascist government's conciliation of the state bureaucracy, and willingness to work through career officials who were competent, and satisfied the broad tests of political loyalty established in the measures of 1925–26.

In some important ways this situation probably inhibited the 'fascistisation' of provincial society. The prefect appointed or recommended the appointment of a large number of local public and official posts, including the *Podestà*. The Interior Ministry recognised that the prefect should consult the local party on nominations to such positions, and in most cases this happened. But the party's opinion was not binding, and in making appointments the prefect often placed criteria of competence and general acceptability before the date of party membership or record of past services to Fascism.

This generally seemed to be the case with the *Podestà* appointed by the prefects. While it remained an unpaid post, it was likely to be filled by the local worthies or in some cases by reputable and neutral candidates such as retired military and policemen. Unsurprisingly, in the north and the centre, rural communes and major towns in mainly agricultural provinces were run by local landowners, many of them also aristocrats in Tuscany. These men were returning to positions of municipal leadership they had lost to the Socialist mayors and councils in 1920. Many of these were certainly Fascists or sympathisers from the days of provincial squadrism, but they were not usually the archetypal Fascist young ex-officer professional men who had led the squads, or the squadrists themselves. However, the increasing number of paid *Podestà* during the 1930s did suggest a shift towards officeholders of an urban middle-class white-collar or professional background.

Like the prefects, the police forces of the Interior Ministry remained a largely career service, the Chief of Police from 1926 to 1940 being a career prefect, Arturo Bocchini. The Militia set up its own political investigation units in 1926, but these never became a party political police. Indeed, operationally responsible to the prefect, they specialised in reporting *on* PNF affairs, and were never more than auxiliaries to the state police.

Although important, perhaps too much can be made of the relative immunity of the Interior Ministry and its officials from the PNF's methods and personnel. Career prefects still had to oversee and implement the Fascist government's policies in the provinces and the police had to enforce Fascist laws. There was no party terror or police terror to replace it, as a result of the PNF's subordination to the state from the late 1920s. But the police's preventive and repressive powers were now so extensive and pervasive as to create a real climate of fear and repression. Police harassment and surveillance became habitual and continuous, affecting even the most mundane areas of daily life, especially in working-class districts. In the early 1930s the political police alone were taking about 20 000 actions weekly, leading to hundreds of arrests, detentions and sequestrations. There grew up a vast network of informants and agents acting for the political police, particularly the notorious OVRA, the special inspectorate initially created to investigate and combat anti-Fascist activity. Policing increasingly came to involve information-gathering and comment on practically everything that talked or moved. In the enforced absence of any real public opinion in a repressive system, police reports constituted the regime's and historians' only regular, if compromised, account of shifts of the popular mood. Repressiveness was not the most distinctive feature of the Fascist 'totalitarian' system, but it was an essential and inescapable component of it. As we shall see, the regime's organisations and initiatives, which aimed at generating support and 'consent', operated in the context of a repressive atmosphere that gave a sense of compulsion to any involvement in activities sponsored by the regime.

Turati regarded his party reforms as preliminaries to the PNF undertaking new functions within the Fascist state. The party could not now expect to direct political matters and decision-making, certainly not at the centre of government where Mussolini was supreme, and less so in the provinces, where the prefect's authority to run affairs was usually respected after 1927, at least nominally if not always in practice. Its transformation into a 'civil and voluntary force at the orders of the State' carried a change of function as the executor rather than the framer of the state's will. It was 'the capillary organization of the regime',[7] conveying the state's will to the people by organising and indoctrinating them. This gave the PNF a wider social and controlling role, to reform the Italian character and mentality so as to secure a positive commitment to the Fascist state. Turati's Secretaryship saw the steady growth of 'capillary' organisations, extending the party's interests in youth activities, leisure, culture, sport, social welfare and syndical affairs, a trend accelerated under his successors.

3. SYNDICATES AND CORPORATIONS

The Matteotti affair and the 3rd of January speech encouraged the Fascist syndicates to be more militant in their continuing circular pursuit of the industrial working-class support which would oblige employers to take them seriously as workers' representatives in contractural negotiations and labour disputes. During the general crisis of confidence in Mussolini's government in late 1924, there were signs and fears of revived working-class agitation, stimulated as well by rising inflation which fed into higher wages demands in early 1925. Anti-employer militancy was also fuelled by the party's offensive under Farinacci against Fascism's lukewarm and opportunistic fellow-travellers, including businessmen unsympathetic to dealing with the syndicates.

Both Farinacci and Rossoni initially supported the metallurgical workers' strike for higher wages and union recognition rather improbably called by the Fascist syndicates in Brescia under the guidance of the provincial *ras*, Turati, in March 1925. The spread of the strikes throughout the industry brutally revealed the dilemma of the Fascist syndicates' position. The strike took hold only because the CGL-affiliated metalworkers union, FIOM, called out the bulk of men who remained loyal to their non-Fascist unions. What Mussolini called 'the race to be the reddest'[8] exposed the persisting isolation of Fascist syndicates among workers, and was contributing to the resurgence of labour agitation led by the old unions. The strikes were the final and fatal demonstration that the syndicates could not capture industrial workers or impress employers, using trade-union tactics in a normal competitive situation. They depended on the support of the party and state authorities to achieve the monopoly of labour representation they wanted.

The strike's settlement by PNF and state mediation, pointedly excluding the FIOM, anticipated in microcosm the general arrangement between the Fascist syndicates confederation and *Confindustria* in October 1925. The so-called Palazzo–Vidoni pact made explicit what had been intimated in the 1923 Palazzo–Chigi agreement. The industrial employers recognised the Fascist syndicates as the sole representatives of labour. The workers' elective factory councils, which had socialist and communist majorities as late as 1925, were abolished. Significantly, the employers would not agree to them being replaced by the syndicates' own *fiduciari di fabbrica*, factory 'trustees' or agents. This meant that the syndicates had no presence beyond the factory gates, and managerial authority in the factories was preserved.

The agreement was effectively written into the institutional structures of the Fascist state. Rocco's April 1926 law on the judicial regulation of labour relations stipulated that only the single organisations legally recognised by the state could negotiate collective labour contracts binding on the relevant branch of production as a whole. These, of course, in industry were *Confindustria* and the Fascist industrial syndicates. The syndicates' minority position on the ground had been transformed into a legal monopoly of workers' representation. Other organisations could exist as *de facto* bodies under Rocco's law, but deprived of the legal right to negotiate labour contracts they simply atrophied. Both the CGL and the CIL dissolved themselves in 1927. Catholic Action kept alive a semblance of Catholic labour organisation under the guise of training and welfare, while allowing Catholics to join the syndicates. The Rocco law also made illegal strikes and lockouts, the normal levers of pressure for workers and employers in a liberal economy. Instead the law created labour courts as the final stage of a process of compulsory arbitration of labour disputes.

The Rocco law and the way it was implemented reflected the balance between various social and economic forces being incorporated into the framework of the Fascist state and, in particular, the power of the industrialists' interest group, *Confindustria*. Since as a result of the Matteotti crisis a Fascist 'totalitarian' dictatorship was being created, *Confindustria* recognised that they would have to enter some formal, institutional relationship with the Fascist state. Their aim was to safeguard their interests within the new structures. This meant consolidating definitively the gains arising from the Fascist defeat of the Socialist Party and labour movement, and also maintaining their organisational independence against 'integral syndicalism'. Industrialists were as much afraid of the syndicates' reliance on party and state support as their reviving labour militancy in 1925. State intervention in and regulation of labour relations and economic matters might threaten the autonomy of private enterprise and the freedom of business to make its own decisions about production.

The syndical law and what followed indicated the extent to which Mussolini's concern to secure industry's support and co-operation with the government compromised the corporatist drift of Fascism. The gradual and piecemeal evolution of the corporative system, rather than its systematic, once-and-for-all establishment, was itself a mark of *Confindustria's* successful resistance to the realisation of the corporative idea. Rocco's law actually dealt with labour relations and the negotiation of collective contracts between separate organisations of workers and employers in each area of production. It was not really a full-fledged corporative reform, with 'mixed syndicates' or corporations, unitary bodies bringing together under a single hierarchy all the people involved in production, employers, workers and technical-managerial staff, and actually organising and planning production. The law allowed but did not oblige the setting up of fledgling corporations as 'organs of co-ordination' of the syndical associations. This was perhaps enough to suggest that a corporative system was in the making. But the facility to form corporations was never actually exercised nor contemplated by industrial employers, before the legal creation of corporations in 1934.

Corporative hopes were rather vested in the new Ministry of Corporations, set up in July 1926. This was meant to supervise the legally recognised syndical bodies and facilitate the stipulation of collective labour contracts. The nominal Minister was Mussolini, and the Under-Secretary between November 1926 and September 1929, when he was made Minister, was the ex-revisionist, Bottai. He intended to make the Ministry the state's central economic planning and co-ordinating body, managing a corporatively organised economy staffed by Fascism's new technocratic and administrative élite. Predictably enough, Bottai's parvenu and predatory Ministry was obstructed and ostracised by the existing Economics Ministry. He found it difficult to take the Ministry's activity beyond the bureaucratic regulation of the syndical bodies' affairs and the conciliation of labour disputes, while the corporations had no legal standing or existence. Between 1926 and 1934 there was a Ministry of Corporations with no actual corporations to direct.

Bottai was given the job of producing the 'Charter of Labour', defining Fascism's social principles. But the final draft approved and publicised by the Grand Council in 1927 was Rocco's work. It once again mirrored that balance in favour of employers limiting the scope of the syndical law. The Charter spoke of corporations organising production as if they already existed; recognised private enterprise as the most efficient way of production; and outlined some workers' rights in terms of employment and social insurance and welfare provision. Far from meeting Rossoni's demands for a full and definitive statement of legally binding workers' rights, the Charter was a general indication of intent, having the force of suggestion rather than the force of law.

Bottai, however, with the support of the PNF and *Confindustria*, was instrumental in bringing about the *sbloccamento* or dismantling of Rossoni's national confederation of workers' syndicates in November 1928. This was fragmented into a number of separate confederations covering workers in the various branches of the economy. From Bottai's perspective, it was a 'corporative' reform, since it broke up a large labour confederation of nearly three million members still organised on class lines and with a class mentality. Forming several workers' associations, which were exactly symmetrical to employers' organisations in industry, agriculture and the services, would apparently facilitate inter-class co-operation and the co-ordination of the different sectors of production under the state control of the Ministry of Corporations. This was a profound miscalculation, later regretted by Bottai. He assumed that corporative planning under the state's auspices would involve the state's direction of *both* employers and labour. But the *sbloccamento* clearly weakened the political and economic muscle of labour organisations with respect to the employers. Most immediately, it deprived the workers' syndicates of the full weight of a unitary confederation in settling labour contracts and disputes. It contributed more generally to the imbalance in favour of employers which would mark the composition and operation of the corporations, when they arrived.

The Rocco law quite deliberately attempted to draw the sting of class conflict by transferring labour issues from the factory, where employers and workers actually confronted each other, to another plane, that of the law and legally recognised organisations. These were susceptible to state and political pressure for the harmonisation of capital and labour in the interests of national production. Wage agreements and the settlement of disputes arising from them were increasingly brokered by the party or the Ministry of Corporations, or a combination of both: the outcome of a bureaucratic exchange rather than the competitive interaction of employer and workforce.

There was an underlying 'productivist' rationale to the legal subordination of class-based and interest group organisations to the overriding will of the state. This inevitably skewed labour relations in favour of employers and to the detriment of workers. The main criterion was always what was best for or most likely to maximise production, and hence the economic strength of the nation. It was the production rather than the distribution of wealth that really mattered. Employers could argue that wage cuts or the introduction of different and more exploitative work practices were necessary to maintain efficient and continuous production. Italy's industrial base was probably not strong enough for a high-production, high-wage economy on the American 'Fordist' model. But anyway, Rocco's law was first enacted during the government's revaluation of the lira in 1926–27, introducing almost a decade of deflationary economic policy straddling the Great Depression. Almost the first acts of the newly legalised workers' syndicates were to endorse wage reductions in both agriculture and industry, so that production costs could be accommodated to the new value of the currency while retaining competitiveness.

The government's refusal early in 1929 to countenance an attempt by the workers' syndicates to relaunch the *fiduciari di fabbrica* came after *Confindustria's* successful lobbying of Mussolini. Only a direct syndicate presence on the shopfloor could ensure that an employer was keeping to the terms of the collective labour contract governing pay and conditions in his industry. But the industrialists said that any challenge to or restraint on the employers' absolute authority to manage their firms would risk damaging production. Again almost without exception, the same 'productivist' criteria were applied to the party and government mediation of labour disputes, and in the decisions of the labour courts on the relatively rare occasions when a dispute actually reached that advanced stage of the arbitration process. Class collaboration in a 'productivist' framework invariably involved one-way collaboration.

4. THE FASCIST CONSTITUTION

The other 'most Fascist' laws which marked the formation of the Fascist state system were more properly constitutional measures, since they affected the relations of government to parliament and to the king. The law of December 1925 invented a new position of Head of Government, replacing the previous designation of President of the Council of Ministers or Prime Minister of the cabinet. As Head of Government, Mussolini was accountable not to parliament for government policy but to the king, who alone could dismiss him. Since the Head of Government also decided what parliament could and could not discuss, the law effectively negated the principle of responsible parliamentary government and removed from parliament the right to initiate legislation. From January 1926 the Head of Government could issue laws by decree. Even though such decrees required eventual retrospective parliamentary ratification, executive and legislative powers were now practically combined in the same position and person.

A law of May 1928 formally reshaped parliament in a quasi-corporative direction. The Senate, whose members were appointed for life by the king, was unchanged. But the Chamber of Deputies was to be made up of 400 deputies, chosen by the Grand Council from 1000 candidates nominated by the national syndical confederations and other public bodies. The one list of candidates was simply approved *en bloc* by the voters in a form of plebiscitary election. This arrangement was another halfway house. It was far from genuine corporative representation, with parliament as a corporative lawmaking assembly of producers. The PNF and government controlled the syndical bodies making the nominations, and the Grand Council sifted the nominations. This was yet another demonstration that the real point of corporative reform was to extend state control over the organised economic forces of the country.

With Rocco's law of December 1928 the Grand Council became a legal organ of state. It was to deliberate on all major matters of government and party policy, and controlled the party's organisation and leadership. These simply formalised functions it had assumed as a *de facto* organ. It was also supposed to designate candidates to fill vacant ministerial posts and to succeed Mussolini as Head of Government and discuss the succession to the throne. This was a significant challenge to the authority and powers of the king as head of state. What had started as a party organ was now being given constitutional powers to ensure the permanence and continuity of Fascism beyond the lifetime of Mussolini.

The Grand Council's powers, however, remained potential rather than actual from the moment they became law. As Head of Government, Mussolini controlled the Council, its membership, when it met and what it discussed. In contrast with its often busy schedule between 1922 and 1929, Mussolini chose to call the Grand Council much less frequently during the 1930s. It was not even consulted on all major policy decisions, such as the Conciliation with the Catholic church and Italy's entry into the Second World War, which Mussolini took himself. The Council's designation of his successor, which conditioned the king's right to appoint the Head of Government, was never taken seriously. Mussolini refused to allow the consideration of alternatives to himself. By a 1929 amendment to the Grand Council law, Mussolini took from the Council and vested in himself as Head of Government the power to appoint the top PNF leaders and draft its statutes. The Grand Council's increasing marginalisation was a striking example of the way Fascism's own new constitutional order, the basis, after all, of Fascism lasting beyond Mussolini, could be subverted by the workings of a personal dictatorship.

The concentration of government powers in his own person was exemplified in the almost ludicrous accumulation of ministerial posts held by Mussolini from 1925 onwards, except for a temporary period of delegation between 1929 and 1932. In 1933 Mussolini was Head of Government and held seven of fourteen cabinet posts. Government came to resemble Mussolini in endless dialogue with himself. The outcome of personal government of this kind was hardly efficient administration of the country's affairs, since it divorced power from responsibility. The accumulation of offices fed the image of an omnipotent and omniscient *Duce*. But it left Mussolini with the nominal responsibility for running ministries over which he could hardly expect to exercise real control, if only because of all the other calls on his time and energy. Management passed to the Under-Secretaries. But they could not employ the full weight of ministerial authority nor feel they were able or required to act decisively while Mussolini was their titular head.

Unlike Hitler, Mussolini just could not delegate, because he was congenitally suspicious and contemptuous of his subordinates, and could not stand any leader of ability potentially overshadowing his own leadership qualities. In a curiously circular and self-defeating way, which undoubtedly inhibited the emergence of a corps of dynamic and competent leaders at the top of the regime, the demonstrable incapacity of his subordinates only served to confirm Mussolini's misanthropy and distrust of others. He knew about their incompetence and the corruption which often accompanied it, but tolerated them, since the knowledge confirmed his superiority as a leader and increased his subordinates' dependence on him, personally. Why else, but for future blackmailing purposes, did Mussolini keep in his personal secretariat files on Roberto Farinacci, the unreconstructed *ras* of Cremona, a copy of the wholly plagiarised dissertation for the law degree which allowed Farinacci to pursue a lucrative career as a lawyer?

The very different management styles of the two fascist dictators, which reflected very different uses of personal command and authority, go some way towards explaining the relative differences in regime performance. For in Fascist Italy, the result of this circular passing of the buck was probably that things did not get done. Italy's deficiencies in military planning and preparation during the lifetime of a regime committed to territorial expansion and war could in part be attributed to the in-built inefficiency of dictatorial government: Mussolini was head of all three armed service ministries from 1924 until 1929, and again from 1933 to 1943.

These various reforms amounted to a violation if not an absolute elimination of the Constitution of liberal Italy. Meaningful parliamentary government had given way to a centralised and unaccountable system of executive rule, vested in Mussolini and the state bureaucracies. Significantly, the personal will and power of Mussolini as dictator undermined the operation of Fascism's most characteristic constitutional innovation, the Grand Council, designed to ensure the continuity of Fascism.

But even these institutional changes represented a kind of balance between Fascism and the monarchy, respecting the king's support through inaction for Mussolini's government which went back to October 1922, and continued during and after the Matteotti crisis. There can be little doubt that Mussolini ruled Italy and made the major policy decisions. Although the king was a political cipher, he retained, just, the latent but decisive power to appoint and dismiss the Head of Government. The monarchy had not been abolished as a national institution and head of state. Mussolini had quite evidently calculated that it was too risky to eliminate the monarchy at a stroke. He had attempted through the constitutional changes to find a diminished place and role for the king within the Fascist system of government. This sort of institutional compromise with a force which was still too strong to confront definitively was used to consolidate and stabilise the dictatorship. It dovetailed, for instance, with the party's subordination to the state. Retention of the monarchy and its neutralisation by incorporation into the Fascist system widened the acceptance of the Fascist regime among important groups such as the armed forces and the state administration. They still looked to the monarchy as at least a symbol of national unity, tradition and state authority.

5. THE CONCILIATION WITH THE CATHOLIC CHURCH

Much the same strategy was applied to the 'co-ordination' of the Catholic church in the evolving Fascist system of rule. Formal and bilateral negotiations between the Vatican and the Fascist government for a church–state agreement began in August 1926. The timing was significant, as Fascism was in the process of erecting the 'totalitarian' state. The

Vatican needed to enter into a comprehensive and lasting relationship with the new state which would guarantee and preserve the church's position in society. This was exercised exclusively through Catholic Action's network of lay associations, now that the PPI and the CIL were on the point of extinction.

The specific cause for alarm was the government's establishment of the National Balilla Agency (ONB) in April 1926, a body initially dependent on the Interior Ministry and led by the *ras* of Carrara, Renato Ricci. Created to organise and indoctrinate children and adolescents in broadly the eight to seventeen age groups, it demonstrated how from a very early stage the Fascist government intended to monopolise the formation of young people and 'fascistise' them. This could only be achieved by squeezing out its rivals in the field. The Catholic Boy Scouts were dissolved by the prefects in early 1927 in small- and medium-sized communes, forcing the Vatican to close them all. The formation of other youth groups was banned, as was the provision of sporting and athletics activities by groups not affiliated to the ONB. By *force majeure*, the members of Catholic sports clubs drifted over to the Balilla organisations. A proposed general ban on all non-ONB youth organisations stalled the church–state talks for a while in 1928, and they only resumed on Mussolini's decision to exempt Catholic Action's youth clubs. The Vatican's need to ensure Catholic Action's survival against the depredations of the 'totalitarian' state was both the reason for breaking off negotiations with the government and for pushing them towards a definitive conclusion.

The Lateran agreements of February 1929 formally reconciled the church to the Italian state which it had condemned at the moment of national unification. A treaty involved the mutual recognition of the Italian nation-state and the Vatican city-state, while a financial settlement compensated the church for the loss of the papal states during unification. But the part of the package to which the Pope attached the greatest importance was the Concordat regulating church–state relations in the country. Mussolini made significant concessions in the Concordat which both recognised and legalised the church's special position in Italian society. Church marriage now had civil force; religious education taught by priests, already part of the curriculum in elementary schools under the 1923 Gentile law, was introduced into state secondary schools; and Catholic Action was allowed to exist, becoming the only non-Fascist organisation legally operating within the 'totalitarian' state.

The Vatican and Mussolini approached the agreement from different perspectives. Pope Pius XI hoped that the church's privileged position, recognised and buttressed by the Fascist state in the Concordat, would allow it to extend its influence throughout Italian life, a platform for the clerical reconquest of state and society. Mussolini's view was equally instrumentalist. He had always acknowledged the importance and strength of Catholicism as the religion of most Italians and as an organisation with a national network of social, economic and cultural bodies inspired by religious ideals. The church was so rooted in Italian life in a civil as well as religious capacity that it could not be challenged directly and immediately without endangering the government's stability and survival. Mussolini rejected both before and after the Concordat any party anti-clerical campaign: 'A holy war in Italy, never; the priests will never bring out the peasants against the state.'[9] The reverse was, of course, true. An agreement ending the church's official alienation from the state would reconcile Catholics to the regime which brought it about. It could help to harness the support of the church and Catholics denied to the liberal state, in both internal and foreign policy.

In this light, the Conciliation was probably the most important contribution to the consolidation of the Fascist government in power on a wider basis of support and consent. It brought Mussolini and Fascism enormous internal and international prestige. It temporarily killed off active Catholic anti-Fascism at home and abroad, because the church, through the pacts, was seen to be endorsing and legitimating the Fascist regime. The ex-PPI and CIL men who had passed to Catholic Action, an organisation closely controlled by the Vatican and bishops, 'could not conspire against a regime constantly backed by the blessings of the Church'.[10]

Catholics could now rally unreservedly to Fascism, and Catholic priests and organisers could be expected to involve themselves and their flocks in support of Fascism. This was demonstrated immediately in the plebiscitary elections of 1929. Bishops and clergy publicly urged Catholics to vote for the single government list of candidates, in the knowledge, of course, that the new parliament would have to ratify the Lateran agreements. But the explicit endorsement was repeated in the 1934 elections, and reflected a more general alignment of the church with many of the regime's economic and social policies. It was difficult to see how else Mussolini could have reached an agreement with the church. But the Conciliation traded the short-term broadening of support for the regime, for the longer-term risk of the 'totalitarian' state recognising an alternative and rival for the control and organisation of the country.

The Fascist dictatorship had been built by 1929 around the position of a single leader, Mussolini, and a highly centralised system of government. It was founded on the primacy of state authority, to which were subordinated both a purged and reconstructed single party and the syndicates. At this stage of its development, the Fascist state did reflect and formalise a series of compromises and a kind of power-sharing with institutions which had helped or tolerated Fascism's coming to power in 1922 and its retention of power during the Matteotti crisis. The dictatorship recognised and rested on important centres of power and influence, the monarchy, the armed forces, the state apparatus, *Confindustria* and the Catholic church. Mussolini had estimated that they were too strong to challenge head-on and simultaneously. It was best to co-opt and incorporate them as far as possible into the Fascist state, if only because this contributed to the regime's stabilisation.

6. THE REVALUATION OF THE LIRA

The construction of the 'totalitarian' state coincided with economic difficulties, which led to the Fascist government's first serious intervention in economic policy. The government's actions and the laws and decrees setting up the new state did not run in parallel, but intersected. From 1925 Fascist policies were being aligned with the kind of governmental system which was evolving.

Mussolini proclaimed in the parliamentary debate on Rocco's syndical bill in December 1925 that 'I consider the Italian nation to be in a permanent state of war... To live for me means struggle, risk, tenacity... not submitting to fate, not even to... our so-called deficiency in raw materials.' He said that the nation's 'permanent state of war' necessitated, as in the First World War, the end to labour conflict and a state conciliation apparatus through which 'we will achieve the greatest possible productive efficiency of the nation'.[11] This speech contained all the characteristic elements of Fascist rhetoric and style, applying the language of struggle and conflict to the resolution of the country's economic problems. It clearly echoed the 'battle for grain' which had been launched that summer, and the 'battle for the lira' soon to be engaged. The ethos of squadrism was being applied to economic policy. Objective economic weaknesses could be overcome by acts of political will which defied caution and rationality. The wartime model and analogy signified Fascism's 'totalitarian' aspirations: permanent war meant permanent mobilisation of the nation, internally disciplined by and around the regime in defence of the national interest.

The speech addressed a bill which would become a fundamental law of the regime, putting organised economic groups under state control to maximise the nation's economic strength. But it also connected the establishment of these permanent structures of state control to the solution of a long-term weakness of the national economy, which was being exposed during the current economic difficulties confronting the government. How the government interpreted these economic problems and how it tried to tackle them were the first real exercise in 'totalitarian' control.

The economic problems of 1925–26 were rising inflation and growing deficits in the balances of trade and payments. Partly due to a poor 1924 harvest, grain imports rose rapidly, along with those of industrial raw materials which manufacturers were accumulating to offset the effects of a simultaneous devaluation of the Italian currency. This was caused by the revaluation of the dollar and sterling, and continuing uncertainty over the payment of Italian war debts to Britain and the United States. The lira's devaluation contributed to general price inflation in 1925–26 and to stock market speculation which in turn accelerated the lira's decline in value.

The dramatic rise in grain imports at high international prices prompted the government's launching of the 'battle for grain'. The aim was to increase Italy's production of wheat and cereals to the point of self-sufficiency. The successive wheat tariffs of 1925, 1928 and 1929 were the traditional recourse to government protection of home producers. But the programme was given a Fascist intonation by the enormous propaganda campaign. Farmers and the public were mobilised behind the regime's self-proclaimed efforts to emancipate the country from the 'slavery of foreign bread'[12] and achieve national economic independence in the event of war. Italy produced enough grain to feed itself by the late 1930s. But the 'battle' was won at the cost of reversing the diversification into export cash crops. It protected the unproductive southern *latifundia* as much as it benefited the entrepreneurial farmers of the north and the centre.

The lira's eventual stabilisation was largely dictated by the deflationary demands of the US and British governments and financial markets, and Italian industry's concern to gain access to these sources of capital and investment. Some of the way was cleared by the Italian government's negotiation of war debt repayment settlements with the United States and Britain in late 1925 and early 1926. Linked to these settlements was the release of large US loans and investments, which went to Italian industry and to the Italian government to stabilise the currency. A stable lira was itself a stimulus and security to further profitable US investment in the Italian economy.

The Fascist government's monetary policies were being largely determined by Italy's subordinate place in the international economy dominated by Britain and above all the United States. But again, Mussolini transformed the Italian economy's adjustment to general deflationary trends into a Fascist 'battle' for the country's economic independence. Mussolini quite deliberately hitched the prestige of the regime to the fate of the lira. In a speech at Pesarò in August 1926, he launched the 'battle for the lira', which was to be revalued at the rate of 90 lire to the pound, the currency's level at the time of his coming to power in 1922.

Most industrialists were convinced of the need to revalue, but 'Quota 90' was probably higher than what they desired or expected. The dispute over the level of revaluation soon faded. The government compensated those large industries producing for the domestic market, introducing higher protective tariffs, placing orders and cutting wages. It also underwrote the bigger firms' takeover and merger of smaller businesses least able to sustain the lower profit margins of a deflationary policy.

Nevertheless 'Quota 90' was Mussolini's political decision, dictated in part by prestige rather than economic rationality. The 'battle' to real-ise the rate was achieved in late 1927. It was conceived as a national mobilisation for economic survival, in which the PNF, now being reorganised by Turati, and the newly legalised syndicates performed their first services as instruments of the Fascist state. The PNF took the lead in announcing as a matter of national necessity wage reductions in both agriculture and industry in 1927. These cuts were to align pay to the revalued lira, and should have been matched by an end to inflation and a lower cost of living. In fact, the fall in wages occurred more rapidly and steeply than the fall in prices, especially in agriculture and textiles, which meant that the costs of deflation were met by workers and consumers.

To ensure that the officially imposed wage cuts were implemented and that corresponding action was taken to lower prices and rents, Turati extended to all provinces the Party's Intersyndical Committees. An equivalent organisation at the national level was also established.

These had already sprung up on the initiative of some local PNF federations to oversee the stipulation of labour contracts and conciliate labour disputes, which were really matters for the Ministry of Corporations, in the wake of the syndical law. Presided by the provincial PNF secretary, or *federale*, these committees were liaison bodies bringing together the representatives of the provincial employer, traders and worker syndicates. As the regime's 'corporative' presence at the local level, with a labour relations role and now assuming responsibility for wages and prices control, they were potentially an important lever of the PNF's influence and interference in economic and social life.

It was difficult to say how effectively the committees carried out the task of carrying the regime's economic 'battle' to employers, traders and workers. In some areas, it made a difference that as *de facto* bodies their decisions were not legally enforceable, a let-out for employers unwilling to recognise their authority in labour disputes. With no statutory control over prices, they certainly found it hardgoing setting accurately and fairly the retail prices of essential foodstuffs, which usually found their own market level. As with the whole campaign, the committees, whose pricing functions lapsed in 1928, were more effective in enforcing cuts in wages than in prices. The committees remained in existence, however, as instruments of PNF political control of the syndicates and their cadres. They assumed a near-permanent role in the arbitration of labour disputes, almost to the point of replacing the syndicates altogether.

The revaluation campaign was important both for its effects on the economy's general orientation under Fascism and for the way it was staged. A revalued currency made trading more difficult for Italy's agricultural and industrial exporters. Together with the government's protective measures against cheaper imports, it generally favoured those large concerns in the chemicals, engineering, iron and steel and agribusiness sectors producing mainly for the home market. It also encouraged import substitution, of which the 'battle for grain' was the clearest example. Only with the Great Depression from 1929 did the Italian economy, like others, become progressively isolated from international trade and finance. But there was an increasingly autarchic feel to the shape of the economy because of revaluation. This was consistent with the government's projection of its economic battles as the struggles of a nation unified around the regime and mobilised into action by the PNF, to revive the country's economic strength and independence against foreign 'domination'.

7. 'RURALISM' AND POPULATION POLICY

The 'battle for grain' anticipated and became part of the Fascist government's more general campaign to 'ruralise' Italy. Self-sufficiency in cereals was meant to ensure that the country had enough food in the event of war. On the same lines, Fascist 'ruralism' was connected to population concerns and from there to Fascism's longer-term aspirations to create an empire for Italy.

Both 'ruralism' and the demographic 'battle' were announced officially in Mussolini's keynote 'Ascension Day' address to the Chamber of Deputies in May 1927. Mussolini gave a universal and global resonance to these concerns in an equally important 1928 article in his newspaper *Il Popolo d'Italia*, entitled 'Strength in Numbers', where he prophesied the swamping of the white races by the yellow and black races and the decline of 'Western civilisation' unless they addressed what he later called 'the problem of problems',[13] falling birth rates. Demographic stagnation was recognised as a major issue in all European countries from the early twentieth century. But in the inter-war period, only Fascist Italy and Nazi Germany and, of the democratic countries, Sweden, made it central to overall government policy and attempted to deal with it in a comprehensive way. Only the two fascist powers linked the issue so emphatically to questions of future national power and aggrandisement, and to a crisis of 'civilisation'.

So in these two important statements in 1927–28, Mussolini asserted that what determined the political, economic and moral strength of the nation was the size and growth of its population. Numbers, quite literally, meant power. A growing population was both the reason for and means of achieving imperialist expansion. Settlement colonies were an outlet for surplus population, and a large army was needed to conquer them. This was a self-justifying, circular and anachronistic argument for empire, and a lopsided view of what constituted power to wage modern wars. But Mussolini took his own formulations seriously and made them the basis of policy.

The reason Mussolini gave for a declining birth rate in Italy and elsewhere was industrial urbanisation. It was in the cities that he thought changing work patterns, including high levels of female employment, and changing life styles and expectations in the materialistic and consumerist culture of urban life induced couples to control their fertility and choose to have fewer children. The city was marked with the negative moral valuation of a corrupting hedonism. In Mussolini's formulation, the urban way of life unmanned Fascist Italy, both literally and in terms of the virile, war-minded culture Fascism wanted to create. So, to be populous and hence powerful, Italy had to protect and promote agriculture and its fecund peasantry, turning out the peasant soldiers who would win and colonise the empire. The hackneyed exaltation of the superior values and virtues of rural life clearly mirrored Fascism's own large social base among the small farmers of northern and central Italy and its suspicion of the industrial proletariat. Mussolini admitted in his speech that workers were 'still distant, and if not opposed as they once were, absent'.[14]

These concerns lay behind a whole swathe of co-ordinated, or at least connected, government policies in the late 1920s, which continued and developed in the years to come. It is important to grasp that the regime's demographic concerns, a consistent feature of its policies from the late 1920s onwards, were the line which drew together its expansionist and imperialist goals, its 'ruralist' agricultural policies, its social welfare initiatives, and its policy towards the family and women. They also gave an impetus to the extension of the newly declared 'totalitarian' state, which now claimed the right to control and shape according to Fascist imperatives the private sexual, reproductive and family lives of ordinary Italians.

The regime's projected solutions to 'the problem of problems' were a mix of legal and police coercion and repression, welfarism, negative and positive pronatalism, and agricultural improvement. Various pronatalist measures favoured early marriage and large families. From 1928, employed married men enjoyed tax breaks on procreating seven surviving and dependent children if they were state employees, ten children if they were not. These benchmarks for large families were so high that any tax concessions could hardly have compensated for the additional costs of bringing up that many children. From 1929, appointment to and promotion in state jobs went preferentially to married men with young families, part of a drive which became general with the impact of the Depression to remove women from the paid labour force. A notorious and lucrative tax on bachelors, first levied in 1927, funded provision for the improved healthcare of mothers and infant children through the *Opera Nazionale di Maternità ed Infanzia* (ONMI, the National Agency for Mothers and Children), set up in 1925 to look after illegitimate and abandoned children and becoming the regime's agency to promote and monitor proper pre- and post-natal care for mothers and their children.

Abortion was made illegal, punishable by imprisonment and significantly redesignated as a crime against the state, along with the dissemination of contraceptive aids and information, a ban unlikely to hit the target when the usual method of birth control was *coitus interruptus*.

An 'empty the cities' campaign launched by Mussolini in the autumn of 1928 was backed up by the prefects and police being given powers to prevent temporary and permanent migration to towns and cities. Such repressive measures were accompanied by concrete action to make rural life more attractive and agriculture more productive. It involved a shift in public spending to the agricultural sector to fund a vast programme of *bonifica integrale* or comprehensive land reclamation and improvement, established in the law of 1928. The scheme was designed to provide public works employment in infrastructural improvements and extend the land area under cultivation to be settled and worked by new small farmers.

The key to the success of the regime's 'battle for births' was women, or rather, the extent to which women could be coerced or induced to limit their lives to the reproduction and rearing of future soldiers for the nation. There was a real sense that Fascism's demographic anxieties allowed Mussolini and the male leadership of Fascism to translate into official policy their misogyny and stereotypical assumptions of women's 'natural' gender role as wives and mothers, passively inferior and subordinate to men in both the home and the state. For Mussolini, having children was to women's nature what making war was to man's nature.

'Ruralism' was clearly tied to the conquest of empire, and to that future period of 1935–40 which Mussolini had identified in the Ascension Day speech as when 'we will make our voice heard and see our rights finally recognised'. The campaign was also a response to the impact of the lira's revaluation on the economy. The anti-urban police measures came just at the point when another rural exodus was threatened, as deflation affected the agricultural sector far more severely than the government expected or wished. Keeping people on the land or, rather, keeping the unemployed in the countryside and not in the cities made the growing social problem of unemployment less visible and more easily policed.

Historians have often been rather puzzled by the 'ruralism' campaign. Some regard it as a gigantic bluff or sleight of hand. It has been described as the way Fascism disguised the onset of serious economic problems in agriculture, 'ideological compensation for crisis'.[15] It was supposedly how the regime deliberately masked the transition Italy made during Fascism to a mainly, if not predominantly, industrial and urban economy, and its subordination to the interests of industrial and financial capitalism. For once, it seems that the policy of 'ruralism', and the demographic policies of which it was a component part, are best understood by separating the reasons behind it from its actual effects.

The measures to restrain urban growth, increase the population and stimulate an agricultural sector of small peasants were certainly largely unsuccessful, on all counts. Literally too much was being asked and expected of demographic policies, which proved unable to stem, let alone reverse, long-term trends of a declining birthrate and the shift to urban and industrial habitation and employment. In fact, the regime's own policies in other areas moved on the trends behind fertility decline and urban-led economic development.

Women had long been workers in both the agricultural and the industrial sectors of the economy. The impact of the Depression and a more general compression of working-class living standards and incomes characteristic of Fascism's economic policies as a whole were bound to lead workers to limit their families to what they could afford, and to rely on women, whether they had children or not, working to sustain the family's earnings. The regime's own efforts to increase autarkic and war production from the mid-1930s brought women back into the industrial labour force, a trend accelerated during the war, when women replaced conscripted men on the farm and in the factory. One has to say that in face of these economic realities for the family, women were not prepared to change their behaviour nor restrict their activities according to the propagandised model of the rural-living, fertile, compliant child bearer and household manager.

Again, the rural economy became less 'rural' under Fascism. It was increasingly penetrated by industry and finance, in the shape of the near-monopolistic chemical and machinery firms supplying fertilisers and tractors under the regime's own 'battle for grain' and *bonifica integrale* programmes.

'Quota 90' certainly improved the purchasing power of the relatively fixed incomes of large parts of Fascism's urban middle-class constituency among public officials, professional men and property owners. Revaluation ended a ten-year cycle of inflation starting during the war, which they associated with the erosion of their own living standards and the material and political advances of the working classes. But currency stabilisation also devastated many of Fascism's own rural supporters, especially those newly established peasant proprietors and tenants who found their debts being revalued upwards at a time of falling land and agricultural prices. The regime showed a clear propagandistic preference for agricultural sharecropping during the 'ruralisation' campaign. *Mezzadria* purported to embody a kind of social solidarity between peasant and owner, and necessitated large and stable family units to work the land under such contracts. But the spread of sharecropping was not only a result of upgrading landless labourers, and hence cutting the ground from under rural socialism. It was also the outcome of proprietors and tenants moving downwards to farm under far more onerous and exploitative forms of sharecropping.

Bonifica integrale, especially in the south and the islands, often went no further than the infrastructural improvements at public expense. The 'partners' in *bonifica*, the landowners, refused to make and pay for land improvements, and the government lacked the political will to expropriate them and disrupt the alliance that had eased the Fascist 'conquest' of the south. This situation not only reduced the amount of newly cultivable land available for prospective farmers, but those that did make it were also saddled with the financing and undertaking of such improvements themselves in burdensome tenancy contracts.

Even as demographic policy, *bonifica integrale* demonstrably did not work, and probably could not work. The new farmers of reclaimed land were meant to be carefully selected for their hardworking and childbearing qualities, a demonstration that on the high profile projects like the *Agro Pontino* near Rome, the intention was to 'colonise' more than the land. The settler families came not so much from the south, as might be expected, as from the landless labourers of the high population density, high birth rate and high social discontent Po Valley provinces of Venetia in the Northeast. In all, perhaps 80 000 people were transferred from overcrowded rural areas to the new lands during the 1930s, about 30 000 of them settling on the *Agro Pontino*. But this figure, however much it was deemed to show a more fertile agriculture in all senses, was nowhere near the tens of thousands of the natural population increase in the original overpopulated areas and of the spontaneous countryside to town migration which continued each year, unchecked by police measures.

If the effects of these policies were inconsistent with their aims, one has to admit that the government's agricultural policies often also had contradictory goals. It was difficult to see how the countryside could be repopulated and agriculture made more productive – the intention of both the 'battle for grain' and *bonifica* projects – when wheat was best cultivated extensively and in a labour-intensive way. It was no surprise that the farmers who made the real killing in the 'battle for grain' were the large-scale commercial farmers of the Po Valley. They increasingly employed machines rather than men, in switching from cash crops whose prices were falling to the safety of the protected grain market. So it appears unlikely that 'ruralism' did or could have had the anticipated impact on Italian agriculture. Nevertheless it remained one of the abiding themes of fascist propaganda and policy, and had its logic in Fascism's wider concern to shape a nation which would be populous and independent enough economically to found and rule an empire.

Part II
The Fascist Regime, 1929–36

4 The Years of the Great Depression, 1929–34

1. THE PARTY AND THE *INQUADRAMENTO* OF THE NATION

It is tempting to say that Fascism did not evolve beyond the point in 1929 when the construction of a repressive dictatorship was largely completed, based on centralised and extended state power administered by the existing state apparatus. Certainly, one of its major rationales both as a middle-class mass movement and in power was the permanent destruction of working-class organisations and the post-war threat of a significant advance in the political and social position of workers. This was the lowest common denominator of the compromise or alliance of Fascism with the institutions and forces of the existing order. The advantages to that order of the Fascist state's disciplining and control of labour were apparent in the way the government had handled the revaluation crisis. But the development of the Fascist regime during the period of the Depression indicated that Fascism was something more than a repressive conservative dictatorship.

Coercion alone was insufficient as a means of control. It was inadequate to keep the lid on a society marked by deep social, economic and political divisions and where both industrial and agricultural workers were used to being represented by their own independent organisations. The regime needed a base of 'consent' broader than its middle-class constituency if it was to survive, be stable and, most importantly, perpetuate itself. Yet the Fascist state was founded on the denial and repression of the free articulation and satisfaction of social and political demands. No political parties were allowed other than the PNF, no unions other than the syndicates. In this context, 'consent' had to be 'manufactured' through the development and extension of the regime's own organisations and structures, particularly the party and its auxiliary agencies. Already under Turati the PNF was becoming a 'mass' party with an organisational network beginning to reach into the localities and involve large numbers of people in a wide range of activities sponsored and controlled by the regime. This incipient process of 'fascistisation' was called *l'inquadramento*, meaning something between organisation and regimentation, with the sense of framing, enclosing and integrating.

Allied to the 'totalitarian' imperative of attempting to create 'consent' in an unfree situation, there was a more immediate and contingent incentive behind Mussolini's injunction to the party to 'go resolutely to the people'.[1] *L'inquadramento* was a response to the actual and potential popular distress and discontent arising from the effects of the revaluation crisis, and then the Depression from 1929. The basic aims of *l'inquadramento* were combined to varying degrees of emphasis and intensity in all of the regime's organisations, which expanded greatly from the late 1920s. They were to erect a more efficient organisational apparatus for exercising control and surveillance over the population; to generate a wider basis of 'consent' for the regime; and to mobilise and identify the population with the regime's policies and goals. The organisations responsible for the attempted 'fascistisation' of Italian society were at least potentially and in intention a way of giving independence and permanent life to Fascism. They were the models and agencies of a new social and moral order which might eventually supersede the compromises and bargains struck with non-Fascist institutions. They were the basis on which Fascism could reproduce itself, and arguably made the PNF the most important organ of the Fascist state in the 1930s.

The party had been geared up for its tasks in the Fascist state under Turati. But the outcome of his reorganisation might well have hampered its performance. It would be difficult to activate a party that was subject to centralised discipline and control, where internal debate and self-government had been stifled. The PNF had also lost some of its earliest and most combative members, and its leaders, appointed from above, could be treated as itinerant public officials. Giovanni Giuriati, like Turati, whom he succeeded as Party Secretary in 1930, retained the idea of an élite party, maintaining the official closure of party ranks which restricted entry to graduates of the Fascist youth organisations.

But Achille Starace's Secretaryship, from December 1931 until October 1939, inaugurated the mass party, removing the boundaries between the party and the nation. The reopening of the party to new members deliberately coincided with the public celebrations of the tenth anniversary of the 'March on Rome', and the sense of the regime's triumphant consolidation they were meant to convey. Enlargement of the PNF would formalise the identity of Fascism with the nation and its general acceptance by the nation. Membership leapt from about one million in 1932 (2.4 per cent of the national population) to over 1 800 000 in 1934, and after another pre-war influx of members in 1936, reached 2 600 000 (6 per cent) by 1939. Decrees of 1932–23 made PNF membership indispensable to gain employment in local and central government, eroding the voluntary character of membership.

It was perhaps hard to see how a party weighed down by such numbers could be active and dynamic, especially when many members were not committed volunteers but conscripted by the requirements of their job. But the party's bureaucratisation and consequent devitalisation can easily be assumed or overemphasised. Making the party bigger facilitated the 'totalitarian' control of more of the population. Greater demands could be made of someone who was inside rather than outside the party. This was recognised by the Pope in his famous encyclical, *Non Abbiamo Bisogno*, at the height of church–state conflict in 1931. He allowed a kind of mental fingers-crossing when it was difficult to reconcile being both a Catholic and a party member. Party leadership at all levels remained the preserve of 'first hour' Fascists or those who had entered the party through the youth organisations.

Some of this inner core of activist leaders were clearly capable of maintaining and enhancing a vigorous and influential party presence which owed something to past squadrist traditions. They often did so, as in Florence and Bologna, by associating the party with the revival of the local economy and the development of a strong sense of municipal pride and public achievement in culture and sport. Some provincial PNFs intervened extensively in local economic life through the intersyndical committees, settling labour contracts and intervening in labour disputes, and assuming responsibility for the control of consumer goods prices, in the 1930s. In doing so, the party committees practically supplanted the state's provincial corporative organs which were meant to work in these areas. Under Starace particularly, who had a simplistic 'totalitarian' vision of the party covering every square yard and every person in the country, the PNF was constantly widening and deepening the scope of its activity and competence in society. Where the party went and who it organised in its empire of dependent and auxiliary bodies were more important than the affairs of the party proper.

So, the party expanded its functions from the late 1920s and through the 1930s in the attempt to undertake its role in the Fascist state, to 'fascistise' Italian life and society. Duplication of activity with state bodies was inevitable. Although state authority and state organs were officially meant to prevail throughout the Fascist regime, in practice Starace's predatory and expansion-minded PNF contested and questioned the actions of state authorities. The persistence of an informal but real party–state dualism in the 1930s suggests that the Italian Fascist regime was closer to the Nazi German model of 'totalitarianism' than most of us have thought.

2.   THE ORGANISATION OF THE YOUNG, WELFARE AND FREE TIME

The regime's efforts to control the formation of the nation's children and young people became more intensive and focused from 1929, in part to mitigate or minimise the effects of the Concordat's concessions to the church. Indeed, in his speech to parliament on the ratification of the Lateran agreements, Mussolini quite brutally emphasised the Fascist and 'totalitarian' nature of the state, and its exclusive right to mould the mind and character of the young through an 'education for war'.[2] This crudely formative view of the educational process under Fascism was carried over into the Ministry of Public Instruction's change of title to Ministry of National Education in September 1929. The ONB became a branch of this Ministry, with Ricci as the Under-Secretary for youth and physical education.

   The ONB provided pre-military physical training in the form of drilling, gym and callisthenic exercises, and crucially, sports activities. It intended its work to be integrated into the school curriculum and time-table. School teachers, especially physical education staff, were expected to become local ONB organisers and instructors. The fusion of school and ONB was actual and complete in the thousands of small rural schools run directly by the agency between 1928 and 1935. The ONB's direct connection to the school system facilitated recruitment and access to equipment and premises, membership always being heaviest among children up to the age of twelve, the statutory school leaving age until it was theoretically extended to fourteen under the 1923 educational law. It also accelerated the 'fascistisation' of the personnel and pedagogy of the elementary schools in particular. An oath of loyalty was required of elementary and secondary school teachers from February 1929. As public employees they were subject to the later decrees on obligatory PNF membership to join the profession. The first Fascist textbooks for obligatory use in all schools, public and private, were ready for introduction in the 1930 scholastic year. They and their successors were designed to impart an education which was nationalistic and militaristic in tone and content.

The PNF itself only retained direct control of the university students associations (GUF) on the formation of the ONB in 1926. It always resented the ONB's special status and argued in a long series of jurisdictional disputes with the ONB that only a party organ as opposed to a state body was suitable to inculcate the Fascist spirit and mentality in the young. Were Fascist youth to be left to a 'lazy bourgeois bureaucracy, which after thirteen years of the regime, remained more or less what it was?' complained Starace to Mussolini in 1935.[3] Under the irascible *ras* of Lucca and party Vice-Secretary, Carlo Scorza, the PNF founded the Young Fascists' organisation in October 1930. It was deliberately aimed at plugging a real gap in the joint ONB and PNF regimentation of young men. These were the eighteen to twenty-one year olds already at work or attending trade or vocational schools but who had not gone on to higher education, the same age range but a different social class to most university students. These young peasants and workers were to be a new source of PNF members and lower level cadres. Their premilitary training came from the Militia and their political education in special courses of political preparation. Their often unruly behaviour and aggressive demeanour, vented to the full in the attacks on Catholic youth clubs in 1931, were the nearest the party got to recreating the bravado of the squads.

But it was clearly among university students that the regime expected the next generation of Fascist leaders to emerge. Here, it was grudgingly recognised that the formation and selection of the new Fascist élite required some attempt to engage them intellectually and politically. A certain latitude to debate and criticise without it was hoped, breaking the bounds of Fascist orthodoxy, was allowed in student circles if denied elsewhere in society. Held annually between 1934 and 1940, the *Littoriali* or student games were a good example of the atmosphere of repressive tolerance in which the regime raised its prospective ruling class. Attending something between a student conference and academic talent show, students competed for the title of 'lictor' in a wide range of examinations for the creative arts and discourses on various themes of Fascist doctrine and practice. Prize-winners and participants could expect to be earmarked for jobs in the burgeoning bureaucracies of the party, syndicates and corporations.

The Young Fascists' motto, 'Believe, Obey, Fight', gave a sense of the kind of 'new Fascist man' the regime hoped to forge in the controlled environment of the educational system and the youth organisations. Essentially, the Fascists wanted to create an Italy made in their own image, a nation of ready-made warriors, physically fit, mentally agile, disciplined, courageous and obedient, committed believers and fighters in the cause of the nation. To achieve this, Fascist propaganda and indoctrination projected a series of images and models of the kind of conduct and behaviour for the 'new' Italian to emulate. To diffuse a culture of warlike and patriotic endeavour, the regime could draw on and propagate the virtues of some of Fascism's own heroic figures, the First World War combatant, the squadrist and, of course, Mussolini himself. The slogan 'Mussolini is always right' was first coined and employed by the party under Turati. He used the idealisation of a single, undisputed and infallible leader to cover the imposition of a centralised order and discipline on the party itself in the late 1920s. Under Starace, the cult of the *Duce*, the charismatic, omnipotent figure shaping the nation's destiny, assumed ludicrous proportions in the 1930s.

But increasingly the prevailing myth on which Fascist propaganda focused was that of ancient Rome, which identified Fascism as the recreation of a glorious and exalted past, and also justified imperialist expansion. The setting of Fascist Italy to the image of imperial Rome allowed the regime to convey and legitimise its desire to make Italy great and powerful, through the foundation of a new empire and as the carrier of a new 'civilisation'. It combined the will to found an empire with the 'making of Italians': the aim was to mould a nation of citizen-soldiers which would be fit to conquer and rule an empire. It was easy to get carried away with all this, and Fascist pretensions now appear hollow and unrealisable. But it is important to recognise that when Fascists talked of 'revolution', they usually meant a 'spiritual' revolution, not so much a transformation of socio-economic reality as its sublimation in a changed national consciousness. The idea was to reshape attitudes, mentality and perceptions, to change the way people thought and behaved. Even what would become during the Depression Fascism's claim to universality, a new social and economic order in corporativism, was given an ethical as much as a 'productivist' dimension. The corporations supposedly brought all kinds of producers together in a collaborative system of production. They were the practical training ground where through the experience of organised co-operation, employers and workers would exchange a class and sectional outlook for a national awareness. This was why the PNF, as the guardian and apostle of national values and the national interest, was always represented on each corporative council. Changing Italy then involved changing the character of Italians in a controlled educative process; hence the priority which the regime gave in the 1930s to propaganda and organisation.

One of the most important aspects of the 'going...to the people' campaign during the Depression was the party's organisation of welfare. By late 1931 the party's welfare agencies (EOAs) had added to their operation of summer health camps for young children, the running of a winter relief programme coinciding with the worst months of seasonal unemployment. This lasted until the dissolution of the EOAs in 1937, when responsibility for winter welfare passed back to the local authorities and the summer camps went to the PNF's new unified youth organisation. There was, of course, nothing exceptional about a government providing emergency aid to alleviate the distress of those suffering most from the effects of a deep and prolonged economic crisis. For one thing, welfare was a way of trying to head off the likely repercussions for public order of widespread economic distress. But the party's involvement gave a Fascist imprint to the provision of welfare, and a further impetus to 'totalitarian' organisation which lasted beyond the actual period of the Depression. Party-run welfare was regarded as an act of 'civil mobilization' and 'a most effective means of propaganda and penetration of the people'.[4] In the rhetoric if perhaps not the reality of Fascist welfare, it was a demonstration of class collaboration and national solidarity, because the party was collecting contributions from all who were able to give and distributing aid to all who were in need. Such was the Fascist moral community in the making, the outcome of the growing connection between people and regime through the medium of the party. This certainly strained the moral significance of the way the party actually collected the funds for winter relief. Much EOA funding came from a kind of party levy on the syndical bodies of employers and workers and the Fascist associations of schoolteachers, railwaymen and other public employees, and similar subscriptions extracted by party pressure on local banks and credit institutions. So workers would find that their syndicates had agreed to them donating a certain proportion of their wage to the EOA. In the spirit of class emulation, employers in the same economic or professional category contributed at least the same amount.

Perhaps more important was the way welfare provision could be used to 'penetrate' areas of the country and parts of the population which might otherwise be untouched by the regime or anyway unresponsive to more overtly political contact. The provincial EOAs were umbrella organisations for various private and public bodies working in the welfare field, through which the party monopolised the collection and distribution of relief funds for the unemployed and their families. The centralised collection of funds and pooling of resources was matched by the decentralisation of welfare distribution to the area groups into which the *fasci* of towns and cities were territorially subdivided. Welfare was synchronised with the spread of the party's 'capillary' structure. From the early 1930s, the area groups were encouraged to establish 'sectors', in turn subdivided into 'nuclei', corresponding to groups of streets or individual streets. Each sector or nucleus was to have a party social-worker, who made home visits to assess and report on need in her patch.

Winter welfare became one of the regime's largest organisations. The Padua Party, for instance, was providing regular welfare for about 19 000 families, affecting 80 000 people in city and province, the equivalent of about 1 in 20 of the total provincial population, in March 1935. Starace's official global figures were that nearly 1 750 000 families or almost three million individuals received daily welfare in the 1934–35 winter.

The party organisation of welfare stimulated the development of the women's *fasci*. Significantly again, the party's drive to create a female section alongside each male *fascio* started with the onset of the 'going...to the people' campaign launched in 1931. The regime's demographic concerns and policies relegated women to the role of child bearing and raising and home management. The involvement of women's *fasci* in various forms of voluntary and welfare work was the natural organisational extension of this child-caring slot for middle-class women with time and energy to spare. From them came the neighbourhood social workers, the women who prepared and distributed the clothing and cooked meals for winter relief, who helped out at the summer camps, the 'fascist Epiphany' and other 'fascistised' popular festivals. Welfare organisation during the Depression quite literally gave the party access to the backwaters of town and countryside. By providing the moral and material benefits of welfare, the party was extending the regime's network of control and surveillance of the population.

Along with welfare, the regime's efforts to provide for people's free time through its national afterwork agency, the OND or *Dopolavoro*, was characteristic of the 'mass' organising of the Depression years. The OND matched welfare in the large numbers of people it reached and involved including groups hostile and indifferent to, or simply ignorant of Fascism, and in what followed from this, the apolitical nature and appeal of its activities. The OND was originally set up in May 1925 as a state agency responsible to the Ministry of National Economy, with the job of unifying and running the workers recreational clubs established by the Fascist syndicates and taken over from the Socialists. The OND became a party auxiliary in 1927. Thereafter its national president was the PNF Secretary, the provincial counterparts were the *federali* and its local administration was staffed by party cadres. Turati's takeover of the OND was part of the PNF's mobilisation for the 'battle for the lira', offering social welfare and rest and recreation facilities for blue- and white-collar workers in a difficult economic situation. Already the largest adult organisation by 1931, with 1.75 million members, it moved beyond the initial phase of affiliating and 'fascistising' existing Socialist and democratic working-men's clubs to build up a new network of sections during the Depression. By 1939 the OND had about 3.8 million members. It retained the character and function of its PNF relaunching during the revaluation crisis, providing some compensation in the form of facilities and services for the low pay and living standards which prevented many workers from becoming serious consumers. The OND's cumulative impact was probably to alleviate and divert some of the social distress and discontent arising during the Depression years.

The regime's organising drive crossed with and reinforced employer paternalism and 'scientific' management practice which saw a healthy and rested worker as a more productive one. Industrial employers also encouraged the OND in order to isolate and marginalise the Fascist syndicates among their workforce, since however toothless, they remained class-based organisations defending workers' interests. Most of the OND's industrial workers' membership and a good part of its white-collar members belonged to occupational sections organised around the factory, firm and branch of the state administration. The territorial sections at the level of the communes were meant to catch the families and the whole population of the area. The typical OND section had a library, a radio, a sports and recreation ground and a clubhouse in which to socialise. It organised sporting activities and local festivals of a folklorist character, and arranged showings of films and performances of the OND-sponsored travelling theatres. It offered to its members rail and other consumer discounts, welfare and social insurance benefits and, probably the most patronised activity, subsidised trips and excursions, a kind of low-level, low-cost tourism. The OND was introducing and spreading forms of popular mass leisure and recreation, which in other countries were occurring more spontaneously as part of the stirrings of a 'consumer society', rather than under the auspices of a 'totalitarian' state.

The OND clearly also played a part in persuading the regime of the utility of modern means of mass communication: the cinema and, especially, radio. These were increasingly incorporated into a more refined propaganda apparatus as the 1930s went on. Organisationally, this was reflected in the constant upgrading of the government bodies made responsible for the control and manipulation of opinion. The Press Office of the Council of Ministers, primarily concerned with the meticulous daily control of journalists and newspapers, was enlarged in 1934 into a sub-ministry for Press and Propaganda. This assumed overall control also of radio, cinema, theatre and tourism. On its elevation in 1935 into a full Ministry, there began a concerted attempt to shape popular culture through the controlled use of mass communication media.

Cinema-going certainly increased, partly because it was facilitated by the regime's own organisations like the OND. There were a few historical and contemporary film dramas conveying something of the Fascist message and style. But the fare was mainly diversionary entertainment provided by both American and Italian-made films. What official propaganda there was, came in the obligatory showing in all cinemas of the weekly documentary or newsreel produced by the government-controlled film agency, LUCE. Their output obviously dramatised the regime's major achievements and policies, placing some emphasis on rural and imperial campaigns and themes.

Rural life was also the focus for radio transmission, which from the start was controlled by a government-run public agency. Radio was clearly a more flexible way than a relatively low circulation press to convey the regime's presence and message to rural populations traditionally indifferent to government and its agencies and isolated by illiteracy and distance. Radio quite literally spanned these social and geographical distances, and was capable of delivering a single, uniform message to many different places simultaneously. The poverty of the Italian domestic market for consumer goods, accentuated by the regime's own economic policies compressing wages and purchasing power, constantly inhibited the diffusion of radio. This was to an extent offset by the government providing what the individual often could not. A special rural radio agency (ERR) was set up in 1933, and significantly was presided by the PNF Secretary, Starace, from late 1934, reflecting the party's drive to control all the channels of contact between regime and people. Besides operating as a programme network for specifically rural audiences, the ERR distributed sets to elementary schools and other outposts of the regime in the countryside, like the communal OND. These sets had to service the whole community: collective listening in public places and premises was another improvised response to the problems of access.

3. THE ORGANISATION OF CULTURE

The study of 'culture' under the Fascist regime, or rather, perhaps, the study of Fascism as 'culture', has dominated the recent historiography of Fascism, for better and for worse. 'Culture' probably provides one of the keys to understanding what Fascism, or what some cultural historians annoyingly call the 'Fascist project', was actually about. Nationalism, and the attempt to realise its core nationalist 'myth', involved Fascism in efforts to 'make' Italians, and Italians as Fascists, out of what it saw as the refractory selfish, individualistic and aimless human material it inherited from the liberal era. If Fascism's goal was the creation of a morally and spiritually regenerated national community collectively assembled and unified around the *Duce*, then the goal was expressed in and through 'culture'. The point of organising people in the regime's monopolistic organisations, and the regime did practically nothing else internally except organising in the 1930s, was to transform and reshape their consciousness. 'Cultural revolution' conveys exactly what Fascism tried to achieve.

Fascists, then, adopted a very broad and 'totalitarian' definition of 'culture'. Understood by them as a set of values, a conception and way of life, 'culture' was to inform and permeate all areas of the Italians' existence. In what came nearest to the official statement on Fascism, Mussolini's and Gentile's co-authored *Doctrine of Fascism* in 1932, the Fascist 'totalitarian' state was described as the 'ethical' state, precisely to indicate that its function was to impart Fascism's values to the people, and so 'deliver' the people to the service of the state. 'Culture' incorporated not only 'art', in its various conventionally understood forms of painting, sculpture, writing, music, and not only the more low-brow consumerism of popular leisure and recreation activities. It also involved what the army of cultural historians, anthropologists and psychologists home in on as Fascist 'culture', the regime's use of public space to convey its 'nationalising' message through staged ceremonies, spectacles, marches and parades. Taken in its totality, 'culture' took in all the areas where the regime could expect to 'fascistise' the Italians and affect their conduct and behaviour, from the educational system to the PNF's ever-proliferating sectoral organisations, to the corporations. Demographic policy, which ran as the connecting line of the regime's social and economic policies from the late 1920s, was also 'cultural' policy, since it expected and required for its success women to return exclusively to the way of life of wife and mother.

Fascism's cultural policies in the area of 'art' were launched following Mussolini's decision to set up the first ever 'totalitarian' state in 1925–26. One important aspect of them was the attempt to realise a new role for artists and intellectuals in the Fascist state. It was no longer to be a matter of 'art for art's sake', of elitist ivory tower intellectualism, but of artists serving the state and of art becoming one of the ways which connected the wider society to the state. Being, or becoming, what one of the official voices on Fascist culture, Gentile, called 'political peda-gogues',[5] meant that artists were seen to play a crucial part in realising Fascism's national myth, in forming the 'new Fascist man'.

Much flowed from this recasting of the artist's position in society from the detached, autonomous, freely creative and, by Fascist definition, selfish and egotistical individual to the socially and politically engaged educator of the nation. Predictably enough, the regime progressively extended its centralised bureaucratic control and regulation of cultural producers and cultural production. This process ranged from the take over of private and municipal cultural bodies as National Institutes of Fascist Culture (*Istituti Nazionali di Cultura Fascista, INCF*) to the organisation of artists and intellectuals in sectoral and confederal corporative bodies, and from the creation of a specific public body to regulate the radio airwaves, the Italian Radio Agency (*Ente Italiano Audizioni Radiofoniche, EIAR*), to the evolution of a full-fledged Ministry of Popular Culture.

A corollary of the perception of the artist as educator was that art should cease to be something created by élites for élites, and become popular and accessible. The Fascist regime deliberately sought to break down the barriers between 'high' and 'low' culture and bring a broader public to 'art', partly by encouraging more and more people to 'consume' art through the promotion of the forms of the new mass culture, radio and especially cinema. A concrete sign of this popularis-ation of culture was the way, over time, under the aegis of one of the regime's most enduring cultural bureaucrats, the ex-Nationalist Antonio Maraini, head of the Fascist syndicate of artists, the Venice bi-annual (*Biennale*) exhibition of art was transformed from a privately and municip-ally-run elitist high cultural and social fine arts event to a state-run national multi-media showcase of official culture, incorporating both high and mass culture forms.

Making art popular and accessible carried a real danger for a regime which wanted to determine what people consumed as 'culture'. It involved giving space to, or using another of the post-modern culturalists' pet terms, 'negotiating', with that other 'totalitarian' god of modern life, the market, a commercial consumer culture which was expanding everywhere in the 'developed' world, even in Fascist Italy. If art was to reach the masses, then it meant accepting art as diversion and entertain-ment, to an extent allowing a commercial market to operate as markets do, both creating and feeding popular demands and tastes. The Fascist government did, for instance, move towards protecting and funding an Italian film industry in the late 1930s, setting up a state-of-the-art film production complex, *Cinecittà* (Film City), and achieving a kind of cultural 'autarky' during the Second World War, which naturally dried up the supply and distribution of foreign films. But in 1937, 87 per cent of all cinema box-office takings were for the showing of foreign, mainly Hollywood, films. Italian publishers translated and sold in large num-bers contemporary American novels throughout the 1930s. Reading Steinbeck might not necessarily have polluted young Fascist minds, since much of the content was critical of contemporary US society. But he was available because he sold, and was good business for Italian publishers, as were Hollywood films for an Italian cinema industry which even if increasingly regulated by the state, remained largely in private hands and was run for commercial profit.

A more dependable and long-term way of influencing cultural production and output was for the Fascist state itself to become the major patron of the arts, and this manoeuvre was what Fascist cultural policy practically amounted to. To show in exhibitions, to receive and compete for commissions, in other words, to secure an audience for their art and a livelihood, artists had to belong to the appropriate official corporative bodies brought together in 1928 in the National Confederation of Fascist Professional and Artistic Syndicates. Increasingly in the 1930s, the government, syndicates, corporations and the PNF became the paymasters of culture, staging the exhibitions, organising and judging the competitions, and providing the commissions for public works financed with public money.

There was the basis of a 'deal' between the Fascist regime and Italy's artists and intellectuals, here. The Fascist state patronised artists, and in return artists participated in state-run exhibitions, competitions and projects. The relationship was a seductively unequal one, since the regime created the conditions which allowed artists to be artists; only 'aligned' artists could expect to receive public exposure of their work and a living. Because they wanted their kind of architecture to secure the big public commissions, Rationalist architects were bound to premise their 1931 exhibition on the claim that their 'moral mission' was 'serving the Revolution' in expressing the 'character of masculinity, force and pride of the Revolution'.[6] Whether this was a show of external conformity or a sign that they had internalised the regime's message on the educative role of artists and intellectuals scarcely mattered in practice. The architects knew that they had to produce designs and plans which the regime, as patron, would accept. From this perspective one begins to see the point and sense of the Fascist regime choosing not to choose one particular artistic style or school to be 'official' Fascist art, something which many commentators take as an indication of weakness, ideological vacuity and inconsistency. The effect of allowing different artistic genres to exhibit, and to jostle alongside each other in competition for commissions and for the status of 'official' art, was to co-opt or align practically all of Italy's best artists with the Fascist regime.

Whether exponents of the *Novecento* (Twentieth Century) or *Strapaese* (Super-provincial) cultural movements, or of Rationalist architecture, their output conformed to Mussolini's own broad and relatively inclusive definition of 'Fascist Art' in 1926, as 'traditionalist and at the same time modern, that looks to the past and at the same time to the future',[7] the blend of 'old' and 'new' which was the ideological nationalistic essence of Fascism. So the regime's initial cultural eclecticism was not the inevitable by-product of having no cultural policy at all; it *was* the policy, and it worked brilliantly. Both established and new artists of various schools contributed to exhibitions and to official culture, and there were hardly any enforced departures of artistic talent from the country until after the enactment of the anti-semitic race laws in 1938.

More than that, popular audiences for official cultural events, which combined propaganda, stimulation and entertainment, expanded considerably. The Fascist regime had developed in the course of the late 1920s and early 1930s an effective and nuanced way of reaching both the producers and consumers of culture, which until the late 1930s was very different from the rigid, didactic and prescriptive cultural policies of Nazi Germany and Stalinist Russia.

To make the same point in another way, there was one informing principle behind 'Fascist' art, which in practice could be expressed in a range or variety of artistic styles. That principle was 'aestheticised politics', pioneered by the Futurists whose practitioners made the most insistent claim to be the 'official' Fascist art throughout the *ventennio*. So, arguably, what defined Fascist art was its conception of art as 'aestheticised politics'. This meant that art was seen as 'political' and had a 'political' value and function, a point already made in relation to the regime's recasting of artists as educators of the nation. It also meant that 'politics' should become 'art', be made 'beautiful' and aesthetically appealing, so as to engage people's emotions and feelings and bind people sentimentally to Fascism. It was a world of 'aestheticised politics' which the regime was attempting to realise in all the public spectacles it organised, giving an orchestrated event the spontaneity of a 'happening', where simply by attending people would be given an emotional or 'spiritual' charge, a sense of involvement and participation in the national 'community'.

In this way, all the artistic styles which found a place in Fascism's relatively tolerant cultural scene could be regarded as 'official' Fascist art, because they transmitted the core nationalistic values of Fascism applying the common principle of 'aestheticised politics'. The style itself was immaterial, since the various styles shared the same aesthetic goal of projecting the common nationalist myth. In other words, in the field of culture, the Fascist regime aimed to convey the one nationalist message, using not one, but many messengers.

Two of the ways in which Fascist culture was conveyed deserve particular mention, the one an 'event', the other a recurring and dominant motif of Fascism's nationalist myth which inspired a whole series of cultural 'events'. The 1932 Exhibition of the Fascist Revolution (*Mostra della Rivoluzione Fascista*), staged to celebrate a decade of Fascism in power, epitomised Fascist art in its eclectic phase. Commissions were extended to artists and cultural bureaucrats representative of all the artistic schools, and the outcome was an innovative fusion of styles, a daring display of Fascist relics and artefacts set in an experimental mix of various modern art and design formats. It bridged mass and élite culture attracting nearly four million people, nearly one in ten of all Italians, in its two years of opening, even though, typically, attendance was in part a matter of 'organised spontaneity', with people coming as members of various Fascist organisations on discounted travel excursions. Most of all, the *Mostra* was 'aestheticised politics' in action. Its dramatic synthesis of styles and forms, including Futurist-inspired collage and photomontage and Rationalist architectural design, was meant to provide an affecting, even disorientating, experience for the many people who went to see it. Even just looking at the still photographs of the various stages of the exhibition, you can almost believe that attending such a show might actually crystallise, even change, people's perception of Fascism.

The central theme of Fascist propaganda and cultural production was the myth of Ancient imperial Rome, of *Romanità* or 'Roman-ness'. It was made to infuse much of the urban renovation and planning both undertaken and contemplated by the Fascist government, which was the financier of such large-scale public projects, dignified religiously in 1928 by Michele Bianchi, the Minister of Public Works, as 'documents of our faith'.[8] Architects and town planners, indeed, were the real cultural entrepreneurs of the Fascist period. Their elevation as 'revolutionary heroes' was partly because, self-evidently, any political regime wants to convey and represent its power and achievement in a way as permanent as it itself hoped to be, through buildings. It was also, again, a matter of a 'totalitarian' state being a planner's paradise, since the state's very existence assumed a purpose of an all-round reordering of people's lives and the lure of changing people by transforming their physical and living environment.

Thirteen new towns were designed and built between 1928 and 1940, the most emblematic of which were constructed on the reclaimed and regenerated land of the previously malarial and under-cultivated marshy areas around Rome. The 'Roman' linkages were explicit. In deliberate mimicry of the colonising initiatives of the Ancient Roman empire, and in pursuit of a future expanding population of farmer soldiers and colonists, the new farms were settled by First World War veterans and their families from the overpopulated and underemployed Northeastern provinces of Italy, and serviced by 'rural' towns the grid of which recalled that of the early Roman military colonies.

The city of Rome itself became the show case of Fascist 'ideological' landscaping, combining the 'old' and the 'new' in the attempt to restore the archaeological sites of Ancient imperial Rome and expose them to public view in the very modern settings of new roads and motor cars. Quite deliberately but incongruously with Fascism's overall demographic policies, the Rome of the near future was to be an imperial and capital city with an expanding population and motorised traffic flow. The physically and 'morally' unhygienic Medieval and Renaissance residential areas of the city's historic centre were bulldozed and its feckless urban poor transferred to 'healthy' semi-rural, in effect half-finished, settlements on the edge of the city. In their place were constructed in the late 1920s and early 1930s the *via del mare* (road to the sea), connecting the central location of Mussolini's government offices in the Piazza Venezia to the coast, and the *via dell'impero* (imperial way), an imposing flattened avenue from Piazza Venezia to the Colosseum and thence to Ostia at the seaside, passing through the newly exposed Roman sites and providing a huge new public arena for parades and ceremonies celebrating Fascism's own empire and 'civilisation' in sight of the remains of the old.

If I am beginning to sound like a Fascist town planner, then you can still see for yourself in today's Rome what this piece of urban vandalism was meant to convey. You can also study the historical Fascism in the dysfunctional state archives building located in EUR, a 'clean slate' green field site partially developed in the late 1930s and early 1940s in the then prevailing neo-classical Roman monumental style as the intended show piece of Fascist Italy's new imperial 'civilisation'. The planners and architects also had a field day in Fascist Italy's other 'clean slates', the newly pacified and newly settled colony of Libya in North Africa and the newly conquered colony of Ethiopia in East Africa. Here, there was applied the same metropolitan combination of the excavation and exposure of Ancient Roman ruins with the extensive remodelling of crowded city centres into expansive broad avenues, together with the additional ingredient of overseas empire, spatial segregation of the races.

The intended symbolism of all this planning and construction should now be pretty clear. The glorious past, the glorious present and the ever more glorious future were being brought together in the one urban space. The renovation of the old imperial Rome was connected to the emergence of a new 'Roman' empire, the present and future legitimated by the past, and for both imperial Romes 'empire' signified order, authority, civilisation.

The idea of 'aestheticised politics' leads the historian onto interesting but very difficult ground. It is used to sustain an interpretation of Italian

Fascism (and of German Nazism) as a 'political religion', which has been done most recently by Emilio Gentile for Italian Fascism, and Michael Burleigh for German Nazism.[9] This interpretation draws on Fascism's own representation of itself, and this is enough to provoke a hostile reaction from some historians. The 1932 Doctrine of Fascism spoke of Fascism as a 'religious concept', offering an all-embracing system of belief. Since the Doctrine was written by Mussolini and Gentile, these words were an official endorsement of the earlier injunctions of Fascist Party leaders like Turati 'to believe in Fascism, in the *Duce*, in the Revolution, just as one believes in God'.[10] So, in this reading of Fascism, the 'secular religion' of Fascism was nationalism, and 'aestheticised politics' was how the Fascist regime expressed and promoted this 'religion' of the nation.

'Religion', here, seems to function as an analogy: Fascism was not actually a religion, but operated like a religion. A religion, after all, deals in 'truths' which are revealed to humankind by a divine, other-worldly being, even though their transmission may be through humans. Fascists were decidedly of this world and were offering national redemption now and not in some after-life, through very human agencies, themselves, and a set of beliefs devised by themselves, not God. This was why in certain moments of lucidity, the Catholic church recognised that Fascism, and fascism, were fundamentally anti-Christian and condemned them for their pagan statolatry, while at the same time seeking an agreement with the 'totalitarian' rival and enemy.

As an analogy, the comparison with religion can be made to work productively for historians. Fascism was like a religion because it had an all-inclusive value system which was meant to inform and inspire every aspect of life, and because it made use of religious language and religious-like ritual, symbolism and ceremony in order to touch people's irrational and intuitive senses and feelings and so create the kind of popular consent it wanted, the blind enthusiastic faith of the believer, the convert. Some cultural historians go even further, seeing Fascism, and fascism, as meeting the universal 'need' of people for a sense of belonging and identity, filling the emotional void left by the decline of organised religion in modern, secular societies, which locates inter-war fascism in a very long historical process indeed.

Putting the Fascist acculturation of the Italian nation in these terms immediately raises the stakes of the Fascist 'project'. The kind of consent and approval ratings actually secured by the Fascist regime's organising and propagandising efforts of the 1930s have to be measured against the 'totalitarian' aim of getting people to act and behave as if inspired by a religious zeal.

In what is an in-built danger of the 'culturalist' approach, cultural historians often tend to take how Fascism represented itself, its 'self-narration', as the actuality. Fascism was what it said it was. They assume that the onslaught of Fascist ritual and ceremony must have changed people, and was bound to have worked, if only because it met the primeval need for community and belonging no longer catered for by religious religions. One wonders quite how and whether the emotional collective bonds temporarily generated by the Fascist parade or ceremony lasted beyond the event itself. An industrial worker in Turin or Milan whose wages and living standards were compressed throughout the life of the Fascist regime might not have felt an integrated member of the national community as a result of his young son enjoying two weeks at the seaside with the *Balilla*. Pressing socio-economic realities might not have been transcended or sublimated by the workings of Fascist 'culture', though that was undoubtedly the aim. A credibility gap might well have become evident as aspiration encountered reality, the outcome of, in more post-modern 'culture-speak', 'negotiations between public discourse and private reception'.[11]

There was also an inherently self-deluding dimension to the attempts to spread a Fascist culture, which tended to take the 'form' as the 'substance'. Understandably enough, the Fascist regime was happy to take the external appearance of the 'new Fascist man' as the sign of that internal transformation of consciousness that Fascist propaganda and organisation aimed to bring about, and even to use the externals as a way of changing the inner man. Civil servants were required to wear a uniform instead of a suit at work in the late 1930s, in the expectation that a civilian would have started behaving like a soldier. To repeat a point, the historian can be reasonably certain about the sheer, frightening ambitiousness of Fascism's 'cultural revolution', but less certain about how the human targets of 'cultural revolution' responded to it. The next section tries to deal with these issues in more concrete terms.

4. THE IMPACT AND LIMITATIONS OF 'TOTALITARIAN' CONTROL

Assessing the actual impacts of the great expansion of the regime's 'capillary' organisations and initiatives during and after the Depression is a far harder task than defining Fascism's 'totalitarian' goals and the mechanisms it used to achieve them. One is always struck by both the unique scale and extent of the regime's organisational achievement in the 1930s and how far it nevertheless fell short of what the regime claimed. The runt in the litter of Fascist organisations, the workers' syndicates, legally represented all workers after the 1926 syndical law, but organised barely half of the country's waged labour force in 1930, as little as 15 per cent in the highly industrialised Milan province. The situation did improve partly because syndicate membership was useful if not compulsory for gaining and keeping a job. But industrial workers especially never warmed to the syndicates when they were generally if not uniformly ineffective in, for example, upholding the terms of labour contracts against the constant spoliation of employers. Perhaps it was an achievement to survive at all as a class organisation in a regime wedded, at least rhetorically, to the overcoming of class conflict and class loyalties in the national interest.

It was scarcely accidental that the syndicates were increasingly bypassed in favour of the OND, the regime's main point of contact with an industrial working class which Mussolini continued to recognise as hostile to or distant from Fascism. Here again, the figures were impressive without being 'totalitarian'. By 1936 the OND had as members about 9 per cent of the national population, including an estimated 20 per cent of all industrial workers, who represented at this point about 70 per cent of total OND membership. In 1939, 40 per cent of industrial workers were in the OND. But the OND was the 'mass' organisation of the lower middle and middle classes, both in terms of relative membership levels, the people who ran it, and the atmosphere pervading it. In 1936, 80 per cent of all state and private-sector salaried employees were enrolled in the OND.

Then again, the OND's profile was culturally lowbrow, folksy and geared to providing popular entertainment, leisure and recreation rather than explicit propaganda and indoctrination. When a zealous *federale* complained that the OND was not being used to proselytise actively among workers, Mussolini replied that 'the important thing is that people are able to meet in places where we can control them'.[12] The OND's neutral approach was both its greatest advantage and its greatest limitation. Workers and their families could join in order to enjoy what it offered, without having to make any uncomfortable political choices about their general view of Fascism. Involvement in the OND contributed to what the analysis of oral testimony seems to indicate as a 'mix' of attitudes in workers' families: a pragmatic acceptance of benefits coexisting with other critical or indifferent postures. But it was unlikely that the OND, precisely because of its popularity, could instil or reflect in its activities the militaristic ethic of Fascism. Despite its cross-class membership the OND did not even necessarily foster a sense of national community. If not class specific, its activities were often class separate: the manual workers did things together, but apart from the group activities of the white-collar workers.

The Fascist organisation of women certainly expanded, though never at the pace and to the extent of the male and catch-all organisations. Specialised and neglected groups of women were enrolled in the euphemistically named Rural Housewives' organisation, set up in 1935, and in that for female domestic and industrial workers founded two years later. This still left urban working-class housewives and mothers outside the organisational net. But it was always difficult for the regime to give the same attention and resources to female as to male organisations. Its warlike values were so evidently masculine, and organising women at all might remove them from their officially located place in the home, giving birth and bringing up the family.

There were also regional, social and gender nuances to the overall picture of youth organisation. A sizeable minority of children and adolescents in the eight to eighteen age range, perhaps between 30 and 40 per cent, did not join the ONB at all. The ONB was so intertwined with and dependent on the school system that membership was inevitably concentrated among children of statutory school age, and membership did sometimes lapse once children left school. This was both cause and effect of the greater degree of overt 'fascistisation' of the teaching staff and curriculum in elementary schools. But the ONB always regarded the considerable presence of women teachers as a hindrance to its work of forming the young. Since those children who continued their schooling were usually of middle-class parentage and boys rather than girls, the absentees from the ONB were mainly working-class teenagers and particularly young females. The membership of GUF simply reflected the overwhelmingly middle-class background of university students.

Whatever the less than 'totalitarian' coverage of youth organisations, there was little doubt that the young were the most susceptible to Fascist propaganda and indoctrination. For many of the young people growing up after 1925, there were no alternatives to Fascism, no pre-Fascist precedents or memories unless they could be transmitted by their family. Fascist regimentation was accepted as the norm. The Fascist regime was the only permissible outlet for and source of youthful idealism, political ambition and activity, career opportunities and more mundanely, services and facilities from sport to welfare.

For the PNF itself as well as its dependent and auxiliary organs, membership and activity generally declined from north and centre to south and the islands. Part of the explanation was that Fascism started from a lower organisational base. In many areas of the south, Fascism was unknown before 1922 and scarcely established by 1925. Starting from scratch, the PNF lacked the already high membership and proven organisational network of its strongholds in some northern and central provinces. In other cases, the party found that backwardness had built in obstacles to organising southern populations which were difficult to overcome. Getting the PNF off the ground meant confronting problems of physical remoteness, inadequate communications, the general lack of resources and facilities, low school attendance because of agricultural child labour, a lack of tradition or experience of organisation and public activity among peasants, especially for women.

But basically Fascist organisations in the 1930s were paying the price for Fascism's renewal of the 'transformistic' deal by which Mussolini's government extended its political control to the south. Fascism's putative organising effort among peasants and their families cut across the support it had won in the south from the local notables, now in Fascism, who controlled the levers of patronage and clientelism. In some rural communities, for whom the state had always been no more than the policeman and the taxman, organisations like the OND at least presented a more benign face to state authority. But in much of the south the Fascist government was too associated with the large landowners, who were the ones favoured by its agricultural and 'ruralistic' policies. Fascism would not have appeared to peasants as anything other than the continuation of a socio-economic order which had always been buttressed by the state's policing and judicial apparatus.

The most important limitation or obstacle to the regime's 'totalitarian' pretensions was self-imposed. The 1929 agreement with the Catholic church gave a fresh impetus to Catholic Action, whose membership reached one million in late 1930. Under the terms of the Concordat this appeared to the church as a legitimate extension of clerical organisation and influence in Italian society. Mussolini recognised the undoubted contradiction of an autonomous non-Fascist body operating within a self-declared 'totalitarian' Fascist state. He expected it to be overcome by the PNF's superior competitive organisational powers and by the annexation of the church's moral and social authority and presence to serve the state's ends. In a way, this approach simply restated the contradiction. Making, for instance, parish priests the chaplains of local ONB sections was a kind of co-option by association with Fascism. But using the church's prestige and status among the population as a form of guarantee that Catholics would support the regime and its organisations naturally allowed the clergy to continue and extend their contact with the people.

Fascist organisations registered with alarm the post-Concordat Catholic activity and the presence of ex-PPI organisers within Catholic Action, and tried to retaliate in the way Mussolini anticipated. The PNF's foundation of the Young Fascists was a response to the low incidence of membership in Fascist youth organisations among Catholic young men. But the open conflict between church and Fascist state was precipitated by the Fascist syndicates' press attacks in March 1931 on Catholic Action's formation of occupational groups among Catholics. These 'professional sections' were with some justification seen by the syndicates as embryonic rival unions infringing their legal monopoly. The issue was particularly sensitive because of the deepening economic crisis and attempts to exploit it by clandestine anti-Fascist groups. The church was also staging an international public celebration of the fortieth anniversary of Pope Leo XIII's famous encyclical on Catholic social policy. This, and the present Pope's restatement of the Catholic position in his May 1931 encyclical, *Quadragesimo Anno*, more than implied that the Church had a superior version of a new economic and social order.

In late May Mussolini brought the simmering conflict to a head by ordering the prefects to dissolve Catholic youth organisations, after a wave of PNF and Young Fascist attacks on Catholic premises and members. The Pope's response, the encyclical *Non Abbiamo Bisogno*, formally drew back from a condemnation of Fascism 'as such'.[13] Nevertheless it exposed the real basis of ideological dispute, rejecting the state's 'totalitarian' claim to abrogate the rights of individual, family and church in the education of the young.

Neither side was prepared to push the conflict to the point of 'holy war'. The September 1931 agreement banned former PPI leaders from holding positions in Catholic Action, whose centralised national structure was dismantled for a diocesan basis of organisation. Catholic bodies were to have a strictly moral and religious character. This stipulation confirmed the earlier prohibition on youth organisations engaging in sports and athletic activities, and apparently pre-empted the transformation of 'professional sections' into unions. The sections were to ensure that the Fascist syndicates 'conform more and more to the principles of class collaboration, and to the social and national object-ives which in a catholic country, the state seeks to achieve through the corporative system'.[14] Did this mean a Catholic endorsement of Fascist corporativism, or an opportunity to influence it in a Catholic direction? It could be read all ways, as could the settlement as a whole. Mussolini obviously felt that the restrictions on the content and scope of Catholic activity would allow the regime to press home the organisational advantage and squeeze out the rival Catholic bodies, while continuing to make use of the church in support of the state. But the church regarded all its activity as 'moral and religious' and all its lay organisa-tions, whatever their function, as having 'moral and religious' ends. So in the general revival of Catholic Action activity from 1934, 'profes-sional sections' re-emerged under this rubric. Catholic youth groups were not abolished, as Giuriati and Scorza demanded. The return of their confiscated premises allowed their reconstitution, and they remained as an alternative to the ONB for Catholic young people. Article 43 of the Concordat was still intact.

These Janus-like agreements pointed to the overall complexity of the working relationship between the Fascist regime and the church in the mid-1930s. The church never really shook off its role as both an ally and a rival of the Fascist state. The Pope's theoretical reservations about Fascist statolatry, revealed in the 1931 incidents, made little practical difference to relations between church and state, and between Catholics and government. The 1931 events might well have forced the Vatican to revise its hopes of a clerical reconquest of state and society. But there had been and would be plenty of occasions for the church to express its support for the regime and its policies. Anti-communism remained the constant and central element of the common ground between church and state. It assumed an international importance for the Vatican with the apparent spread of atheistic communism and its persecution of the church by the Popular Front governments of France and Spain. Italian intervention to support the military rebellion against the anti-clerical republic in Spain from 1936 was portrayed as the struggle of Catholic Europe against Bolshevism. The church wholeheartedly backed and participated in the regime's demographic and 'ruralist' campaigns from the 'battle for grain' onwards and its attendant efforts to relegate women to their allotted gender roles. In doing so, it stereotypically evoked the disappearing world of a sober, prolific and god-fearing peasantry, set against a sterile, materialistic urban-industrial society, the corrupter of religion and morals. This was the complementary spiritual equivalent of the regime's own more secular assumptions and expectations behind its promotion of rural life. The church also willingly associated itself with the myth of a civilising imperial and Catholic Rome, made actual in the conquest of Ethiopia. Even Fascist corporativism could be generally welcomed and accepted as an imperfect stab at realising Catholic social teaching, though these affinities were not usually recognised or acknowledged by Fascists themselves.

A Catholic slant was always given to these expressions of support for Fascist policies, which could be backed because they approximated to Catholic ideals and models. At times, particularly with the philofascist intellectuals and teachers of the Catholic University of Milan, there was a sense that Catholics were inventing a Fascism which would match their hopes of realising a Catholic society through the regime. All this indicated an apartness and a concern to avoid total identification with Fascism, embodied concretely in the jealous preservation of a separate body for Catholic laity in Catholic Action. But the evident symmetry between the policies and outlook of the regime and the church must have satisfied Mussolini's instrumentalist view that it was more advantageous to get the church on the regime's side, than push their differences to the point of rupture.

For De Felice, the Italian historian writing an encyclopaedic and sometimes opaque 'life and times' biography of Mussolini, 1929–34 were the years when the Fascist regime was most stable and enjoyed the greatest 'consent'. His provocative intention was to show that the relationship between workers and the Fascist regime was not necessarily nor always one of mutual hostility and antagonism. The view of the regime enjoying popular consent was, in other words, a challenge to the 'anti-Fascist' historical 'orthodoxy' which saw Fascism as a criminal minority in forcible occupation of the country. At first sight this is a questionable proposition, because no government could expect to have the people's support during a period of economic depression. Certainly in Italy, clandestine anti-Fascist activity undertaken by Communists, Socialists and a new liberal-socialist group called 'Justice and Liberty', was more intense in 1930–31 than at any other point before the war. These groups were very efficiently broken up by the police. Only sometimes could they be connected to the incidence of popular disturbances, including illegal strikes, of which there were 101 according to official records in 1933, the highest figure for the Depression years. The Vatican, along with others, was expressing doubts in 1931 on the regime's ability to survive the impact of the economic crisis. They did so hardly from the view point that they wanted the government to fall. It is at least arguable that 1930–31 were years of 'dissent'.

What De Felice appears to mean by 'consent' in relation to workers' attitudes to the Fascist government was an absence of political opposition to it. This, he explains with reference to the police's undoubted efficiency and to the regime's largely successful efforts to mitigate the effects of the crisis in its 'going ... to the people' campaign conducted through the PNF's organisations. The whole debate cries out for greater rigour in the use of the concept of 'consent', and of the idea of 'consensus', often used interchangeably with 'consent' as if it means the same thing. Who exactly was 'consenting' to what, and how and when? 'Consent' can best be understood as a continuum of attitudes, ranging from, yes, the lack of dissent to enthusiastic commitment. It is ephemeral, varying in quality, intensity and location through time; 'consent' over one issue often evaporates over another. 'Consensus', as employed by sociologists, is a more nuanced explanatory concept which seeks to understand whether a given society is stable or not by examining a range of social relationships and patterns of human behaviour, one of which would be the attitudes of the governed towards their government, the usual field of enquiry for locating 'consent' and 'dissent'.

This kind of analysis is a quagmire for the historian and sometimes of doubtful utility. How do you actually gauge whether 'consensus' exists, at all? Exactly how do you measure 'consent' in a repressive Fascist dictatorship, which prevented any free expression of popular opinion? About 17 000 people were sent to *confino*, or internal exile, under Fascism, and police files contained the names of about 160 000 Italians who were under surveillance or police restraint. Does this convey a climate of 'consent' or conformity? But the figures were deceptively large precisely because Fascist Italy was a 'totalitarian' and police state, and demanded and prohibited more than in other systems. Under Fascism the police had very wide powers, hence almost infinitely enlarging the compass of actually and potentially unacceptable behaviour. To take an example already mentioned, banning abortion as a state crime criminalised an act of birth control which many working-class Italian women regarded as a perfectly acceptable way of family limitation in difficult economic or personal circumstances. The continuation of the practice made many women 'opponents' of 'Fascism'.

The difficulty if not the futility of assessing 'consent' and 'dissent' under Fascism should now be apparent. But the question raises some important points about the distinctive nature of the Fascist 'totalitarian' system. The context of life in Fascist Italy was repressive, and necessarily so. No alternative or contradictory viewpoints to those put out by the regime were allowed, and where they appeared they were repressed. The police state created a kind of blank space of opinion, clearing the ground for the attempted indoctrination of the population. This indoctrination could only be the outcome of an organising process. The Fascists expected to change people by putting them through the experience of being organised in the regime's own bodies. There was an inescapable element of compulsion and dictation in this process, which permeated all the regime's initiatives. In the case of the PNF's provision of welfare through the EOAs, what was portrayed as the spontaneous display of national solidarity bringing together the haves and the have-nots was in fact the result of organisation. By leaning on its own members and other bodies it controlled to subscribe on a regular and systematic basis to winter relief, the party was organising 'spontaneity'. There was an obligation to contribute, though clearly not one marked by violence.

The contradiction of 'orchestrated spontaneity' was clear also in the attempt to indoctrinate. There was a real debate or dispute within the regime, never entirely resolved, over the kind of formation the young should undergo in the youth organisations. Bottai and his journal *Critica Fascista* constantly argued that Fascism's future leaders should be allowed the relative freedom to discuss, and even criticise, within the party's framework. This was the only sure way of producing an élite with a sincere and enthusiastic, rather than conformist and opportunistic commitment to Fascism. Scorza, the head of the Young Fascists, emphasised instead the regimental and blind faith approach. The *Duce* and Fascism 'do not need political brains which lose their way in the esoteric', but 'an army organised in closed ranks: huge and imposing, firm and disciplined, masculine, unshakeable in faith, irresistible in its advance: in short, an armed religious order'.[15] The combination of the two sets of attributes was the ideal, according to the official aphorism, 'Book and Rifle Make the Perfect Fascist'. But all the regime's mass organisations havered between functions of control, surveillance and regimentation, and mobilisation to gain support, consent and participation, a unique and paradoxical combination of force and consent.

Historians of any political system will continue to speculate on the extent and degree of harmony between government and governed. But the accepted polarities of 'consent' and 'dissent' are generally extrapolated from the experience of democratic and pluralist systems. They are not easily applied to the analysis of the methods and goals of a regime which aspired to be 'totalitarian', mobilising 'consent' in a context of repression and dictatorship. The Fascist 'totalitarian' state was novel in its attempt to keep control of and win active support from the population. To secure the identification of people with the regime, society was aligned to the state through the state's organisations. The party did organise among social, age and gender groups, many of them previously untouched by Fascism. But there was a considerable gap between 'totalitarian' claim and performance in the 1930s, not only in terms of the numbers organised. In its organisation of the population the party could never overcome the contradiction, inherent to the 'totalitarian' system, of exercising both a repressive and educative role. A consciously willed acceptance of Fascism was unrealisable within the system erected to create it.

If all this seems plausible, then it is an important conclusion to reach. Scorza's remarks about the point of organising young men made it clear that Fascism was not satisfied with a low level, passive 'consent'. The regime wanted the committed enthusiastic 'consent' of the religious convert. Judged by its own measure of 'consent', then, success was unlikely, because of the very nature of 'totalitarian' mobilisation. This is a point worth pursuing, even though it may only reinforce the power of paradox and play of unintended consequences in history.

Take the position of women in the Fascist regime, which has already been looked at. There was an innate contradiction in the regime's attempt to impose, or re-impose, on women a conventional gender role of passivity and subordination within a framework of 'totalitarian' organisation. Women were organised on an unprecedented scale. But how exactly could the regime mobilise women to passivity? The self-confident trained young women graduates of the Fascist physical education academy at Orvieto, set to be instructors in the Fascist youth organisations and role models to a generation of Italian girls and teenagers, were ludicrously labelled 'virile, but not masculine'[16] by the regime, and hardly conformed to the Fascist ideal of the resigned and doting wife and mother. Even as humble 'rural housewives' (*massaie rurali*), peasant women, urged to tend their kitchen gardens and raise poultry in the name of national production and autarky, would, as a result, in some small way have had some access to a 'market' economy and some limited exposure to the world of 'consumerism' which the regime affected to despise. Their organised trips to the local national monument or to an official exhibition or parade in a city were steps towards a broadening rather than a limitation of horizons. These are pretty banal and micro-cosmic examples. But they were how many 'ordinary' people would have experienced the regime, on a personal level.

Perhaps the conclusion to draw was that there was likely to have been a mismatch between the intentions behind all the propagandising and organising, and the outcomes. We need to know how women, and everybody else, responded to the regime's injunctions and policies. Did they adopt or adapt? Did choices still remain in a system which aimed to remove choice? How do historians actually find out, when the reporting of popular reactions, whether a matter of 'consent' or 'dissent', was carried out by the regime's own agencies, the PNF and the police, who were unavoidably commenting on their own activities on behalf of the regime?

Some historians, or rather sociologists and anthropologists, have made imaginative use of the oral testimony of 'ordinary' Italians looking back on their experiences during the Fascist era. There are certainly methodological problems in using historically this kind of evidence. But the oral accounts, even when they do not touch on overtly political matters, do reveal a regime which was difficult to keep at a distance and required some kind of interaction with it beyond the routine repressiveness existing in most working-class neighbourhoods. People appeared to behave pragmatically and selectively, accepting some of the things which the regime had to offer, for lack of alterna-tives, like the night out with the *Dopolavoro*, the free or subsidised holi-day at the seaside for their children in the *Balilla*, while rejecting other blandishments such as actually joining the PNF themselves. In other words, rejection of some of the regime's services could have co-existed with the enjoyment of others. This many-sided 'mix' of popular attitudes and reactions is inadvertently quite close to the De Felician reduction of 'consent' to the lack of 'dissent'. Certainly, there was nothing here which remotely challenged the grip of the Fascist regime and its continuation in power. There was no absolute rejection of the regime, nor of its 'right' to rule. However far short it was of the partici-patory enthusiasm desired by the regime, this ambivalent 'mix' of popu-lar attitudes and responses might well suggest or be construed as a kind of 'consensus'.

5.   CORPORATIVISM AND THE GREAT DEPRESSION

Mussolini's personal dictatorship was strengthened by his ministerial shake-up of July 1932. This undid the apparent delegation in 1929 of important government office to prominent figures of the regime other than himself. Rocco went from the Justice ministry, Grandi from Foreign Affairs and Bottai from Corporations. Mussolini personally reassumed headship of the latter two, and in further reshuffles in 1933 once again became the nominal minister for all of the armed forces. The changes probably ran deeper than Mussolini's congenital suspicion of collaborators who knew their own mind. They clearly reinforced the reality and the impression that Mussolini was, effectively, the government and that the regime's future was ultimately dependent on himself and what he achieved. The depersonalised figure of the cult of the *Duce*, a leader of more than normal talents and qualities, above and beyond the fray, did correspond in some way to Mussolini's self-imposed solitude in government, and reinforced his sense of being a man with a mission.

The self-elevation of the *Duce* coincided with the first serious official attempts to launch Fascism as an international phenomenon, which were clearly related to the deepening of the worldwide economic Depression. Its severity, duration and extent gave ample scope and justification to Fascist claims that it marked the crisis *of* liberal capitalism and parliamentary democracy, and the start of the fascist era. The formal statement of Fascist doctrine was published under Mussolini's name in 1932. Fascist movements were emerging in other European countries and the Nazis were on the verge of power in Germany, lending credence to Mussolini's prediction that Europe would shortly be fascist or 'fascistised' on the model of Fascist Italy. The officially sponsored international Volta conference in late 1932 discussed the 'universal' aspects of fascism. It anticipated the regime's effort to create a fascist 'International' of European movements recognising the primacy of the Italian version. The launch and, as it turned out, culmination was a multinational conference in Montreux in December 1934. This gathering attracted some obscure fascist adventurers keen to get Italian patronage and funding, as well as fascist movements of some significance, such as the Romanian Iron Guard. It agreed, albeit in the loosest terms, that a defining element of international fascism was corporativism. The Fascist 'corporate state' was projected as a new social and political order, a 'Third Way' alternative to both the socially unjust and self-evidently dysfunctional liberal capitalism, and the state collectivism of communist Russia. As such, Italian Fascism exercised during the Depression years an appeal and fascination in European politics that was not confined simply to fascist movements.

Corporativism occupied a major place in Fascist ideology and propaganda in the Depression years, and significantly remained largely a matter for international consumption. In Italy itself the corporative structures reflected only too well the balance of forces and compromises underpinning the foundation of the regime. In 1929 Bottai had urged on the Grand Council the actual enactment of a provision in the 1926 law setting up his Ministry, for a National Council of Corporations. Established in March 1930, it was made up of seven large sections, corporations in embryo, bringing together the employer and worker organisations covering the main branches of the economy, which also met in a general assembly and were represented on a Central Corporative Committee. The National Council appeared to have normative as well as consultative functions, which suggested a role in the co-ordination and planning of production itself. This was carried over into the 1934 law which finally created twenty-two corporations for the productive cycles of the major sectors of industry, agriculture and services. The corporations could fix the prices of goods or rates for services in their own areas and issue norms 'to regulate economic relations and the unitary discipline of production'.[17]

Such provisions were for self-governing, inter-class organs of producers which could manage production in the various branches of the economy and also co-ordinate production between sectors. In practice, they were inoperative. Deciphering what the corporations actually did was, to reapply Gaetano Salvemini's phrase, like 'looking in a dark room for a black cat which is not there'.[18] But there was a basic unreality to the idea of producers' self-management of the economy in the conditions of Fascist dictatorship.

The corporations were basically councils where workers' and employers' representatives met in the presence of PNF or Ministry of Corporations officials embodying the 'national' interest. Only one side, however, was genuinely representative. Members of the employers' organisations were usually technically equipped managers actually chosen by the employers. Despite confirmation in 1934 of the barely observed principle of election to major syndical posts, the representatives of workers' syndicates in the corporations were generally not workers or men close to workers and the environment of work. The ex-revolutionary and interventionist syndicalists had given way since the *sbloccamento* of Rossoni's national workers' confederation in 1928 to a new breed of middle-class and careerist syndical officials drawn from the PNF and the Ministry of Corporations. There was little possibility of the corporations becoming a real forum for the harmonisation of all producers when representation was so unbalanced. Those who were most strongly represented won out. Without some equivalence of interest representation, the corporations were easily dominated by employers and by the pro-employer 'productivist' rationale which informed every government measure in the field from the 1926 syndical law onwards.

Again, the corporations' formal powers of economic co-ordination were deliberately circumscribed by the government. All deliberations of the corporations had to be approved in the National Council of Corporations assembly or, after 1935, by the Central Corporative Committee, whose convenor and president was the Head of Government. Corporative regulations only had effect when issued as a decree of the Head of Government. It was the executive's ultimate control which reassured *Confindustria* that economic decisions would be a matter for Mussolini and the government and that the corporative system would not become an economic planning mechanism interfering in production. This really revealed that the corporative ideal of delegated economic decision-making by self-run producer organisations was incompatible with the centralised state authority at the centre of Fascist 'totalitarianism'. As party leaders liked to point out, Mussolini led a Fascist not a 'corporate state', and political control was not to be passed down to even the regime's own permanent economic organisations.

Practically all the government's economic measures during the Depression years were proclaimed as advances of the corporative economy. But in reality, as Bottai and other Fascist corporatists realised, these were mainly emergency and 'acorporative' actions, a response to the depth of the economic crisis. Industrial production in Italy and worldwide was at its lowest point in 1932. It was at this juncture that the government intervened in a way that continued the policies of the revaluation crisis of the late 1920s. In June 1932 a law made the formation of consortia or cartels obligatory where a large majority of firms in any sector favoured it. By dividing up a shrinking market among existing producers, cartels deliberately limited competition and held up prices in a depressed economy.

The January 1933 law setting up a licensing scheme for new and expanded industrial plant could have become a lever for state direction of industrial investment and development. But it worked in the same way and served the same interests as government-endorsed cartelisation. Competition was restrained to protect the current market share of existing firms. Industrialists applied for authorisation to set up new factories and then did nothing, simply to pre-empt the entry of any potential rival firms onto their patch.

The government connived at this use of its economic rescue package, even when these emergency measures were eventually integrated with the corporative structures. From 1935 the corporations supposedly supervised consortia established in their areas. In 1937 they were responsible for the running of the licensing system, having always been expected to give an opinion on new plant applications. The Ministry of Corporations anyway in practice relied on *Confindustria's* technical expertise in the evaluation of applications, while the employers' dominant position within the corporations ensured that 'productivist' criteria prevailed. There was a real sense here of the private use of public power, of business or its biggest exponents carving up the domestic market with official endorsement.

The intrinsically Fascist character of the regime's economic crisis management was in the continued coercion of labour through the PNF and syndicates. As in 1926–27 there were more officially imposed wage cuts between 1930 and 1934, heavier in agriculture than in industry, which prevented employed workers from enjoying the full benefits of falling prices during the Depression. A forty-hour week was similarly enforced in industry in October 1934 in order to create more employment. Industrial workers with large families were in part compensated for loss of income through shorter working hours, by the introduction of family allowances, a measure soon subsumed under the regime's continuing demographic 'battle'.

The government's resistance to the lira's devaluation throughout the Depression meant a constant revaluation of the currency, as, crucially, the sterling and the dollar were devalued in 1931 and 1933. An overvalued lira contributed to a growing balance of payments deficit and the outflow of Italy's foreign currency and gold reserves during 1933–34. It was this situation which led the government in early 1934 to set up yet another special agency, the Institute of Foreign Exchange, through which it could both monopolise and regulate foreign exchange and currency trading. From February 1935 quotas were imposed on imports, in relation to the availability of foreign currency to pay for them. This gave a further impetus to import substitutionism and autarky.

The most important government salvage operation during the Depression occurred completely outside the corporative framework and was never even formally accommodated to it. A special feature of Italian capitalist development from the late nineteenth century had been the interlocking of the major banks and industries. Banks lent to and invested in industry and held industrial shares as collateral. The crisis in industrial production was so severe during the Depression that the stability of the country's banking system was also threatened. The banks had lent money to now ailing industries, whose shares in the hands of the banks were declining in value.

A series of attempted rescues of banks and industries using public money was made in 1931. Mussolini in late 1932 delegated the working out of a definitive salvage operation not to the Ministry of Corporations, but to the Finance Minister, Guido Jung, and Alberto Beneduce, a technocrat with feet in both private industry and state-run credit institutions. The outcome was the establishment of the Institute for Industrial Reconstruction (IRI) in 1933, a kind of giant state holding company. IRI took over the industrial share assets of the three banks, in return for paying off the banks' enormous debts to the Bank of Italy, incurred during the unsuccessful operations of 1931. This colossal public payment of private industrial and banking losses finally ended the connection between the banks and industry. It was the start of a reorganisation of the entire banking and credit sector culminating in the 1936 banking law. The banks were restricted to supplying normal short-term commercial credit, while for medium- and long-term capital investment, industries went to the stock market and mainly state-owned financial institutions.

These were very significant and lasting changes in the organisation of the capitalist economy in Italy. But it was probably not the original intention to make IRI anything other than a temporary dispensary for sick industries in extraordinary economic conditions. IRI was meant to reorganise, rationalise and reprivatise the industries whose shares it now held, and this happened in the case, for example, of the profitable electricity companies. But not all of IRI's holdings were as attractive to private enterprise. IRI's existence during and beyond Fascism rested on its continued responsibility for administering the loss-making industries which the private sector would not touch, especially the iron and steel, shipbuilding and navigation companies. With IRI, state intervention in the economy took on a new institutional form. Through the entrepreneurial public body, the state had a sometimes majority share-holding in many firms which retained the structure and management of private companies. The boards of IRI's companies were filled by the same men who were on the boards of businesses in the increasingly monopolistic private sector.

All this ran parallel to the corporations and resembled a 'consortial' rather than a 'corporate' state. It was clear that the government was not prepared to entrust its economic rescue measures during the Depression, which had to be rapid and functional in effect, to the complicated mechanisms of the corporations. The problem was how to reconcile the corporative apparatus with increasing state direction of the economy. The government resolved it by ignoring the former and developing an alternative network of public bodies with economic functions.

State economic intervention was initially made necessary by the severity and duration of the Depression, and then by the imperatives of Fascist foreign policy. By late 1934, planning and spending for the conquest of Ethiopia was under way. The various public agencies which had originated as emergency measures of the Depression were now used to regulate an economy being geared up for war. Italy's growing isolation from the international economy was reflected in the collapse in value of its foreign trade. As for other countries which sought some kind of refuge in protected domestic and imperial markets, this was a consequence of the Depression and also in Italy's case, of the government's refusal to devalue. But in the end it was the Fascist government's military and imperialist foreign policy, and the knock-on effect of directing the economy towards autarky, which finally scuppered the corporative system as a way of organising society and the economy.

5 The Creation of the Fascist Empire, 1935–36

1. IMPERIALISM, REVISIONISM AND THE LIMITS TO FASCIST FOREIGN POLICY IN THE 1920S

From its inception, Fascism was imperialist. Mussolini had cynically abandoned D'Annunzio in Fiume in 1920, calculating correctly that Fascism's opportunity lay in combatting 'the enemy within'. But the movement consistently had as its declared aim a general commitment to realising the grandeur of Italy, specifically through the foundation of an empire. Self-consciously drawing on the legacy of interventionism and the war experience, Fascism claimed that under its rule Italy would at last be recognised as a major power and achieve hegemony in the 'Italian' sea, the Mediterranean.

Recognition as a Great Power and Mediterranean expansion should, of course, have been the natural outcome of Italy's participation on the winning side of the war. But in the Fascist view Italy's 'mutilated victory' was plain to see in the peace treaties of 1919, which had not delivered the anticipated gains in the Adriatic, the Near East and Africa. Responsibility rested with the pusillanimous liberal governments, both cause and victims of the country's deep post-war internal divisions, which were unable to defend the country's national interests. Blame was shared with the ungrateful ex-Allies and already well-established imperialist powers, France and Britain.

This reading of the war and its outcome was hardly original. It regurgitated wholesale the Nationalist position, whose war aims Mussolini had practically adopted as his own during 1918. From the Nationalists too, Mussolini and Fascism took the notion of the struggle between rival imperialisms as an inescapable fact of international relations, and of war as the inevitable and even desirable test of a nation's will to power and expansion. There existed a ready-made Nationalist rhetoric about international 'class war' between up and coming 'proletarian' nations and satiated 'plutocratic' ones, for the redistribution of territory and resources. It was employed regularly by Mussolini in the late 1920s, even if the realisation was delayed until the 1930s. From the very start then, Fascism was tendentiously bound to be 'revisionist' of the Versailles settlement, anti-pacifist and anti-internationalist. It had little time for the principles of parity and respect between countries which purportedly inspired the new international order enshrined in the League of Nations, even though Italy was a member.

Revisionism seemed to put Italy at odds with France in particular, since France regarded the retention of the post-war territorial settlements as a guarantee of security against Germany. France had built up in the early 1920s a network of alliances and agreements with Czechoslovakia, Poland, Romania and Yugoslavia, the beneficiaries of the treaties and of the collapse of the Austro-Hungarian empire in Central, Eastern and Southeastern Europe. The lands bordering the Adriatic were not only the focus of Italian irredentism, but a bridgehead for the spread of Italian influence in the Balkan and Danubian regions now that the Habsburg empire was gone. Control of the Adriatic was also seen geopolitically as crucial to the wider goal of Mediterranean hegemony, the realisation of which was again hindered by French and British colonial possessions and mandates in North and East Africa and the Middle East.

It is obviously dangerous to divine the actual diplomatic and military alignments of 1940 in the grandiose pretensions of early Fascism, as if one was the logical and inevitable outcome of the other. There was much ground to cover before the outbreak of a general war of the fascist powers against the 'plutocracies', and some historians, notably De Felice, try to argue that Italy's choice of allies and enemies was still open as late as spring 1940. But whether it was expressed in political and economic influence or military conquest and direct control, Fascist foreign policy always went in two directions, towards the Balkans and Danubia, and to Africa. Both prongs potentially cut across France's European and imperial interests. This was not so much Fascist as Italian foreign policy, or at least that of conservative liberals and Nationalists both before, during and after the 1915-18 war. Fascist foreign policy could be seen as conventional or the extension of a certain tradition. The continuity with much of what had gone before helps to explain why the Fascist government's policy was for a long while broadly supported by Italy's establishment, including the monarchy and the top career diplomats in the Ministry of Foreign Affairs.

Italy was a small power in European and world terms, lacking the kind of economic and military muscle which would allow the country to be an independent player in international power politics. Italy's attempted economic penetration of the Balkan and Danubian countries, one of the arms of its diplomacy in the area, always met superior competition on the same ground from richer nations. This came from France in the 1920s and early 1930s, and then later from Germany during the late 1930s and into the period of war and occupation. Such inescapable and objective weakness meant that it was difficult for Italy to contemplate going it alone. She always needed the help of other major powers, or the opportunity to exploit to her own advantage the balance, tensions and rivalries among these more powerful countries. Italy's entry into the First World War was a classic demonstration of this kind of makeweight diplomacy. Although formally allied to Germany and Austro-Hungary in the Triple Alliance, the Italian declaration of neutrality in 1914 indicated that she was open to offers from both sides at war. Even continuing neutrality would have a price. Italian irredentism might well have been pushing the country towards intervention against Austro-Hungary. But the decision to fight alongside France and Britain in 1915 was clinched by the secret Treaty of London, where the Western Allies were able to offer the better territorial deal.

Mussolini's first dramatic foreign policy coup in government was his provocative escalation of a dispute with Greece over the delimitation of the Greek–Albanian border. The bombardment and occupation of the Greek Adriatic island of Corfu in the late summer of 1923, the prelude to its expected annexation, was not only an example of Mussolini's exhibitionist, bullying and bellicose style. It showed the extent of the Fascist government's aspirations to dominate the Adriatic and its Balkan coast, and the then insuperable barrier to their achievement. Although Mussolini managed to avoid mediation by the League of Nations, to which Greece had referred the dispute, the island was evacuated under the implied threat of British naval action in the Mediterranean.

This was a demonstration of where real power lay, and an increasingly forward policy in the Balkan and Danubian regions in the late 1920s could not really shift the reality of Anglo-French domination of European affairs. The resort to largely secret and 'dirty tricks' political activity in the area was both a recognition of the situation and a sign that Mussolini was prepared to use undiplomatic and unconventional methods in foreign policy. As Secretary-General of the Foreign Ministry, the top position in the career service, Salvatore Contarini has been credited with both restraining Mussolini's natural mischief-making in foreign affairs during his first years of government and in rallying the career diplomats to Fascism. His resignation in March 1926 was basically in protest at Mussolini's conduct of foreign policy, which barely respected the norms of diplomatic activity.

Mussolini sought to extend Italian influence in Southeastern Europe by meddling in the internal politics of countries. He attempted particularly to exploit their ethnic and national antagonisms. These had been fuelled rather than dampened by the corrupted form of national self-determination inspiring the 1919 peace treaties, where strategic and economic as well as ethnic criteria had been used to determine national territorial boundaries. Involvement in the dynastic rivalries of the Albanian royal family had reduced Albania to an informal Italian protectorate in 1925-26. A footing in Albania was also a wedge into Yugoslavia, with its own Albanian minority. Destabilisation of the new Yugoslav state was again actively pursued through aid to the separatist and fascistic Croatian Ustasha movement from early 1929, and similar support to Macedonian nationalists from 1927. In defiance of the treaties Italy also secretly armed and supplied Hungary, which had revisionist territorial claims against all its neighbours, including Yugoslavia.

Subverting states from within might not have been new, but both fascist regimes made it a regular instrument of policy. Mussolini applied it in North Africa and the Middle East against the British and French empires, as well as in the Balkans. As early as an official visit to the Italian colony of Libya in 1926, Mussolini declared himself the defender of Islam as an incitement to native anti-colonial nationalism in French and British territories bordering on the Mediterranean. At the time the Italians were engaged in their own nasty internal pacification of Libya's Arab population. Mussolini's intermittent interest in Zionism was again related to the concern to shake the British hold on its Middle Eastern mandates and its place in the Mediterranean. The abortive destabilisation of Yugoslavia anticipated the highly manipulative Nazi dismemberment in 1938-39 on the phoney grounds of national self-determination of Czechoslovakia which, as Mussolini liked to say, was not simply 'Czecho-Slovakia' but also 'Czecho-Germano-Polono-Magyaro-Rutheno-Romano-Slovakia'.

As a revisionist country herself, Fascist Italy was in league with the other revisionist countries, specifically Hungary. The regime's contacts with some sections of the revanchist German right in the 1920s pointed in the same direction, even though such a revisionist axis created other contradictory tensions, notably over Austrian independence and the German-speaking population of the Italian alpine border region. Revisionism also indicated a growing ideological convergence and division in Europe. Antipathy to France, the barrier to Italian influence in the Danube and Balkans, was heightened by Fascist anger at democratic France 'harbouring' Italian anti-Fascist emigration. The Fascist government had dealings with the right-wing opposition in Weimar Germany and sponsored imitative, violently nationalistic groups to undermine the Yugoslav state. It co-operated with a succession of rightist if not fascist governments under Admiral Nicholas Horthy's regency in Hungary, again to attack the democratic beneficiaries of the peace treaties. With the rise of the Nazis in Germany, Mussolini could see in a 'fascistising' Europe the extension of Italian power and influence on the continent.

It seems difficult to describe Fascist foreign policy in the 1920s as basically one of peace and reconciliation. Some historians do see incidents like that of Corfu in 1923 as aberrant interruptions to a decade of calm in Fascist foreign policy, a period of good conduct largely determined by the need to consolidate power in Italy itself, which required a low profile internationally to reassure both foreign and domestic opinion. Italy, after all, was with Britain the co-guarantor of the 1925 Locarno agreement bringing Germany into the League of Nations and securing the French and Belgian borders with Germany, which contemporaries regarded as cementing peace between former enemies. But we also know that Mussolini was hardly an initiator of Locarno, and tried and failed to link it to a European guarantee of the Italo–Austrian frontier. He eventually participated with bad grace, seeing it at most as a recognition of Italy as a Great Power arbitrating the fate of Europe in a way which anticipated the abortive four-power scheme of the early 1930s. He certainly shed no tears over the dispelling of the illusions of peace nourished by Locarno and indeed contributed to this through his revisionist actions in Eastern Europe from 1926.

No Eastern Locarno here; imperialism and revisionism were consistently held and publicly declared goals, and both meant changes to the post-war territorial settlement. Such changes could occur peacefully, of course. A 1926 Italo–British agreement slightly modified the border between Somalia and Egypt in Italy's favour. But Mussolini's predilection was to make trouble wherever he could and disparage the forms of conventional diplomacy, using methods of internal political subversion as covert, undeclared warfare on countries he regarded as Italy's enemies.

The point is not that Mussolini could be credited with a decade of good behaviour in foreign policy, but rather that the damage he could do in the 1920s was limited, because of Italy's intrinsic economic and military weakness, and the lack of any counterbalance to effective Anglo-French dominance in Europe which Italy could exploit.

In the late 1920s this external and objective obstacle to the realisation of Great Power aspirations was reinforced by international political economy. The Fascist government's revaluation of the lira in 1926–27 was achieved as part of a wider currency and economic stabilisation involving other European countries, and was arranged and funded by the American and British governments and financial markets. Although Fascism had just embarked on the construction of its own system of government in the form of 'totalitarianism', Italy was still integrated into and dependent on an international economy dominated by Anglo-Saxon finance and capital. It was difficult to run a foreign policy which ignored these realities of economic and financial dependence, which were only transformed by the impact of the great Depression.

2. THE 'TOTALITARIAN' STATE: INTERNAL POLICY AS FOREIGN POLICY AND VICE VERSA

In another very important sense, too, Fascist foreign policy could not be regarded as essentially peaceful or demonstrating 'realistic' restraint. It is usual for historians to separate their treatment of a country's foreign affairs from the analysis of domestic policy. This chapter, dedicated to international relations, shows how difficult it is to kick the habit of considering foreign policy as an autonomous, even superior, field of governmental activity. We conventionally see foreign policy as being relatively stable and consistent through time in both line and approach. This is because the 'national interest' of any country can apparently be defined in relation to certain constants, such as its economic and military resources and potential, and its geographical and strategic position. So far this chapter has handled Fascist foreign policy in a similar way and argued that broadly comparable constraints shaped the diplomacy of both liberal and Fascist Italy, hence establishing a basic continuity between the two. As 'the least of the Great Powers', an Italy governed by liberals or Fascists had generally the same aims, oscillating between the Balkans and Africa, and employed some of the same means, oscillating between the Great Powers, the perpetual makeweight. To an extent the traditional approach holds up, as we shall see in the later discussion of the invasion of Ethiopia. But the customary separation of foreign and domestic matters is artificial and distorting, in both fact and interpretation, for Fascism. Internal and external policies were explicitly linked, and they interacted in a synchronised way.

It was not just simply a matter of Mussolini using dramatic foreign policy coups to enhance his own and the regime's internal popularity and prestige. This was one of the earliest views of Mussolini's diplomacy, argued out with some verve by the exiled anti-Fascist historian, Salvemini. He described a gadfly foreign policy, inconsistent, volatile and surprising, because its only rationale was the constant pursuit of momentary advantage and success for primarily home consumption. The patriotic tub-thumping over Corfu in 1923 was certainly designed to demonstrate to the Italian public that at last Italy had a government which stood up for and defended the nation's interests. But this was not all that the Corfu incident represented. Focusing exclusively on the internal clamour gives the whole affair a sense of improvisation, which disguises the longer-term drive to realise control of the Adriatic and Mediterranean. Also, the use or abuse of foreign adventures to build up prestige internally or to save the skin of governments floundering on the domestic front was and is hardly the preserve of fascist regimes. It is the last resort of all kinds of government, as the recent experience of the Falklands War would indicate.

The interdependence of domestic and foreign affairs lay also in the connection between the Fascist 'totalitarian' state and an imperialist foreign policy. Mussolini made this linkage explicit in the speech of October 1925 where he first used the term 'totalitarian' publicly. He spoke of the party imposing the 'discipline of a state of war' on the nation, unavoidably caught up in the continuous 'competition between peoples in the arena of world civilisation'. 'The present century must be the century of our power' and the 'magic key' to national spiritual and material power was 'the disciplined will'.[1] Once again, this was a reworking of the Nationalist perspective that internal policy was the premise and preparation for an expansionist foreign policy, which provided the incentive and reason for internal discipline and order. The deliberate association with the 'totalitarian' state showed that the intention was not to preserve and reinforce the existing order. Only a new internal political and socio-economic order, unifying and concentrating the nation's resources through 'totalitarian' controls, could enable the country to fight and win its battles in the international arena.

The Fascist 'totalitarian' state thus gave concrete and practical form to the fusion of domestic and foreign policy. Put simply, the purpose of the 'totalitarian' state was to equip Italy and Italians for war. This was evident in the government's policies and actions from 1926 onwards, described in the previous chapters, however partial and contradictory they were in effect. The single-party state put an end to the divisive and competitive political parties which placed factional and sectional interests before those of the nation. From its monopolistic position the PNF could organise and mobilise the nation in support of the regime and its goals, re-educating and forming the 'new Italian', a breed capable of founding and civilising an empire. Demographic and 'ruralist' policies were intended to move the country in the same direction. A 'productivist' corporative system would organise and discipline all 'producers' in the overriding interest of national production so as to make Italy economically independent of other countries and materially strong enough to expand.

This is admittedly a tidied-up and perhaps over-rationalised reading of Fascism's conduct of the country's affairs, which deals with intentions rather than effects. The interplay of events at home and abroad which lay behind the invasion and conquest of Ethiopia was more complicated than that suggested by the schematic relationship between internal and external affairs represented above. The full interaction of domestic and foreign policy distinctive of the Fascist way became more evident from 1936.

3.   THE DEPRESSION AND FASCISM'S OPPORTUNITY

If not the aim, then the opportunity for and timing of Italy's imperialist war was undoubtedly consequent on changes in the international situation during the years of the Great Depression. For one thing, the international economic context in which all countries worked out their economic and foreign policies was rapidly changing under the impact of the Great Depression. By 1934 the interdependence of international finance and trade had largely broken down, as had the various attempts to manage the Depression through multilateral co-operation. The United States had abandoned its pivotal position in the world economy, looking to protectionism, devaluation of the dollar and internal pump-priming to revive its economy. United States tariff protection provoked similar countermeasures elsewhere, as countries developed their own variants of autarky and economic self-help, Britain and France in tightening exclusive links with their empires.

By defending the value of the lira at the cost of reducing its gold and foreign currency reserves, Italy could at least pay off its dollar debts on advantageous terms and more rapidly. Even before 1934 Italy was trading less with the United States and more bilaterally with Central and Eastern European nations, including Germany. Italy was increasingly no longer a part of or dependent on a framework of international trade and finance dominated by the United States, and such a dependence could no longer inhibit the pursuit of a more forward foreign policy. Italy's weaker economy meant that it would be difficult to avoid another form of dependence on a stronger economic power. But her trading and economic links were less and less determined by her place in the international economy, and more by the drift towards autarky and the realisation of nationalistic goals. The collapse of international trading and financial connections during the Depression encouraged or facilitated in Italy's case the matching of economic policy and trade patterns to the direction of her foreign policy.

Also, the growing strength of the Nazis in Germany, the largest single party in the German parliament by mid-1932, raised the imminent prospect of a revanchist Germany challenging the 1919 settlement and the Anglo-French domination of European affairs. Makeweight diplomacy had some prospect of success in a situation of equilibrium rather than hegemony, and the emergence of Hitler's Germany provided the balance which Mussolini thought to exploit.

The hope was to prey on Franco–German conflict, avoiding binding alliances and blackmailing both sides for Italy's gain. Grandi, Foreign Minister between 1929 and 1932, gave a characteristically Fascist intonation of bellicosity and opportunism to his summary in 1930 of Italy's position as the so-called 'determining weight': 'With everybody and against everybody. Arming ourselves and isolating ourselves even more, in order to sell ourselves at a high price at the time of future great crisis.'[2] For a while Grandi tried to work through the League of Nations and for disarmament, as a way of bringing about a parity between France and Germany which would allow Italy to oscillate between the two. He seemed to appreciate the potential risk as well as the opportunity of German revisionism, not least for its likely impact on Italy's position in the Balkans. A Franco–Italian agreement on colonial questions, and a tacit restraint on Germany in Central and Eastern Europe, almost exactly what eventually emerged in 1935, was a possibility in 1931–32.

The prospect temporarily disappeared once Mussolini replaced Grandi in the Foreign Ministry in July 1932. Mussolini disliked giving any credibility to the League and wanted to push the German lever even harder.

His idea of a four-power pact in 1933, which came to little in the end, envisaged a kind of Great Power directorate to rearrange European affairs. Part of its purpose was to get Italy recognised as a major power alongside Britain, France and Germany, bypassing the League. Its talk of Great Power collaboration to revise Versailles, German equality in armaments, and co-operation on colonial issues was a scarcely coded attempt to use Germany against France, while intimating to all sides that Fascist Italy was Nazi Germany's minder and patron. The idea of reintroducing a revisionist Germany to European affairs under the auspices of an Italian-sponsored arrangement among the Great Powers did not survive Hitler's unilateral and simultaneous decisions in late 1933 to withdraw from the League of Nations and resume rearmament.

Hitler's actions were a clear warning that German revisionism would be a difficult horse to ride. Relations with Germany deteriorated also as a result of the activities of the Austrian Nazis, perceived as the long arm of the German Nazi government. To defend Italy's own frontiers against the weight of German revisionism, Mussolini became the protector of Austrian independence. The murder of the Austrian dictator, Engelbert Dollfuss, in an abortive coup by Austrian Nazis in July 1934 intended to precipitate union with Germany, might well have tipped Mussolini towards the kind of understanding with France which he had earlier resisted. There was nothing explicit in the written record and agreement of Mussolini's talks with the French Foreign Minister, Laval, in January 1935. But the nature of the tacit bargain was understood on both sides. Italy could have a free hand in Ethiopia, and in Europe it would join France in resisting *Anschluss*.

4. THE INVASION AND CONQUEST OF ETHIOPIA

What we know of the planning and preparation of the Ethiopian conquest is at least consistent with the view that changing international circumstances gave Mussolini the opportunity to achieve Italy's and Fascism's empire in East Africa. Actual invasion plans were commissioned by Mussolini from the Colonial Ministry and presented to him by the Minister, De Bono, in late 1932. This coincided with the awareness of the unsettling effects on international relations of the prospect of a revanchist Germany under a nationalistic government. The Italian military became involved later in planning discussions, but the definite decision to invade was taken by Mussolini and communicated to civilian and military leaders in December 1934. One of Mussolini's stated premises for war was a period of European stability or balance from 1935. It could scarcely be coincidental that the tacit arrangement linking the containment of German revisionism and action in Ethiopia was made in the Franco–Italian talks of early 1935.

But the internal dimensions of the decision to attack Ethiopia can scarcely be ignored. It is too simplistic to argue that rearmament and war were the only way that the regime could find to stimulate a depressed economy. The worst point of the Depression was 1932, when planning for an invasion started. But the economy was beginning to recover during 1934. That recovery was certainly aided by the government's war-related commissions and contracts, which began to flow in late 1934 and early 1935, coinciding with and consequent on Mussolini's decision to invade and the Italian–French understanding. Preparation for war undoubtedly had an impact on employment, which by the spring of 1935 was down 250 000 on 1934 levels. Some sectors benefited hugely from mobilisation, the war itself and colonial administration, obviously enough those supplying arms, clothing, equipment, transportation and other logistical services for the war effort and the running of the empire. Few industrialists do badly out of a war, but those that profited did so as a result of the government's initiative to go to war, not as the war's prime movers.

The Fascist government had an economic rationale or perception of the war. It was projected endlessly and unoriginally before and during the invasion as that of a 'proletarian' nation fighting for its share of territory and resources at the expense of the richer 'plutocratic' imperialist powers. An empire would guarantee raw materials and markets for Italian industry and agriculture, and its colonisation would satisfy the land hunger of the overpopulated south and islands. This familiar rehash of imperialist rationalisations was not directly concerned with a way out of the Great Depression. Such a poor man's imperialism was couched in more general terms of rectifying an historical political and economic inferiority which had consigned Italy to the second rank of nations.

In economic matters, then, what happened was dictated by the pursuit of the government's foreign policy aims for overseas expansion. But other domestic pressures did arguably help to shape foreign policy decisions. It is again too glib to say that the Ethiopian war was simply a diversionary foreign policy adventure to distract attention from internal political difficulties and recoup support and prestige for the regime. There was certainly no political crisis, arising from the effects of the Depression or not, which seriously threatened the regime's stability. At least internationally, the corporatist 'Third Way' could be taken as a demonstration that it was the liberal democracies rather than Fascism which were struggling to ride the Depression.

But objectively, as we have seen, the regime's corporative reforms had swollen the state's bureaucracy, without changing or affecting much the way the economy and society were managed. *Confindustria's* largely successful evasion or use of the corporative apparatus indicated the strength and persistence of the compromises with conservative interest groups and institutions, on which the regime had consolidated itself in the late 1920s. The prospects of an internal Fascist transformation of society seemed to be on hold, as long as the regime did not challenge the established interests which it had itself incorporated into its system of rule. In foreign affairs, however, Mussolini could act with more freedom than seemed possible domestically, and a dramatic and successful foreign policy coup could unblock the road to the further 'fascistisation' of Italian society.

So far this might appear to be a subliminal or over-rationalised argument, but some indication of its plausibility comes from the way Mussolini communicated his decision to invade Ethiopia in December 1934. He stated that the aim was the total conquest of Ethiopia by war: 'the empire cannot be made in any other way'.[3] This explicitly rejected a diplomatic rather than military solution to Italian claims on Ethiopia. It sat uneasily with Mussolini's apparent willingness to consider a negotiated settlement short of complete annexation in November and December 1935, after the invasion had been launched in October. In the event, Mussolini avoided having to decide whether to accept or reject the compromise terms of the Hoare–Laval agreement of December, which gave Italy part of Ethiopia and informal control of the rest. The British government was forced to disown the deal arranged by its own Foreign Minister. The arrangement rewarded Italy for an act of war and contradicted Britain's public support for and application of limited economic and financial sanctions imposed on Italy as aggressor by the League of Nations.

The Hoare–Laval plan was motivated by the British and French governments' fears that the possible extension of League sanctions to measures which would really bite, including an oil embargo, might precipitate a real war with Italy. Mussolini had every reason to be anxious about League action of this kind, which, if implemented, could seriously handicap military operations in Africa and cause hardship in Italy. It seems likely that Mussolini's openness to the possibility of settlement was his attempt to head off the consideration of more severe sanctions, which would, of course, be made superfluous by victory in the field.

Certainly, the sheer scale of Italy's military preparation and commitment, which ran to an army of 400 000 men to wage a small colonial war, indicated that the intention was to achieve a rapid, decisive and comprehensive conquest of Ethiopia by the overwhelming force of arms. The massive mobilisation leading to war was an end in itself for the regime. The winning of an empire was the opportunity to demonstrate and enhance 'totalitarian' mobilisation and control, to rally and unify the nation around the regime and a Fascist war. The barrage of preparatory propaganda working on the anti-British theme of the justifiable imperialism of the 'proletarian' nation was building up from the summer of 1935, matching the actual concentration of arms, equipment and men on Ethiopia's borders. Significantly, the Under-Secretariat for Press and Propaganda, which under Mussolini's son-in-law, Galeazzo Ciano, was expanding its jurisdiction to radio, films, music, theatre and literature, was made a full ministry in June 1935. The ministry's creeping monopolisation of the making and dissemination of information and control of cultural activity was both boosted and tested during the period of the Ethiopian war, when the regime embarked on a systematic propaganda campaign to rouse opinion in support of the war.

However ephemeral the effects, the regime, milking the sense of outrage at the sanctions imposed by the League from November 1935, did seem to manage to arouse a reactive nationalism and xenophobia among Italians of all classes and backgrounds. As far as this was measurable, the Ethiopian war marked the high point of support and consent for the Fascist regime. One of the peaks of the propaganda campaign was the organisation of the 'day of faith' on 18 December, when the royal family, along with thousands of Italians and with the blessing of the church, publicly and emotionally symbolised their marriage to the nation by ceremonially handing over their wedding rings. An estimated 20 million Italians listened to Mussolini's public radio broadcast announcing the invasion in October and again to his proclamation in May 1936 that 'Italy has an empire at last. . . . a Fascist Empire'.[4] If nothing else, the

Ethiopian war finally convinced the regime of the utility of radio as a means of controlled mass communication.

The conquest of Ethiopia, then, was a Fascist war, even though it clearly drew on Italy's pre-Fascist legacy of colonial aspirations and achievement, and won the endorsement of the country's establishment. It was Fascist in the commitment to victory by force, and in the deliberate exposure of the nation to the test of war, both a measure and justification of 'totalitarian' mobilisation and control. Fascism's new order was the nation in a perpetual state of mobilisation for war, and in this sense Fascist foreign policy was also an act of domestic policy. Mussolini's sneering conclusion to his December 1934 directive to prepare for the invasion of Ethiopia was that 'the remnants of the old world fear the "adventure" because they believe that the war will be conducted with their systems, but they deceive themselves, and besides, politically and socially they count for nothing'.[5] The way in which the regime handled the war as an exercise in organisation and control of the nation's resources and energies indicated that this was not just gratuitous anti-establishment rhetoric. Victory in a war planned for by the regime and using its own 'totalitarian' apparatus to organise and generate support undoubtedly strengthened the position of Mussolini and the regime in the country. The Fascist system had apparently been validated by the achievement of empire. From the sense of the regime's enhanced popularity and control came the confidence and will to push harder on the pedal of 'fascistising' the country, both the premise for and the result of fighting and winning wars. The period after 1936 was perhaps the real 'totalitarian' phase of Fascism, marked by the almost total complementarity of foreign and domestic policy.

Part III
Fascist Expansionism at Home and Abroad, 1936–43

6 The Axis Connection and the 'Fascistisation' of Italian Society, 1936–40

1. THE AXIS WITH GERMANY

Foreign policy decisions were the most important and revealing of the regime's nature and intentions, and must be harmonised with any view of domestic and economic policy between 1936 and 1940. The Ethiopian invasion could be regarded as a successful exercise in 'determining weight' diplomacy. Exploiting the threat of Germany to Anglo-French hegemony in Europe, Mussolini had won what he thought was a free run in East Africa in return for restraint on Germany in Europe, specifically resistance to *Anschluss*. The question is, what options were still open to Mussolini during and after Ethiopia? Could he maintain a position of 'equidistance' in international relations, and did he actually want to?

Except for De Felice and his 'school', most historians see the working out of a kind of 'logic' in the sequence of events leading from League of Nations sanctions against Italy over Ethiopia, through the Axis and then alliance between Fascist Italy and Nazi Germany, to the decision to enter the war on Germany's side in 1940. The 'logic' lay in the force of changing international circumstances apparent even during the Ethiopian campaign and in the nature of the Fascist regime as an imperialistic totalitarian dictatorship. To support his view of Mussolini still pursuing makeweight diplomacy, manoeuvring between Germany, Britain and France, De Felice focuses on Italo–British relations. Mussolini's intention and priority, he argues, was to achieve a general Mediterranean settlement involving British recognition of Italy as a Mediterranean power, which more or less revived Mussolini's idea of a four-power directorate of European affairs. The more conventional view sees Italo–German relations as central to Mussolini's foreign policy in the late 1930s.

There is something in the force of circumstances argument, since the so-called Axis of the two fascist powers had its immediate origins in the Ethiopian crisis. In early 1936, League of Nations sanctions confronted Italy with a degree of international isolation, which left Italy in bad need of friends. Germany obliged. Hitler refused to apply sanctions against Italy and became a major supplier of materials and energy crucial to the Italian siege economy. He simultaneously armed the Ethiopians in secret, presumably to keep the war on the boil and increase Italy's alienation from France and Britain. In return, Mussolini wavered on the Austrian question, the very issue which allowed Italy to straddle Germany and the Western democracies. In 1934–35, Mussolini had propped up the Dollfuss-Schuschnigg regime as the guarantee of an independent nationalist Austria. Now, he indicated to Germany that Austria and Germany should reach agreement on the status of Austria, and later leaned on Kurt Von Schuschnigg to make concessions to Germany and the Austrian Nazis.

The mutual benefits of synchronised action by Italy and Germany were demonstrated by the German reoccupation of the remainder of the Rhineland in March 1935, deliberately timed by Hitler to catch France and Britain with their attention diverted to the Ethiopian affair. Hitler's action broke the terms of Versailles and of the 1925 Locarno treaty, which made Italy and Britain the guarantors of France's frontiers with Germany. But Mussolini, who knew of Hitler's intended coup, declared he would not support any possible League of Nations retribution against Germany. Hitler's move increased the attractiveness of hitching Italy to German revisionism. A German Rhineland pinned France down in the west, made her more worried about her own security and her ability to stand by her treaties with the East European 'successor' states. Co-operation with a dynamic Germany was clearly the best way of hammering concessions for Italy out of a more vulnerable France.

These connections and perceptions of mutual advantage persisted after the Ethiopian invasion. The autumn 1936 talks between the newly appointed Foreign Minister, Ciano, his German counterpart, Konstantin Von Neurath, and Hitler, discussed a range of issues where collaboration was possible and forthcoming. These included Italy's endorsement of the July 1936 Austro–German agreement, set in train by Mussolini himself, which effectively made Austria a 'German' state and eased the way to actual *Anschluss* in early 1938. This surrender of Austrian independence was traded off against German recognition of Italy's new African empire. The two sides agreed on military aid to Franco's rebellion against the Spanish republic, and more broadly, on a common front against communism. These meetings also apparently affirmed respective and parallel spheres of interest, Germany in Northern and Eastern-Central Europe and Italy in the Mediterranean and Balkans, as the basis for collaboration in foreign policy. Italy tried ritually to extract German recognition of this division of labour in subsequent meetings, though it was never formally written into the agreements between the two countries.

These productive meetings enabled Mussolini to declare in November 1936 the emergence of the Rome–Berlin alignment, which was not only a relation between two states but 'an axis around which all the European states animated by the will to collaboration and peace can also collaborate'.[1] The 'peace' aspired to was clearly not meant to be that prevailing at the moment. Mussolini's appeal for collaboration was at face value multilateral and inclusive, but would turn on the two linked and dominant poles of Italy and Germany.

It is just possible to argue that couching Italo–German co-operation in the form of an Axis rather than an alliance still bound Mussolini to no one and did not mark any definitive break with France and Britain. Mussolini did not take up German approaches in 1937–38 to transform the Axis into a full military alliance, which in the nature of a treaty of alliance would be exclusive in its obligations and commitments. It was also the case that despite Italian anger and hostility over the part played by Britain in sanctions, diplomatic contact was resumed in the context of Italy's intervention in the Spanish Civil War. The nebulous 'Gentleman's Agreement' of January 1937 acknowledged the status quo in the Mediterranean. It was followed by the rather more concrete 'Easter Accords' in April 1938, which won British recognition of the empire in return for an Italian promise to disengage from Spain.

But these agreements did not lead to a comprehensive settlement of Mediterranean issues between Italy and Britain, let alone France. If such a settlement was Mussolini's intention, as De Felice says, then one wonders why it was not achieved. Perhaps the fact that it never came about indicates that it was never actually what Mussolini intended to happen. Britain's eventual endorsement of the 'Easter Accords', even when it was clear that Mussolini was not getting out of Spain, was a sign of its hope that if Mussolini was not antagonised, Italy would act as a kind of go-between between the Western democracies and Nazi Germany. The role of middle man was the one which Britain wanted to give to Mussolini. In looking at this post-Ethiopia diplomacy, the De Felician 'revisionists' transfer these British hopes onto Mussolini and rather assume that Mussolini claimed the role of mediator for himself. But a study of Mussolini's *actions* indicates that a general agreement with Britain and France was neither intended nor possible and that the declaration of the Axis marked a new point of departure in Fascist foreign policy.

The Axis could be seen as the blackmailer's card and the continuation of a kind of balancing act, which is how De Felice interprets both the Axis and, incredibly, the alliance between Italy and Germany in May 1939. Closeness to Germany might well be the lever to extract concessions from France and Britain. Yet allowing a *de facto Anschluss* can hardly be construed as using the threat of Germany to win something from the West. It is difficult to see how Mussolini's public declaration of a new international alignment in the Axis could ever, in fact, lead to or make possible Italy's independence of both sides as the 'determining weight'. The Axis, after all, became an alliance of the fascist countries and was not dissolved in the wake of some peaceable and conciliatory accommodation among the European powers. In both timing and content, the Axis indicated that Mussolini had made a choice. It was a statement of a perceived division in Europe between the dictatorships and the democracies, which was accentuated by Mussolini's actions in both foreign and internal policy thereafter.

The Ethiopian conquest was, then, a watershed in inter-war international relations. It was the occasion which brought out a basic convergence of interests between Fascist Italy and Nazi Germany. They were both expansionist and revisionist of the 1919 settlement, and united in their hostility to France and Britain, the beneficiaries and defenders of that settlement which stood in the way of achieving their expansionist goals. Certainly from *Mein Kampf* onwards, Hitler had always regarded an alliance with Italy as central to German revision of Versailles and the attainment of a German racial empire in Europe. The Italian ally would tie down the French on the Alps and in North Africa, and the British in the Eastern Mediterranean, which was exactly the role allotted to Italy in the period of Italian so-called 'non-belligerency' between September 1939 and June 1940.

For his part, Mussolini recognised that only a revanchist Germany would back the Italian challenge to Anglo-French hegemony in the Mediterranean and help Italy become a Great Power. For Mussolini was not really interested in security in the Mediterranean, which could have been achieved by some accommodation and balance between

Italy, France and Britain. It was clear from Mussolini's summary of the international situation and Fascist Italy's aims for a secret meeting of the Grand Council in February 1939 that he aspired to control and dominance of the Mediterranean. Mussolini spoke of war with the Western democracies as inevitable if Italy was to break out of the 'prison' of the Mediterranean and remove the 'bars' and 'guards' of French and British possessions and colonies in its 'march to the oceans'.[2] Mussolini's pacing of this Italian Mediterranean stage-by-stage plan did not anticipate war in 1939, and such a qualification was important. But his keynote address, consistent with earlier and later public and private pronouncements, ruled out any compromise with France and Britain.

This was unlikely, anyway, after the Gallophobic war-scare propaganda campaign deliberately mounted in November 1938, which had Fascist deputies in the Chamber screaming for Corsica, Tunisia, Nice and Savoy, students rampaging outside the French embassy and vicious anti-French articles in the press. The campaign was staged shortly after Mussolini's 'mediation' of German claims on Czechoslovakia at the Munich conference in September 1938. Here, Mussolini had appeared to be the peacemaker, as broker of a deal between Germany and the Western democracies to dismember the country. Was the public airing of Italian grievances and claims against France, Mussolini's reminder to the democracies of the price Italy would exact for 'restraining' Germany in the interests of general peace? If so, it was a clumsy piece of blackmail and led nowhere except to a hardening of the Axis relationship. Vigorous French remonstrations at the campaign, and Britain's support of the French position, showed Mussolini that threats would not extract concessions out of the French and that more pressure needed to be applied, in the shape of an actual alliance with Germany. The events of November 1938 were probably the immediate backdrop, even the immediate incentive, for Mussolini's decision in January 1939, communicated to the German Foreign Minister, Joachim Von Ribbentrop, through Ciano, to proceed to an alliance. Even if we apply here the logic of De Felice's line about Mussolini trying to extract advantage for Italy by straddling the two camps, we are still left with a non-existent 'equidistance'. Mussolini's Mediterranean dreams only actually required France and Britain to give something up, and the 'logic' of this situation impelled Mussolini to an ever greater reliance on Germany, a choosing of sides in other words.

It is important to realise that the Axis, in Mussolini's view, met the *interests* of both countries in the ways outlined above, since historians have been keen to emphasise their differing and conflictual interests, as well as their apparent ideological divergence. The differences were real enough and persisted into the war years in the uneasy and unequal condominium of the Balkans area. But the conflicts of national interest were never insuperable or a cause of rupture in the relationship. They were, to some extent, resolved by the tacit understanding on the Italian side, at least, of separate and parallel German and Italian 'living space'. Austrian independence, apparently so crucial to the security of Italy's land frontier in 1933–35, ceased to be an issue between the two countries once Mussolini had effectively withdrawn his support for it during the Ethiopian campaign. The attempted 'Italianisation' of Italy's German-speaking alpine border provinces rankled with both Weimar statesmen like Gustav Streseman and Nazi pan-Germans as much as German complaints offended Mussolini, whose concern was to secure the nation on a contested frontier. But again, Hitler had decided very early on, in the 1920s, that making the South Tyrol German was not going to endanger an Italian alliance, a commitment he maintained until the later stages of the war.

If the Axis was sustained by a sense of common interests being served by action against common enemies, then it was also sustained by ideology. This was another factor eroding Italy's 'equidistance' from the two sides. There has always been some debate over the impact of ideology on foreign policy. If foreign policy is that function of government which defends national independence and the national interest, however defined, then ideological differences in the political systems of countries should be irrelevant to the conduct of foreign policy. Parliamentary and republican France allied itself to tsarist Russia in the 1890s and to communist Russia in the 1930s, because both countries saw their national interest in taking precautions against a common German threat. From this perspective, the fact that Britain was a democracy and Italy a Fascist dictatorship was no barrier to diplomatic relations between them. So, for all his talk about Mussolini being inspired by the Ethiopian success with a sense of historical mission to realise the grandeur of the Italian nation, De Felice schizophrenically portrays the dictator as a normal player on the international stage in the late 1930s. This approach is comparable to A.J.P. Taylor's view of Hitler as a normal German statesman in his *Origins of the Second World War*, which misses the peculiar and essential dynamic of the foreign policy of a totalitarian state.

Such a simple separation of ideology and interest is difficult to maintain in inter-war Europe, even for the example of the Franco–Russian alliance of 1935, which was the cause of serious political division in France, enough to render it inoperative. Sections of the French right were not convinced that the real danger to the nation came from Nazi Germany. They rather feared that the Soviet alliance would strengthen the position of the French Communist Party internally, fears apparently borne out by the formation of the centre-left Popular Front government which rested on the PCF's parliamentary backing.

The separation is even less justifiable in the case of the fascist powers. The hostility to France and Britain was compounded by the dictators' constantly expressed conviction, confirmed as they saw it by events, that the democracies were on the slope of irreversible decline. Ultimately, they were victims of their own social Darwinist assumptions and propaganda that these enfeebled countries would inevitably give way to the rising, aggressive fascist powers. That the Axis was not open to all, despite its apparent multilateralism, was evident from the sense of ideological affinity which the dictators gave to the relationship from the start. As Mussolini put it in March 1939, the Axis was the 'meeting of two Revolutions which declare themselves in direct antithesis to all other conceptions of contemporary civilization. Here is the strength of the Axis, and here are conditions for it lasting.'[3] This meaning was carried over into the formal alliance, 'the Pact of Steel', which was signed shortly after in May 1939. The text spoke of the basis of the alliance being 'the close relations of friendship and solidarity which exist between National Socialist Germany and Fascist Italy ... closely bound together through the complete affinity of ideologies and through comprehensive solidarity of interests'.[4]

The meshing of interest and ideology can be seen in Italian involvement in the Spanish Civil War between 1936 and 1939. Franco's military rising against the Popular Front government in Spain would not have survived at all without the early logistical and transport support from Italy. Intervention extended to the commitment of about 60 000 Italian troops alongside Franco's forces, some of them camouflaged as Militia 'volunteers'. The deception itself was significant. Mussolini could disclaim any 'official' involvement, and at the same time the sending of the armed guard of the Fascist revolution would show that the struggle against anti-Fascism was now indivisible and Europe-wide. There is no evidence that Mussolini deliberately used the lever of Italian aid to install a Falangist regime in Spain, when the Soviet Union was certainly manipulating its aid to the Republic in order to increase Spanish Communist Party influence on the Popular Front government. But Mussolini clearly backed the rebellion because he wanted the Popular Front government and the parliamentary Republic to fall. He feared an agreement between Popular Front governments in France and Spain, which would allow France to use Spain as the land bridge to its North African empire, and might even introduce communism to Spain and, by extension, the Soviet Union to the Mediterranean.

The Mediterranean was to be the Italian sea, and any strengthening of the French position there had to be resisted. Franco's victory, achieved with Italian support, would increase Italian influence in the Western Mediterranean and give access to Spanish ports and naval bases from which to threaten French North Africa. Many of these hopes were disappointed by Franco's neutrality during the Second World War, and Mussolini certainly did not anticipate the Civil War dragging on for so long. But Italian intervention connected Mussolini's strategic and geopolitical concerns for primacy in the Mediterranean to the particular form of the Spanish government. Who governed Spain and how Spain was governed made a difference to the promotion of Italian interests in the Mediterranean. This, after all, was the rationale of the Axis. A similarity in political systems was some measure of the mutual support which each could expect from the other in the international arena.

The Axis brought together warmongering dictatorships, whose 'totalitarian' structures were designed to mobilise the populations behind the regimes and prepare them for war. Any agreement with the Western democracies not only meant Italy abandoning Great Power ambitions and dreams of Mediterranean supremacy. Peace also made it difficult to continue the Fascist 'totalitarian' state, whose premise and justification was organising the nation for conflict.

The interdependence of domestic and international politics for the Fascist regime was directly and immediately felt on at least two emblematic occasions. At the time of the Czech crisis in late summer 1938, Mussolini was clearly not ready for war, and this partly explains his willingness to 'arbitrate' the dispute at the Munich conference. But his contempt for the democracies was reinforced by his perception that they were capitulating to German demands, without war. Yet Mussolini was equally disgusted at the popular enthusiasm in Italy for his role in avoiding a European war. The response was one of his periodic tirades to Ciano about the unwarlike demeanour of the Italian people, and especially of the country's establishment and bourgeoisie, whose values and conduct were still modelled on those of the pacifist and cowardly democracies. The popularity of peace in Italy was to be a further stimulus to the 'fascistisation' of society, in the shape of the 'anti-bourgeois' campaign confirmed in Mussolini's speech to the PNF National Council in October 1938.

The second, more painful occasion was whether to intervene or not in the war which Germany had started in September 1939. As the ex-Nationalist journalist and senator, Maurizio Maraviglia, confided to Bottai, war was always preferable to peace, since even if with peace the country might be saved, 'the regime goes to the bottom, because it rests on the prestige of military, warlike indoctrination'.[5] 'Non-belligerency' in 1939–40 will be broached later. But there are no starker illustrations of the line drawing together foreign and internal policy in Fascist Italy and simultaneously driving apart Fascist Italy and the democracies. It was literally the case that Mussolini could not and did not contemplate reversing the evident drift of the Axis: estrangement from France and Britain, and proximity to Germany.

2. MAKING SOMETHING OF THE EMPIRE

The inter-war Italian African empire was the only European overseas empire under a fascist state, and empire was central to the very idea of Italian Fascism. The movement was imperialist from the start, and the regime saw empire as the concrete realisation of its own nationalistic myth and the way Fascism would secure its place in Italian history and become a lasting 'historical' force. The possession of a territorial empire was not only justified in the conventional, and by now in the early to mid-twentieth century, anachronistic terms of enabling Italy, at last, to be a Great Power among other, rival Great Powers through the redistribution of land and resources to an under-resourced 'proletarian nation'. The empire was, above all, the place where Italians were 'made', and were 'made' as Fascists, and where a distinctively Fascist 'civilisation' would be forged and demonstrated, and it was a 'spiritual' as much as a territorial empire.

This was why the Fascist regime spent so much time and energy in 1934 and 1935 on preparing the country for the invasion of Ethiopia, and made its invasion and conquest a great exercise and testing ground of 'totalitarian' mobilisation for war. The regime expected, and at least temporarily received, a great surge in Italian patriotic feeling and national consciousness. Before it was the illusion, anyway, of the Fascist national 'community' in action, where individual Italians made personal sacrifices for the greater national collective good, especially in response to the international economic sanctions imposed on the country.

The regime attached great importance, in principle and fact, to the demographic colonisation of Italy's African empire. The language and aspirations of Fascism's internal colonisation, 'redeeming' the land and the people who worked it, were extended to imperial colonisation, on the basis of Mussolini's attempt to portray the rehabilitation of the Pontine marsh lands as an essentially 'civilising' and civilisation-forming process: 'to reclaim the land, and with the land the man, and with the man, the race'.[6]

The 'Fascist' empire was self-evidently that created by the conquest of Ethiopia in 1935–36. But its invasion was both preceded and followed by the 'fascistisation' of the African empire inherited from liberal Italy, which took wing once Fascists were appointed to executive positions in the empire. Mussolini tended to use service in the empire as a kind of punishment exile for Fascist leaders who became an inconvenience in Italy itself, either because of their incompetence and venality, or over-ambition, or both. But these reluctant imperialists undoubtedly gave a kind of Fascist dynamism to colonial rule. Cesare Maria De Vecchi, the pro-monarchist Fascist boss of Turin and one of the leaders of the 'March on Rome', was made governor of the East African colony of Somalia in 1923. He embarked on attritional military campaigns to 'pacify' Somalia's Southern tribes and Northern Muslim sultanates, to make real, in other words, Italy's sometimes nominal authority in the colony. The military outposts he provocatively set up on Somalia's ill-defined and contested border with Ethiopia provided one of the pretexts for war against Ethiopia in 1935.

With hardly coincidental timing, the decision to move from the liberal to the Fascist 'totalitarian' state in 1925 was accompanied by significant personnel changes which indicated a change of direction in colonial policy. Yet another Fascist commander of the 'March on Rome', the colonial military officer Emilio De Bono, became governor of the North African ex-Turkish province of Tripolitania in July 1925, while in November 1926 the intransigent Farinaccian Fascist, Attilio Teruzzi, whose fanaticism matched his incompetence, was made governor of Cyrenaica, the other province which made up the colony of Libya, with a brief to crush the Senussi tribes' resistance to Italian colonial rule. Teruzzi later commanded a Fascist Militia force in Ethiopia and, like De Bono before him, became junior minister and then full minister of colonies, or minister for Italian East Africa (*Africa Orientale Italiana*, AOI) as it was then known, by 1939.

A Fascist rather than a liberal hand was behind the rescinding in 1927 of a post-war 1919 law which had allowed the possibility of Libyans' assimilation through the acquisition of full Italian citizenship. But the most evident sign of a Fascist rule of Libya was, as with Somalia under De Vecchi, actual military conquest and 'pacification' of the colony. This was eventually achieved by 1932 in Cyrenaica by Italy's most 'Fascist' general, Rodolfo Graziani, in a very nasty colonial war, where the Italian army implemented a systematic policy of terror which today would be called 'ethnic cleansing'. The rebels were bombarded with poison gas, tactics repeated in Ethiopia, and most of the area's nomad population of 100 000 people were forcibly removed to concentration camps on the coast, their possible refuge across the desert cut off by the wired fencing of the Egyptian border, while the basis of the nomad economy, their livestock, was destroyed.

This 'civilising' exercise of 'pacification' made possible the attempt to create the model Fascist colony in Libya, carried out by another Fascist leader in exile, Italo Balbo, who became governor in 1934. The argument as to whether colonial emigration was desirable or feasible was hardly a new one; it had exercised the minds of imperialists of all political hues before and after the First World War. But Balbo, as governor, committed himself and the regime to a policy of encouraging and facilitating mass demographic settlement of the newly 'pacified' colony. Before, the state's land concessions had been taken up by companies working large agricultural estates for commercial production and using Libyan labour. Now the state-funded private–public initiative, an agency organised very much on the lines of those responsible for Fascist Italy's internal land reclamation projects, transported and settled Italian peasant farmers and their families on small farms which they would eventually own after paying back in a kind of mortgage the initial state investment.

Balbo's governorship saw a concerted attempt to make Libya an integral part of Italy, a 'fourth shore' to the country's Adriatic, Sicilian and Tyrrhenian coast lines, very much in the same way as Algeria became 'French'. The mass emigration and settlement of landless peasants from the overpopulated and politically volatile Northern and Central agricultural provinces, as opposed to the overpopulated but less politically sensitive agricultural areas of the South and the islands, was clearly meant to change the population balance of an underpopulated colony. The plan was to settle 20 000 colonists a year, 100 000 in all, between 1938 and 1943, and two waves of settler farmers and their families made the relatively short crossing to the 'new' Italy in North Africa, 20 000 in 1938 and another 10 000 in 1939, before the coming of war curtailed the population transfer.

The two areas inherited from the Turkish empire, Tripolitania and Cyrenaica, were administratively unified as 'Libya', with its capital and seat of government in Tripoli. As an even more evident mark of the integration of colony and motherland, the four coastal provinces of Libya formerly became part of Italy in 1939. That meant the full application of Italy's laws in Libya, including the race laws, which effectively nullified Balbo's deviant thoughts on allowing native Libyans to progress to Italian citizenship as part of his idea of 'separate' but 'equal' development of the two 'races'.

There was the intention to make Ethiopia a settlement colony as well. But the conditions which made mass emigration possible in Libya never prevailed in the brief period of Italian rule between 1936 and 1941. Ethiopia was not 'pacified' to an extent which would have encouraged permanent settlement. It took a year after the declaration of the empire in May 1936 for Italian forces to extend their occupation to the whole country, and from the summer of 1937 organised and persistent guerrilla-type resistance by Ethiopian 'patriots' made living and travel outside the towns dangerous and insecure.

The continuing insecurity of life in the colony was the main, if not the only, reason why even the target figures for the colonising agencies were low and why the actual colonisation of about 3000 farming families by late 1940 fell way below the targets. Most of the land allocated to the agencies, restricted anyway by the need to expropriate working Ethiopian farmers, was never farmed by Italian emigrants, and most of the funds granted to the agencies to promote and facilitate settlement were never spent.

Running and creating a colony was a very expensive business, and one is surprised by the fact that the Fascist leadership was surprised at Ethiopia being unable to pay for itself and continuing to be a net drain on the resources of metropolitan Italy. An occupation army of 200 000 men for the internal security and external defence of the colony had to be maintained, and roads had to be built. The development of cash crops for export and the settlement of new Italian farmers both required a high initial investment with few initial returns, and in the meantime AOI still had to import the bulk of what it consumed. What any empire needs is time, and a Fascist regime predicated on war did not give itself time. The new Italian colony was strategically vulnerable, surrounded by the colonies of its enemies, and was reconquered in 1940–41 by British armies invading from British Kenya and Sudan. For five years, Fascist Italy's new empire in East Africa lived a tenuous, high risk, high gain speculative 'frontier' existence, where the 'typical' Italian residents were not the peasant farmers from the Po Valley, but the soldiers and the adventurous entrepreneurs looking to make a quick, if dangerous, buck before moving on.

The British, and even the French, for all their talk of assimilation, had evolved a system of 'indirect rule' in their overseas empires, ruling as far as possible through native élites, which was a rationalisation of an acute shortage of European manpower to service tropical or subtropical colonies. The possibility of doing the same in Ethiopia certainly existed, since the African Ethiopia was itself a recently assembled empire of different territories and peoples. The Italian invasion and conquest had been eased by the fact that it provided the opportunity for some Ethiopian chiefs to escape Haile Selassie's centralising imperial rule based on the Amhara people. If allowed to resume their positions of local authority, these chiefs could have been co-opted as the intermediaries between the new imperialists and their subject populations. But a 'totalitarian' and racist Fascist regime could not share power with its own Italian citizens, let alone the Italians' presumed racial inferiors, without compromising its own nature.

The Fascists did play the ethnic card, deliberately breaking up the African Ethiopian empire and destroying Amhara hegemony within it, creating six regional areas across the whole of Italian East Africa, Ethiopia, Eritrea and Somalia, which broadly corresponded to geographical, ethnic and religious divisions on the ground. These areas were placed under Italian military governors who were nominally responsible to the viceroy in overall charge of running AOI, but who could also communicate directly with the metropolitan Minister of Colonies. This quite deliberate confusion of the lines of authority was, the then Minister of Colonies, Alessandro Lessona's attempt to play off the viceroy against the governors and ensure that policy was decided in and by the Ministry. Other government ministries and the PNF also set up shop in AOI, each of them able to communicate with their own central bureaucracies and heads back in Italy around, rather than through, the office of the viceroy. To an extent, then, the party-state and inter-ministerial rivalries of metropolitan Fascist Italy were translated to AOI.

This was of some importance to the direction of colonial policy, since the in-built administrative turf wars of the 'system' of colonial rule were overlaid and exacerbated by differing conceptions as to how AOI was to be run. The efforts of the king's nephew, the Duke of Aosta, who was viceroy from November 1937, to open up co-operation with Ethiopian élites in the administration of AOI, in marked contrast to the generally repressive 'direct rule' methods of his predecessor, Graziani, were constantly resisted and held back by the colonial ministry. Its under-secretary and then minister, the Party and Militia intransigent, Teruzzi, wanted AOI to be under civilian rather than military rule, but otherwise shared the reliance on force and imposition of Graziani. The only pragmatic, and perhaps unavoidable, concession to a form of 'indirect rule' came at the lower rungs of the colonial administrative hierarchy. Below the governors were district commissioners, whose districts were further sub-divided into residencies. Both commissioners and 'residents' were the usual career military officers or administrators, but they co-opted and salaried compliant local chiefs in the villages.

One of the main reasons for 'direct rule' was, of course, the assumed racial superiority of Italians to Africans, who were regarded as being unfit to rule themselves both now and in the future. The Fascist regime never developed a sense of the 'stewardship' of empire, that it was there to 'civilise' Africans by gradually assimilating them to European standards, which was how the British and the French, however cynically, rationalised their presence in Africa and Asia. Africans, to Fascists, remained racial inferiors to be dominated not cultivated, and colonial policy was, hence, one of 'separate' and 'unequal' development of the races.

There were no avenues by which an African subject could even aspire to become an Italian citizen. Racial superiority was to be marked and reinforced by the principle of racial segregation. Sexual and family relations between the races would clearly corrupt the colonial relationship of domination and subordination, and a mixed race population would clearly undermine what demographic colonisation was meant to achieve, an 'Italian' Ethiopia. Decree laws in 1937 restricted every day contact and sociability between Italians and Africans, and criminalised the live-in 'concubine' relationships between Italian men and African women who were often also maids and housekeepers. This so-called *madamismo* was practised almost unavoidably both before and after the conquest of Ethiopia in colonies which were being run by single men or men living and working in Africa without their families. Even more significantly, the facility to 'Italianise' the children of mixed race liaisons, which existed in Italy's East African empire before the Ethiopian invasion, was withdrawn. Mixed race children took the status of the native African parent, and much to Balbo's disgust this exclusion applied to Libya as well as AOI.

The practice of *madamismo* was, self-evidently, no less a 'colonial' relationship than that of racial separation, since it was a case of the dominant white male 'keeping' the subservient black female. Though the attempt was undoubtedly made, in practice, it was anyway difficult to enforce sexual and social racial segregation, when there was such a huge and sudden influx of unattached Italian men and the security situation in the colony discouraged the emigration of women. Officially approved white female prostitution was not really enough, and *madamismo* and recourse to African prostitutes were often unofficially tolerated, as they were before the invasion.

Direct rule, and the idea of racial superiority on which it was based, meant that co-operation from the Ethiopians was neither desired nor expected. The Fascist regime was caught in the inescapable logic of early 1920s Fascist squadrism that a situation gained by force could only be sustained by force. So it was just as well that Italian colonialism was cut off by military defeat in the war. As colonisers, Italians under Fascism were brutal and racist, and a rule resting on repression came close to realising the grim prophecy of General Guglielmo Nasi, the governor of Harar and then deputy viceroy to the Duke of Aosta, who had apparently come to share the Duke's more conciliatory outlook on governing the colony: 'You cannot construct anything by repression. You make a desert...'.[7] In its colonial practice, then, Italian Fascism was true to its own nature.

3.   FORCING THE PACE OF 'FASCISTISATION'

Between 1936 and 1940 the regime consciously stepped up and intensi-fied its attempts to 'fascistise' Italian society. The structures and organ-isations of the 'totalitarian' state were already in place, of course. It is possible, then, to see what happened in the late 1930s as the continu-ation, extension and refinement of the system of 'totalitarian' controls, though the successful conquest of Ethiopia undoubtedly provided an extra impetus to the process.

The invasion had been the first great test of and opportunity for the controlled manipulation of opinion, using all available sources of information and means of communication. The institution co-ordinating this propaganda effort, the Ministry of Press and Propaganda, was renamed the Ministry of Popular Culture in May 1937. The new title denoted more ambitious tasks, never fully realised before the collapse of the regime. These were to achieve full control of all cultural activity and of the means to transmit an official and uniform culture on a mass scale. What this meant for the regime's relatively pluralist cultural policies will be examined later. Still, 'Minculpop', in name and function, was a further step towards the 'totalitarian' submersion of the private sphere in the public or political domain. Culture was no longer seen as a free-standing, self-generating activity, but as propaganda, produced or directed by the state to serve the ends of the state.

The main prop of the Fascist state was, of course, the party, which more than any other body was meant to ensure the permanence of Fascism beyond Mussolini by creating the 'new' Italian. After years of bickering competition with the Ministry of Education and the ONB, the party at last achieved the complete and integral control of youth organisations that Starace had long regarded as necessary for effective 'fascistisation' of the young. In 1937, the ONB was merged with the Young Fascists to form a unified, party-run youth organisation, *Gioventù Italiana del Littorio* (GIL, or Italian Youth of the Lictors), which organised young people of both sexes from the age of six to twenty-one.

The formation of GIL marked a more 'Fascist' education of the young, both in and after school. GIL's instructors, now increasingly the young Fascist men graduating from the Fascist Academies of Physical Training, ran all the sports activities and physical education in state elementary and secondary schools, as well as that provided in the youth organisations themselves. From early 1938, GIL also organised the pre-military training of the eight to eighteen age group. Racial themes were introduced into the training manuals of GIL, as they were in school curricula and textbooks, coinciding with and marking the regime's incorporation of racism into its 'anti-bourgeois' campaign.

The reforms announced by the Minister of Education, Bottai, in the School Charter of February 1939 were meant to equip schools to provide training in and for life. Bottai's balance between academic study, hands-on experience of manual work and physical fitness might well have stood up outside its Fascist context and provenance. But that was inescapable in Bottai's own stated belief in the merging of GIL and the school system as a 'single instrument of Fascist education'.[8] Whether Bottai felt that the PNF, rather than his own Ministry, should take charge of the process was another matter, but the momentum of party control was difficult to resist. One of the recommendations of a joint ministry-party working group in July 1940 was for a uniform school timetable which would make over every afternoon in the school day to GIL activities. Enactment in wartime conditions was impossible, but it recognised the PNF's more than equal role in what was glibly perceived as a total educational experience. As such, it indicated the scale of the party's growing intrusiveness in school life from GIL's formation, and the increasing emphasis on militaristic and physical preparation of the young to match 'the climate of Empire'.

The party and the corporations, together the most evidently Fascist of the regime's institutions, were also given formal and official standing in the constitutional framework of the Fascist state. In January 1937, the PNF Secretary was given ministerial status, and he could, for instance, by right of office, sit in the Council of Ministers. After consideration of the issue by a Grand Council commission between 1936 and 1938, the law of January 1939 replaced the Chamber of Deputies with the Chamber of Fasces and Corporations, a change in more than name. In its even greater strengthening of the executive arm of government, the law carried on the work of the constitutional legislation of 1925–28. The nominal elective and representative character of the old Chamber disappeared completely. The new Chamber was composed of members of the PNF National Council, the National Council of Corporations and the Grand Council, who were there by virtue of their offices, all of which were nominated by the government. The executive appointed the legislative body, in other words, which was now an assembly of officials, leaving the Senate as the only unreconstructed element.

The timing and purpose of the reform were significant. It was a further attack on the constitutional position of the monarchy, which apparently disappeared from the legislative process altogether. The bill stated that Senate and Chamber collaborated with the government in the formation of the law and made no mention of the king at all. There were other straws in the wind. In a stage-managed wave of enthusiasm which deceived no one, the old Chamber of Deputies had rushed through a bill in April 1938 which created a new honorific title, First Marshal of the Empire, and bestowed it on both the king and Mussolini. This appeared to put the Head of Government on a par with the Head of State. A relatively trivial matter in itself, the incident came shortly after Mussolini's far more serious suggestion to the Senate that he should be the country's military commander in war, and not the king and the generals. On the eve of intervention in the war, he broached the question again with the king, whose fudging compromise was to give Mussolini command of operational, but not all, armed forces. The fact that the king had delegated control just preserved his formal constitutional position as Commander-in-Chief of the armed forces.

These frictions at least give some credence to Mussolini's intention, often expressed in his private conversations with Ciano, to eliminate the monarchy. The Italo–German Axis never allowed the question of the monarchy to go away in the late 1930s. This meant that the attempts to clip the crown's prerogatives could not only be regarded as the resumption of a long-standing campaign of attrition. It was known that the king was critical, or at least sceptical, of Mussolini's pro-Axis foreign policy, even if his reservations did not lead to any overt resistance to that policy, nor appear to make a real difference to Mussolini's conduct. Almost inevitably, this made the king a potential rallying point for others' unease about where the Axis alignment was leading, including, by 1940, Fascist leaders like Balbo, Grandi, De Vecchi and De Bono. None of these men broke with Mussolini and the regime over the Axis, at least not until 1943. But Mussolini was only too aware that the king's residual prerogatives lay precisely in military command of the armed forces and in foreign affairs, including that of the declaration of war. So, insisting that he, like Hitler, should be military commander was a way of ensuring that the country would enter a Fascist war under Fascist command, and that the hoped-for victories of war would redound entirely to the regime's credit. Mussolini expected the conclusion of a successful war to provide the opportunity for a final settling of accounts with the monarchy. This fitted the king's own gloomy assessment of his position in 1940 – that win or lose the war, the monarchy was doomed. If the Allies won, it would be compromised by the 'dyarchy' with Fascism; if the Axis powers won, Mussolini would abolish it. These were prognostications of an unpredictable future. But Mussolini's growing intolerance of the monarchy's existence as a drag on Fascist policy and power was evident in the late 1930s, yet another indication of the nexus between internal 'fascistisation' and the German connection in foreign policy.

The most extraordinary aspect of accelerating 'fascistisation' after 1936 was the grotesque efforts to reform the conduct, habits and attitudes of Italians. The party set the example and spearheaded the campaign, which began in early 1938 but was at its peak in the period between the summer of 1938 and late 1939. The PNF banned the use in its own organisations of the impersonal form of second-person address, 'lei', described as a foreign import to the language denoting servility, and insisted on the more comradely 'voi'. The fraternal 'you' was also formally required of all in state employment from June 1939. Other obligatory lessons in Fascist style handed out in 1938–39 included the abolition of the unhygienic handshake of greeting for the raised arm of the Fascist salute; putting state officials in uniform as a mark of their readiness to serve the nation from their desks; and the introduction of the goose-step (*passo romano*) as the marching step of the Militia and the army.

Some of Starace's initiatives were laughable, and deliberately parodied by Mussolini to show how plainly daft they were. When the PNF Secretary ordered that all official correspondence had to be signed off with a ringing 'Viva il Duce', Mussolini concocted in his presence some imaginary letters: 'Dear Sir, ... you have been dismissed. Viva il Duce!'[9] Not that Mussolini distanced himself from the campaign. He initiated and extended it, and seemed to share Starace's view that the way in which things were done actually indicated some inner spiritual transformation. It was as if forcing the nation to adopt in its daily life the rituals and symbols of the military barracks would put the country on a war footing and make the people warlike: the style was the substance.

The campaign broadened into a concerted attack on the so-called 'bourgeois' outlook and lifestyle, to the extent that the term 'anti-bourgeois' was applied to the campaign as a whole. Many of the slogans used and attitudes conveyed were evocative of the adventurous, dare-devil and violent days of squadrism, and the associations were apparently deliberate. As Mussolini put it to Ciano in July 1938, 'henceforth, the revolution must impinge upon the habits of Italians. They must learn to be less sympathetic in order to become hard, relentless and hateful – in other words, masters.'[10]

The dynamic of Fascist 'totalitarianism' connecting internal regimentation and control to expansion externally was evidently at work here. Fascism needed to accelerate the formation of a nation of 'squadrists', bold enough to rule and extend the empire. In Mussolini's view, time was pressing, especially now that international politics were changing so quickly, and the opportunities for increasing Italian power were correspondingly greater because of Fascist Italy's association with the dynamic 'revisionism' of Nazi Germany. This rapidly evolving international situation justified the intensifying efforts of the regime to create real Fascists out of Italians, so that the nation could successfully confront the inevitable conflict to come.

It could be argued that the anti-bourgeois campaign shared the same basic mystification of the actual squadrism of 1920–22, as well as reviving its myths. The squadrists, after all, glorified and acted out a life of risk and violence, inimical to the outlook of the property owners who payrolled their 'punitive expeditions'. Squadrism gave a revolutionary and heroic veneer to the sordid defence of threatened middle-class social and economic interests. Did the same sublimation lie behind the anti-bourgeois rhetoric, in the sense that it did not really target social and economic inequality, and gave the regime a sense of dynamism while disguising its inability and unwillingness to bring about real social change? Some young Fascists, who took seriously Fascism's pretensions to embody a new social order, tried in their GUF journals to extend the attack to the social and economic privileges of the bourgeoisie. Syndicalists and labour organisers did the same. It may be possible to relate to the anti-bourgeois campaign the government's decision to make official in October 1939 the extension of the appointment of factory agents (*fiduciari di fabbrica*) to most large-scale industrial plants. The Fascist syndicates had long argued before and since the ban on such agents in 1929, that only a live representative of the syndicates on the shop floor could ensure that employers stopped violating labour agreements, and sceptical workers saw some point in the syndicates.

But the brunt of the campaign was certainly directed at the 'bourgeois mentality', not at middle-class wealth. This was consistent with Fascism's own view of itself as a 'spiritual revolution', concerned with the recasting of consciousness and perception of how Italians saw themselves and others. In this light, the term 'bourgeois' was not applied to a specific class, a socio-economic category, but rather to an outlook and a demeanour which the regime condemned as un-Fascist.

Particularly after the Munich Conference, the internal stereotype of the 'bourgeois' was given a foreign incarnation, in order to emphasise that 'bourgeois' behaviour was imported, unpatriotic, and that Fascism's martial values were in fact authentic Italian national values. So the 'bourgeois' was cosmopolitan, defeatist, pacifist not by conviction but for the easy life, complacent, passive and materialistic. Infertility was the consequence of these moral failings, typical of 'bourgeois' egoism and a sure sign of national decline. The 'bourgeois' supported the Western democracies and peace with them rather than war alongside Nazi Germany, and modelled his conduct on the unheroic stance of the French and British people. These images revealed the self-fulfilling nature of propaganda. The Italians would both avoid and prey on the inevitable decline of decadent peoples, because they were being toughened up for national aggrandisement in the hard school of the Fascist totalitarian state. The campaign's focus on mentality was not simply sublimation, then. Because 'bourgeois' was not class-specific but an attitude of mind in need of correction and redirection, it could take root everywhere and in anybody. In an obviously circular and self-justifying way, the anti-bourgeois campaign was the vehicle of the Fascist totalitarian regime and its claim to exercise total control over everybody and every facet of their conduct and personality.

Important strands of the anti-bourgeois campaign were race and anti-Semitism, still a puzzling and contentious episode in the history of Fascism. Many historians see the race issue as a qualitative mark of distinction between Fascism and Nazism. If they accept an ideological dimension to the Axis, then this ideological convergence is regarded as instrumental, adopted for political reasons of state. So in 1933–34 Mussolini's opposition to Anschluss was to keep a revanchist Germany from Italy's frontiers, and also a bridge to an agreement with France in Europe and Ethiopia. Being publicly contemptuous and critical of Nazism's racial policies was Mussolini's way of reinforcing the diplomatic alignments and divisions of the time. Equally his decision to introduce anti-Semitic measures in 1938–39, thereby removing the one major ideological difference between the two regimes, was almost a pledge to Germany that he was serious about the Axis. From this perspective, ideological affinity was the product, not the cause of the closer relations between Fascist Italy and Nazi Germany.

This was exactly how Germans and Italians saw the introduction of the anti-Jewish laws at the time. German state and party officials were caught on the hop by the publication of the Race Manifesto in July 1938. This list of purportedly 'scientific propositions' about race had been concocted on Mussolini's instructions in the Ministry of Popular Culture, using the names and work of fellow-travelling academics and intellectuals. If the Germans were surprised, they were pleasantly surprised, because the Manifesto apparently endorsed a biological view of race. It asserted that the Italians were a pure Aryan race, not something accepted by all Nazi race ideologues, and that the Jews were not of the Italian race and therefore unassimilable. There appears to be no evidence of pressure from Hitler or anywhere in the Nazi system for the regime in Italy to come into line on the race question. However, Nazi German observers were unanimous in their assessment of the international repercussions of such moves: Fascist anti-Semitism would bind

Italy to Germany and make it very difficult for Italy to reach an understanding with the democracies.

Reaction in Italy exactly mirrored the Nazi response. The Pope quickly and roundly condemned the move, to an audience of Catholic students, as an un-Italian imitation of German Nazism which was a further step in the regime's descent to pagan totalitarianism. The Manifesto was popularly stigmatised as 'the Axis Ten Commandments', and from what the police and other sources tell us about the public's view, official anti-Semitism was regarded as Italy's capitulation and subordination to Germany in the Axis. If Mussolini's intention was putting on a show of ideological solidarity in order to make the Axis stick, then it clearly had that effect.

These contemporary perceptions were important, not least because they shaped the Italian people's response to the Fascist regime in the late 1930s. But it is still difficult to be absolutely sure that Mussolini, the undoubted instigator of the race measures, saw and intended them as the necessary cement of the Axis alignment. Or at least, this aspect did not exhaust the reasons for their introduction.

Mussolini seemed to hold rather conventional political prejudices about Jews, sharpened considerably by League of Nations sanctions against Italy and then by the Spanish Civil War. Jews were associated nationally and internationally with anti-Fascism in the shape of Masonry, democracy and communism, and 'controlled' international finance and business. These prejudices came together in the anti-Jewish propaganda of the sanctions period, which portrayed sanctions as the work of the Jewish international conspiracy of plutocracy and Bolshevism. Such simple-minded connections hardened with the emergence of what were portrayed as communist, Jewish-inspired Popular Front governments in France and Spain. Mussolini also appeared to be concerned about the assumed dual identity of Italian Jews as both Italians and Zionists, especially when the totalitarian state made such heavy and inescapable demands on people's loyalty to the nation. The Axis certainly did not help resolve the question hanging over the Jews' divided loyalties. Nazi racism was hardly likely to endear those Jews in military and civilian government service to the idea of an Italo-German alliance.

As a result of sanctions and the Axis then, the Jews in Italy, though small in number, had become a political problem for the regime. The conquest of Ethiopia also brought race issues in general to the political foreground. It gave an added dimension and point to the regime's long standing demographic policies, which had always been related to the stocking of an empire with healthy and well-bred Italians. The first miscegenation laws were applied in the Italian East African colony of Eritrea in 1933. Similar measures to enforce the separation of races were introduced in Ethiopia in 1937, since over-familiarity with the natives apparently undermined the principle of European racial superiority. The race problem could logically be exported from the empire to Italy itself, which explains how the Grand Council could justify its racial measures of October 1938 as the domestic aspect of a general racial problem, rendered acute by the conquest of an empire. If it was wrong on racial grounds for Italians to mix with Africans, then it was wrong for Italians to mix with Jews, as members of a different race. In fact, all the regime's public pronouncements on race from and including the Race Manifesto made a principle of racial segregation, saying that European and non-European races should not mix, and in this general way, connecting colonial racism to metropolitan anti-Semitism.

The jump still had to be made, however. The impetus came from the regime's quickening of the tempo and intensity of internal 'fascistisation' from 1936, in Mussolini's view made necessary by the conquest of empire itself. Italians needed to acquire an 'imperialistic' mentality, a racial consciousness, a sense of their own superiority and fitness to dominate and rule. A general resolution of racial issues emerging in both Africa and Italy after 1936 was therefore made possible and pressing by the regime's commitment to forcing the pace of the campaign to remake Italians. Speaking to Ciano in June 1938 of the imminent unleashing of the Fascist revolution's 'third wave', Mussolini incorporated racism into the anti-bourgeois campaign, as an integral part of the regime's attempt to tone up the population. The connection was even more strikingly made later. In an implicit recognition of the unpopularity of the measures against the Jews, the anti-bourgeois propaganda of late 1938–early 1939 condemned the 'pietism' of especially Catholics' attitudes to the Jewish community. Any trace of compassion, pity or sympathy for the Jews was a mark of the 'bourgeois' mentality and unworthy of Italians being raised in the climate of empire and war.

Perhaps one would expect the regime to insist that anti-Semitism was internal to Fascism, a natural and unavoidable extension of the race issue from Africa to Italy, and deny that it imitated Nazism. The Race Manifesto's biological racism made the charge of imitation difficult to counter. But the package of discriminatory measures announced by the Council of Ministers in September 1938 and the Grand Council in October 1938 was an odd hybrid of non-racial nationalism and biological racism. Besides action against foreign-born Jews resident in or citizens of Italy and the colonies, there was a ban on intermarriage and sexual relations between Italians and Jews, and the exclusion of Jews from the PNF and all public employment, including education, the armed forces and the civil service. Jews were also to be prevented from entering or exercising the professions, and from owning and inheriting property.

But religious and other criteria were used to dilute the racial definition of the Jews subject to these measures. The children of mixed 'Jewish'–'Aryan' marriages who were not practising Jews were categorised as 'Aryan'. No Nazi would have religious beliefs overriding the evidence of blood. The exemptions violated biological determinism too. Patriotic and Fascist Jews and their families, meaning, for instance, war veterans and those joining the PNF early on, were not affected by the anti-Semitic laws. About a fifth of all Italian Jewish families were exempted as a result, probably more after the partial and corrupt way in which the laws were actually applied.

This discretionary rather than deterministic view of 'race' marked the survival of the original Fascist conception of the nation as a 'spiritual' community, unified by and through the consciousness of all its members that they belonged to and identified with the nation. So not all Jews were strangers to the nation. Fighting in its wars and participating in the movement which embodied the best of the nation showed a real sense of being and feeling Italian and validated their membership of the nation. This idea of nation underpinned the whole process of 'fascistisation' within the framework of the 'totalitarian' state. No one was *a priori* excluded from the nation; anyone and everyone could be reformed and 'made' into Italians in the regimented and controlled atmosphere of the regime's organisations. A kind of racism might well have been adopted and adapted by Mussolini for political reasons of state. But these were as much to do with the 'fascistisation' of Italian society as with making the Axis credible as an international alignment.

The race laws were the occasion and one of the causes of the confrontation between the regime and the church in 1938–39. The underlying problem was the Catholic lay organisation, Catholic Action, which the government thought it had contained in the 1931 deal ending an earlier conflict. Catholic Action activity was picking up from the mid-1930s, at the very time that the regime was pushing harder at the 'fascistisation' of the country. In successive administrative changes it had managed to resurrect itself as a unitary, national organisation, when the whole point of the 1931 agreement had been to fragment Catholic Action into separate diocesan pieces.

It was clear that particularly in the areas of youth organisation and quasi-union activity, Catholic Action was the umbrella for networks which duplicated and thus offered alternatives to the regime's own organisations. The church appeared to have cordoned off a section of the country's educated young men in the Catholic university students' federation, its graduates' organisation and various professional associations. The parallel and competitive nature of Catholic Action was evident from the relatively small numbers of its members and leaders who were simultaneously participating in the equivalent PNF bodies. The church, building on its uniquely privileged position in the Concordat, was hoping to continue and extend its influence in society through laymen organised in the church's own orbit. The party and police reported on and urged action against a rival organisation which, to their eyes and not without reason, was assuming the dimensions of an embryonic Catholic movement capable of outlasting Fascism.

Mussolini's preferred response, as always, was to combine low key PNF and police harassment of Catholic activity in order to make life difficult with a belief in the natural wastage of Catholic Action as a result of superior party organisation. A kind of *modus vivendi* was restored in the August 1938 agreement between the party and Catholic Action, which probably took both sides back to the terms of the 1931 arrangement. This was scarcely reassuring from the party's viewpoint, since the commitment to purely religious activity had hardly inhibited Catholic Action. But there was an inbuilt caution to the Pope's jealous defence of Catholic Action, because he never wanted to risk offending the Fascist state to the point of calling the Concordat into question. This became clear from the relatively muted reaction to the race laws, which never lived up to the Pope's vigorous attack on the Race Manifesto.

Racial legislation violated the Concordat in a specific and general sense. The ban on intermarriage made invalid those church marriages involving Jews converted to Catholicism, but the Vatican's protests got nowhere and this 'wound' to the Concordat remained open. On a broader front the laws challenged the church's claims to minister to the needs of all Catholics and to a special and protected position in society based on the Concordat. The laws were to apply to everybody, including Catholics. The abuse heaped on Catholic 'pietism' in that accentuation of the regime's anti-bourgeois propaganda showed they could expect the same treatment as anybody else from a 'fascistising' regime. The

Vatican limited its defence of the Concordat to the specific point of marriage and did not broaden its resistance to defend the Jews against legalised discrimination. This was a measure of the Pope's concern not to allow the confrontation to rupture church–state relations and endanger the very survival of the Concordat, which he continued to see as the guarantee of the church's presence in society.

Concern about how Fascist 'culture' was being transmitted and received, as the attempts at 'fascistisation' intensified, lay behind the shifts in cultural policy in the late 1930s and early 1940s. The balance between the various artistic styles competing for official status moved in favour of the cultural hardliners who had always doubted whether a policy of tolerating diversity of expression could produce a distinctively Fascist culture, and who were drawn to the Nazi German model of cultural orthodoxy and singlemindedness. Their views came to prevail, if never to monopolise the field, as the Fascist regime conquered an empire, moved closer to Nazi Germany and war, and stepped up its 'totalitarian' drive to 'fascistise' Italians.

The introduction of the race laws in 1938 opened up a significant breach in previous policy. No Jewish artists' work could now appear in official exhibitions, which excluded one of Italy's best and best known expressionist *Novecento* artists, Mario Sironi, who had always been attacked by Fascist intransigents like Farinacci for a too subtle and 'distorted' representation of 'Italian-ness' in his paintings. The race laws generally gave licence to some crude Nazi-like verbal and written assaults on all 'degenerate' modernist genres, ridiculed as expressions of Jewish cosmopolitanism rather than proper Italian art.

The outcome of the drift towards 'cultural autarky' was the sponsorship and display of a public art which was monumentally 'Roman' in style, more crudely celebratory and more directly propagandistic and literal in theme and content. Almost inevitably, it was more pedestrian artistically, as demonstrated by the lumpen responses to Farinacci's 1939 Cremona prize for paintings on 'listening to a speech by *Il Duce* on the radio'. By this time, the Fascist regime had as little a sense of humour and a sense of irony as the cultural historians have fifty years on when encoding and deconstructing Fascism's 'symbolic universe'. The shift in artistic format was based on the calculation that the Fascist message was best conveyed in an unequivocal, documentary and educational fashion, when as the cultural eclectics of the late 1920s and early 1930s realised, probably the reverse was true. Attendance at the revised conventional museum display lay out of the Exhibition of the Fascist Revolution in 1937 was way down on that for the original 1932 version. In moving towards art which was blatantly propagandistic, the regime probably helped to kill off the audience's receptiveness to propaganda, the purpose of which, after all, was to persuade.

4. AUTARKY AND ECONOMIC PREPARATION FOR WAR

There was a demonstrably high degree of alignment between Mussolini's foreign policy, increasingly centred on the Axis with Nazi Germany, and the drive to 'fascistise' Italian society. The government's continuing commitment to autarky indicated a similar alignment of economic policy to foreign policy. Mussolini's speech in March 1936 making autarky official explicitly linked a strong foreign policy to economic independence and spoke of the need for a state-run 'regulatory plan'[11] for the exploitation of the country's economic resources to meet the inevitability of war. Mussolini's reference to a planned war economy cannot be taken at face value. It is quite difficult to show that economic and foreign policy were exactly matched, because Italy was not ready for war when she joined it in 1940. This apparent puzzle needs explaining.

Autarky was at the start as much impelled by circumstances as by choice. First, the circumstances were those of the Depression and the universally protectionist responses to it, which destroyed Italian and international trade between 1929 and 1935. Italy's trading position was worsened by Mussolini's political decision to stick to an overvalued lira, but overall Italy's trade declined in the same proportions as world trade. Second, there were the economic sanctions of the Ethiopian war, and the goal of self-sufficiency made a virtue out of the necessity of finding a way around them. Sanctions were lifted in July 1936 and the Depression was easing too, even though this did not automatically involve any return to the world trade of the 1920s. As for foreign policy, the question was whether there was a choice between continuing autarky and returning to the international economy.

For the Fascist regime any such choice was political and ideological, or would have such repercussions. International trade could only revive in conditions of international peace, and if Italy wanted to trade with the United States and Western Europe, relations with them had to improve and continue to improve. It was no wonder that anti-Germans like Fulvio Suvich, Under-Secretary at the Foreign Ministry until he was removed in July 1936, were urging a restoration of trading relations with those countries as a way of slipping out of Germany's embrace. But Mussolini was not interested in international stability and peace, nor in a non-ideological and accommodating foreign policy towards the Western democracies. The Axis exacted a kind of economic price.

After 1936 trade certainly resumed with Italy's usual trading partners, including countries which had applied sanctions. But two things were different. First, trade was increasingly conducted through bilateral clearing agreements, where the value of imports exactly matched the value of exports. For Italy this was a way of curbing and controlling imports, a vital aim of autarky, without paying for them by scarce gold and foreign currency reserves. Connected to this, the government's import licensing system and its control of foreign currency were strengthened and made permanent *after* the lifting of sanctions. The agency it had set up for this purpose, to control foreign trade in preparation for and during the invasion, became the Ministry of Exchange and Currency in November 1937. The lira's belated hefty devaluation in October 1936 to improve exports – another autarkic aim – suggested a return to international trade, except that exports were often part of bilateral deals rather than multilateral exchange.

Second, the clearing arrangements with the countries that had not applied sanctions, such as Germany and Hungary, were more advantageous than the others, which marked a more general shift in the pattern of Italian trade during and after the Ethiopian war. Italy traded more with the empire and the countries of Central and Eastern Europe, and traded less with Western Europe and the United States. German imports were 18 per cent of the total in 1936 and 29 per cent in 1940. Imports from East Africa were small, but Italian exports to the empire were about 25 per cent of the total by 1939, and another 25 per cent went to Germany. Germany supplied coal and industrial goods; Italy sent agricultural produce and labour to Germany. Here were the worrying signs to Italian businessmen of Italy becoming the agrarian client of its powerful industrial neighbour, and clear confirmation that the two economies were drawing together as the Axis hardened into the alliance.

There were other telling indications of an autarkic and war economy. State intervention in the economy continued and increased. IRI, initially the device for banking and industrial salvage operations in the Depression, became a permanent body in 1937. It ran a huge complex of largely public-owned heavy industries through subsidiary holding companies, like Finsider in the iron and steel sector, and had powers to take over private firms where this was justified by reference to national defence, autarky and empire. State-controlled and monopolistic agencies mushroomed and were run like private companies on public money, often, indeed, capitalised jointly by government sources and the near-monopolies dominating the private sector, like Montecatini and Fiat. They were responsible for developing import surrogates, whether through finding and exploiting indigenous sources of energy, metals and raw materials or producing synthetic substitutes. Obligatory requisitioning was introduced in 1936-37 for cereals, beet, hemp, wool and other agricultural foodstuffs and raw materials, in the hope that stockpiling would end market volatility and guarantee a regular supply at stable prices.

Government spending increased wildly, about 30 billion lire in 1934-35, rising to double of that in 1938-39. Middle-class incomes and savings were squeezed to pay for it, through government loans, the renegotiation of Treasury bonds, and four extraordinary direct taxes on property, capital and shareholdings. But even these increased tax revenues did not cover the state deficit, which rose from about 2 billion lire to 28 billion between 1934-35 and 1938-39. The money was going to autarkic and heavy industry servicing the armed forces. By 1939 probably between a quarter and a third of all government spending was on the military, including Spain and the empire. Nearly 80 per cent of the ballooning state deficit between 1935 and 1939 was accounted for by mainly military 'exceptional' expenditure.

Autarky bred abnormal and distorted economic growth, in itself a measure of the priority being given to war preparation. High-cost domestic industries were producing a range of products which could be bought cheaper in the international market. Since the contractor and consumer was the state, it did not matter that this made little economic sense. The goal was not productivity and market efficiency, but producing enough of what the country required for war.

Whether the autarkic economy was a planned economy in the way announced by Mussolini in 1936 is debatable. There was no central planning agency to co-ordinate the six economics ministries and innumerable economic bodies working in specific sectors, unless that job was done by the Commission for Autarky, set up in 1937 and later replaced by an inter-ministerial committee. The main organs of state control or regulation worked effectively enough in their own areas. IRI's Finsider, for instance, had reached the planning stage in 1938 for the co-ordination of production and investment in the iron and steel sector. Foreign trade was covered by the Ministry of Exchange, which by controlling raw materials imports and the currency to pay for them could discriminate between industries dependent on those imports. The requisitioning and stockpiling of cereals was an attempt to plan outside the market, for adequate food supplies in the eventuality of war. A prices policy of sorts was applied to contain the inflationary spiral set off by devaluation and increased public spending. A two-year block on rents and the prices of utilities and basic items was imposed in 1936. But as in the revaluation crisis of 1926–27, the party's pricing committees were unable to stem price inflation. The corresponding award of quite significant across the board pay rises in 1936, 1937 and 1939 was hardly a sign of the control of labour in line with war mobilisation.

Italy's evident economic and military unreadiness to sustain a big war in 1939 might suggest the absence of economic planning for war, or at least a lack of synchronisation between economic and foreign policy. The second position has more validity than the first. It is difficult to deny the connection of autarky to war preparation, and not just because Mussolini insisted on the linkage. There was the evidence of the misshapen economy of the late 1930s, as the government poured public money into military and military-related spending. Much of these economic and military resources were consumed in the local wars and actions undertaken by the regime between 1935 and 1939, from the conquest, pacification and administration of Ethiopia, through the Spanish Civil War, to the annexation of Albania. This was another important reason for the situation on the outbreak of a more general European war in 1939.

Again, autarky was certainly an unattainable goal for a relatively poor and ill-resourced country like Italy, which would always need to import coal, oil and raw materials. But the fact that it was unrealisable in present conditions was the very reason pushing Fascist Italy towards war alongside Germany. Within the Axis bloc of fascist powers, German resources were already making up for some of Italy's economic shortfalls. Whatever the illusions about Ethiopia's economic potential, the empire was an attempt to make Italy economically independent and powerful by war. Future expansion and conquest would achieve that redistribution of territory and resources which had always been behind Fascist 'revisionism'. Talk of 'living space' (*spazio vitale*) was as common in Fascist Italy before and during the war as it was in Nazi Germany.

5.   'NON-BELLIGERENCY' AND WAR, 1939–40

The problem was that the Axis partners were moving at a different pace and according to a different timetable, and Italy was being dragged along by its stronger ally. Partly as a result of this, Italian economic, military, political and diplomatic preparation were put out of joint, and led to Mussolini's humiliating decision not to join Hitler's war in 1939.

This was clear from the extraordinary and irresponsible alliance, the 'Pact of Steel', signed in May 1939. It envisaged permanent political consultation between Fascist Italy and Nazi Germany with a view to agreement and joint action on all matters. It bound each side to automatic military intervention when the other went to war, and planned for military and economic co-operation enabling such automatic military aid to occur. It was an agreement for war, in other words. Mussolini and Ciano had Ribbentrop's verbal assurances about the separate and parallel spheres of interest of Italy and Germany, and that war, though inevitable, would not occur in the immediate future. A breathing space of two to three years, perhaps even four to five, was presumably why Mussolini felt he could enter such an alliance, though none of the German nods and winks about the timing of war were actually written into the Pact.

It was self-deluding not to be aware of the dynamism of the German partner. Already in March 1939 the Czech agreement nominally brokered by Mussolini at Munich had been destroyed by Hitler's seizure of Bohemia and Moravia – without consultation. As a reassertion of Italy's Balkan sphere of influence, the bad-tempered and anxious Italian response was to annex Albania in April, a country already so tied to Italy that it was 'like raping your own wife'.[12] Not that the Germans seemed to mind. The annexation gave the impression of the Axis powers acting in unison and with irresistible force, and kept Italy apart from the Western democracies. Again, immediately after the alliance was signed, which in Hitler's view made it even more unlikely that France and Britain would resist further Axis coups, he ordered the invasion of Poland. Ciano was dismayed to learn in his meetings with Hitler and Ribbentrop in August that a Polish war was not only inevitable but imminent.

The news of German plans for immediate war put Mussolini in a corner. He was bound by the alliance to join Hitler in a war he had not anticipated would happen so soon, and which he knew Italy could not really fight. It was not only a matter of Italy's military and economic unreadiness to sustain a long war. Mussolini and Ciano paraded this in front of the Germans, in order to get them to delay things or at least accept that the alliance could not be activated then. The other reason or pretext for prevarication was the need for more time to make the Axis popular in Italy and prepare the nation politically and psychologically for war.

This was some admission for a regime and a system predicated on war, but it pointed to what some historians have seen as Fascism's 'crisis of consent' in 1939-40. Fascist foreign policy and its complementary internal policy had the effect by 1940 of beginning to break through the crust of compromise under which the regime had stabilised itself in the late 1920s. More evidently Fascist foreign and domestic policies, marked by the Axis, internal 'fascistisation' and autarky, did not now necessarily serve the interests of those semi-autonomous centres of power which had come to terms with the dictatorship. Important sections of the establishment, the church, the monarchy and *Confindustria*, along with some major Fascist leaders, were against the German alliance and appalled at the prospect of war on Germany's side. Their concern, whether communicated privately or occasionally in public, made little apparent difference to Mussolini's commitment to the German connection, except to play its part in heightening Mussolini's sense of national unreadiness in 1939.

Mussolini's own police sources were telling him that anti-Axis feeling was not confined to these areas, and that warlike indoctrination was not taking hold in the country. Indeed, it was probably counter-productive, as 'fascistisation' imposing on people's outward behaviour and conduct invited resistance, annoyance and even ridicule. The anti-bourgeois campaign attacking their values, together with a spendthrift government taxing their income, were a strain on the largely uncoerced sympathies of the middle classes for Mussolini and Fascism. The more Fascist the regime became, the more it put at risk its broad base of 'consent'. Although it did not result in much opposition to the regime, the idea and approach of war made many apprehensive, and the Axis was unpopular precisely because it seemed to be leading to war.

Going to war was a gamble for all sides. The king realised that Mussolini by his actions in 1938-39 was gunning for the monarchy, and acknowledged that war, whether resulting in victory or defeat, could mean the end of the monarchy. The Vatican faced the same basic dilemma. The understanding between the church and regime had produced the Concordat. But again, this would be threatened either by a triumphant Fascism completing its 'fascistisation' of society on the back of a successful war, or in the event of defeat by anti-Fascism taking revenge on those institutions compromised with the regime. Neutrality in the war and Mussolini still in power preserved the benefits of Fascism without incurring the risks.

As for Mussolini and the regime, war was both the test and the gauge of 'fascistisation' and the means of completing it, as was clear from his dark threats to finish with pope and king once the war was won. The dilemma was inescapable. Taking to war 'a race of sheep'[13], who had so far resisted their transformation into wolves, courted disaster for the regime if things went badly. But if the Italians were reluctant fighters and Fascists, then the Fascist solution could not be peace, only exposure to the test of war.

There was an immediate way out of the problem of wishing but feeling unable to go to war. This was Hitler's agreement in September 1939 to Italy remaining in the alliance without actually fighting, providing instead political and diplomatic support and acting as Germany's economic and military 'reserve'. It is important to realise that Mussolini's face-saving declaration of 'non-belligerency' was nothing like neutrality. As in 1914–15, neutrality was 'equidistance', listening to and taking offers from both sides. But Mussolini quickly killed off the tentative idea of a Balkan bloc of neutral countries led by Italy, which the Vatican supported, once France and Britain seized on it as a wedge between the Axis powers. 'Non-belligerency' quite deliberately meant that Mussolini was keeping Italy in the alliance, but there would be no fighting war as yet. In the meantime Mussolini kept alive, at least in his own mind, the hopes of a parallel war, alongside but not subordinated to Germany. This was probably the intention behind Mussolini's letter to Hitler in January 1940, urging him to end the Nazi–Soviet Pact and seek his *Lebensraum* in Russia. Knowing that Hitler was contemplating a campaign in the West, Mussolini wanted to delay matters so that Italy would have the chance to intervene in *its* war against France and Britain.

By the end of March 1940 Mussolini was informing the king that the only issue was the when and how, not the whether of Italy's intervention. Staying out of the war would put Italy at the mercy of whoever won, and reduce the country to the status of a 'Switzerland, times ten'.[14] Even the king could see the logic of that in May–June 1940, when the Germans achieved rapid and crushing victories against France and seemed set to decide the fate of Europe, with or without Italy. For the few weeks up to Mussolini's decision to declare war on France on

10 June 1940, there was temporary unity of Mussolini and the country in the perception that Italy could gain much and risk little by joining a war that was practically over. Since only a short and victorious war was in prospect, with easy pickings, Italy's unreadiness to wage a long campaign was irrelevant. What Mussolini's political journal, *Gerarchia*, called in July 1940 a 'revolutionary' fascist war could begin.

7 Fascist Italy at War, 1940–43

1. THE COLLAPSE OF ITALY'S PARALLEL WAR

War should have been the apotheosis of Fascism. In fact it was its nemesis. Fascism failed the test that it had set for itself, indeed the only standard by which it wanted to be measured, as a mass-mobilising dictatorship preparing the nation for victorious war and conquest. War was what Fascism was about, whatever the opportunism of Mussolini's June 1940 decision to exploit the apparently overwhelming Nazi military gains in Northern and Western Europe. The gamble for Mussolini and the regime was huge, if calculated. The only justification for war was to win it, and rapidly. The losing of a prolonged war exposed the regime's growing unpopularity, already passively evident before 1940 as a result of that combination of accelerated 'fascistisation' and the Nazi German alliance. The wartime experience revealed the inevitable superficiality of Fascist attempts at totalitarian mobilisation and the fatal flaws in the institutional structures of the Fascist state, and completed the dissolution of the broad conservative coalition of interests that had sustained Fascism since the 1920s.

Fascist Italy claimed to be fighting a parallel war within the Axis framework, alongside Germany and against the same enemies but in different areas and for Italian aims. The idea of a separate if connected war effort can be related back to the implicit Axis understandings of the late 1930s for contiguous 'living spaces', the Italians in the Mediterranean basin and hinterland, the Germans in Northern, Central and Eastern Europe. It could also, just, be linked to 'non-belligerency', in the sense that Mussolini had not committed the country in 1939–40 to a war started by Germany and at a time not of Italy's choosing.

The war was also to be parallel in political terms, as the regime attempted to articulate a vision of a Fascist 'New Order' which was in part emulation of and in part a rival to that of the Nazis. In the wake of conquest, itself validating Fascism's superior value system and its claim to universality, European politics and society would be 'fascistised' by implanting the totalitarian state governed by Fascist élites and the corporative social and economic structure. This remodelling of a conquered Europe on the Italian Fascist prototype would be the essential first step in the continent's economic reorganisation, both serving the immediate needs of the Axis war effort in a global conflict and marking out the shape of the post-war order. Opinion differed as to whether a subjugated Europe and its African and Asian hinterlands should be treated as one unified economic bloc managed by collectively agreed Axis policies, or whether Italy should carve out its own separate and autarchic Mediterranean regional economic zone. Both projections were clearly meant to prevent or dilute German hegemony in Europe, especially the more commonly aired second option. A bipolar system, with each of the Axis powers dominating, organising and exploiting its own *spazio vitale*, would be some guarantee of Italian political and economic independence in the new Europe. The regime's propaganda gave Fascist war aims a patina of Europeanism, but the rhetoric of an imperial 'community', to be conquered and then civilised by Fascist Italy, only thinly disguised the intention to dominate.

The Fascist New Order was and remained fanciful stuff, because the military parallel war was over by the spring of 1941. There were demonstrable signs of who dominated the Axis in June 1940, on the defeat of France. Italian territorial claims on metropolitan, insular and colonial France, essential to achieve a redistribution of power in the Mediterranean, were turned aside by Hitler's political argument that the war against Britain would be hindered by the permanent alienation of France at that juncture. Then Mussolini ordered the invasion of Greece from Albania in October 1940. This was entirely consistent with the goal of Mediterranean hegemony, but was improvised in timing, planning and execution. It was precipitated by Germany's unilateral action to secure exclusive control of Romania's oil fields, which was seen as yet another move to monopolise the Balkan and Danubian economies in disregard of Italy's regional sphere of influence. It was hastily carried out, to pre-empt German objections to a Balkan war which Hitler felt would invite Allied intervention and thus compromise his own plans for the invasion of the Soviet Union. Deliberate aggravation of the Albanian minority issue in Greece and the attempted corruption of Greek politicians raised hopes of an easy victory on the cheap. But the Greek army resisted and counter-attacked into Albania before the front stabilised. The botched invasion was a military and political disaster for the regime. It undermined the regime's credibility internally and brought about the subordination of Italy's war to Germany's which it was designed to prevent. Hitler's successful invasion of Yugoslavia and Greece in April 1941 alone allowed Mussolini a part in the dismemberment and occupation of countries in the Italian orbit.

Similar bailing-out operations were necessary in Africa, the other theatre of Italy's parallel war. As early as May 1941, the Italian East African empire of Eritrea, Somalia and Ethiopia was lost to British armies and Ethiopian insurgents, and Erwin Rommel's German force was required to stem and then reverse losses in Libya.

The self-evident failure of the separate war inevitably nullified the parallel Fascist political New Order. As a result of being incapable of winning its own battles in its own recognised spheres of action, Italy simply lacked any political weight in asserting her version of a European order or influencing the course and conduct of the war. This subordination was revealed concretely in both military and political matters. Mussolini insisted in diverting troops and equipment better deployed in North Africa to support the German invasion of the Soviet Union in June 1941. This was for the sake of 'being there' and of confirming Italy's presence in the Axis. But the impression was of Italians fighting Hitler's war in a place where no national interests were served. Italian involvement made little difference to how Hitler conducted the war, there or anywhere else. He was deaf to Mussolini's suggestions from late 1942 for a separate compromise peace with Russia.

Initially the Italians had made pointed comparisons between what they saw as Germany's brutal incorporation of northern Slovenia and their own alleged attempt to 'associate' the Yugoslav territory they controlled. But German pressure and German priorities led inexorably to the extension of German methods of control in occupied and annexed Yugoslavia by early 1943. Italian political and military control of Dalmatia and southern Slovenia and of the supposedly satellite statelets of Croatia and Montenegro was tenuous and short-lived anyway, as Slav resistance was active from the summer and the autumn of 1941. Increasingly concerned that Balkan unrest would encourage Allied landings and endanger the war on the Eastern front, the Germans insisted on co-ordinated repressive action against all Slav partisans and their host local populations, including the nationalist bands which the Italian military had tried to use as a check on the communist formations.

It had been thought that this eventual assimilation of Nazi occupation policy stopped short at the racial question, and that despite German diplomatic pressure and Mussolini's official assurances, the persecution and the deportation of Jews were only implemented once the Germans themselves took over the Italian-occupied zones of France and the Balkans in September 1943. But recent research has indicated a shifting of the Italian position in the areas Italy occupied in Yugoslavia and Southeastern France, before the fall of Mussolini in July 1943. It was certainly the case that Fascist racial legislation was not usually extended to Italian-occupied territories, and that Mussolini's 'no objection' response to German demands for the hand over of local and refugee Jews in Yugoslavia did not bind the Italian authorities on the ground to co-operate in deportations.

Early in 1942, however, the Italians in Kosovo handed over to their deaths some refugee Jews to the German occupation authorities in Serbia. The Nazi 'final solution' was certainly common knowledge among power-holders in Italy and Italian-occupied areas by the time, in the summer of 1943, Mussolini decided to intern Jews in camps, and the Italian police in France were ordered to transfer into German hands those German refugee Jews living in the Italian zone and to repatriate Italian Jews. These decisions, literally on the eve of the first fall of Mussolini in July 1943, were countermanded after his dismissal by the king. Unpalatable though it might be, it seemed that in the summer of 1943, the Fascist government was prepared to consign foreign and refugee Jews to certain transfer to the death camps. The attempt to distinguish between the treatment of foreign and 'national' Jews echoed Vichy France's policies and its claim to be protecting French Jews by sacrificing non-French Jews. But this only postponed and did not prevent Vichy France's eventual participation in the deportation of French Jews. Had Mussolini not fallen from power in July 1943, and Italy not been occupied by the Germans, it was at least likely that Italy's Jews would have suffered the same fate as they actually did under German occupation.

2. THE IMPACT OF WAR AND THE INTERNAL CRISIS OF THE REGIME

Italy's military performance might be taken as an object lesson in the weakness of dictatorial rule. In 1940 Mussolini was Head of Government, minister for all three armed services and commander of the armed forces in the field. He clearly wanted to emulate Hitler's personal control of military matters, but unlike Hitler deprived himself of the support enabling him to manage such a role. Mussolini apparently had all the power, or at least the positions, and took the basic military decisions, but had no staff, office or command organisation to ensure proper briefing and translation of the leader's decisions into operational action by the armed forces. This should have been one of the roles of a General Staff. But its nominal head, Pietro Badoglio, had a nominal staff, and never expected or attempted to co-ordinate and direct the three services according to an agreed military strategy. Things improved when he was replaced as Head of the General Staff in May 1941 by Ugo Cavallero, whose office at least operated as an intermediary between Mussolini as supreme commander and the services.

This serious lack of effective strategic and operational co-ordination between the army, navy and air force had blighted Italy's preparation for war, reflected in inadequate anti-aircraft defences and the failure to construct aircraft carriers. In wartime, even communication between the services was laborious, and the lack of an overall view in individual actions as much as general strategy led to some disastrous military own goals. It appeared as if the three services were fighting three separate wars, with no one, not even Mussolini, capable of co-ordinating them. The point was that the problem was not new, but endemic to the regime's relationship with the armed forces. Mussolini's accommodation with a still largely monarchical officer corps was in part sustained by his tacit respect of the traditional autonomy of the individual services. When it came to that most Fascist of endeavours, war, Mussolini paid dearly for the customary inter-service rivalry which marked the regime's compromise with the armed forces.

In order to explain Italy's military failures, there is also something to the argument that in comparison with the major powers at war with Italy, the country simply lacked the economic resources and potential to fight a long war. The evidence suggests that the country was performing during the war to its productive, financial and physical limits. Industrial production, at least in the war industries, rose, falling away from high levels only during 1942, partly as a result of Allied bombing of the northern industrial cities. Agricultural production too, at least in the north, generally held to its pre-war levels until declining significantly in 1942–43, as the call-up of labour and shortage of fertilisers began to bite. The problem was that agriculture was still not producing enough foodstuffs to meet consumer needs, and wartime blockade and the regime's own autarchic policies cut off imports. Industry, though increasing production, could not supply sufficient arms and equipment for a prolonged conflict, and suffered from an inadequate supply of the raw materials and fuel which Italy had usually imported, even under autarky.

This was what allies were for, and Italy became almost entirely dependent on German coal supplies to fuel its industries, though again such provision progressively declined to a point below sufficiency, forcing breaks in production in 1942. Significantly, Germany began to extract more economically from Italy than she gave, and this changing balance of trade was another facet of Italy's subordination in the Axis alliance. Forced to export labour and agricultural produce to Germany in return for essential but shrinking supplies of coal and iron, the country was penalising its own war effort by 1942. Agricultural exports reduced the availability of food in Italy, depressing consumption levels even further. In February 1942, an estimated 350 000 Italian workers were in Germany, at least half of them skilled industrial workers needed in Italy's own factories. It was bad enough that the war was not leading to that grand redistribution of territory and resources which was its justification and which would raise Italy to the position of a major power. During 1942 the war and the German alliance were actually draining away the country's current and inadequate economic strength.

Moreover, this was perceived and more importantly experienced by almost every Italian during the war, which made all the difference to the regime's will, solidity and credibility. If the economy within its limits met the test of war, society did not. Popular dislike of the war and of the German alliance which had brought it about, temporarily suspended in summer 1940, found constant and concrete reference points in the worsening daily conditions of wartime life. As in the late 1930s, the government tried to meet the spiralling costs of the war economy by printing money, inflation and the diversion of private surplus into public hands by loans and taxes on property and capital. But the country's capacity to pay was not limitless. State taxation was taking perhaps a quarter of national income in the war, but whereas tax revenue met about 60 per cent of government spending on the eve of the war, in 1940–42 it barely covered a third, its value constantly eroded by general inflation. The middle-class taxpayer and saver had had enough. By late 1942 there were declining returns on successive issues of Treasury bonds, the method by which the government borrowed money from its citizens. This was a precise indicator of the lack of confidence that middle-class savers had in the state, undermined by military reverses and a deteriorating economic situation where inflation and shortages made people spend rather than lend or invest whatever money they had.

The rising costs and shortfalls of basic food and consumer goods eating into the real incomes of white- as well as blue-collar workers could be and were directly attributed to the autarky, enemy blockades and priority to military production and consumption associated with being at war. Food shortages were worsened by the inefficient operation of the government's own measures to ensure consistency of supply or at least some equality of sacrifice for consumers. A rationing scheme of sorts existed, but was never intended to cover all food needs. The official normal daily bread ration was nearly halved from 150 to 80 grams in the course of 1942, but the actual rations distributed were always below the official rate. Such a system, which could not guarantee a supply of basic products, was practically an open invitation to the emergence of a black market during 1941, at prices way beyond the reach of most people. The obligatory stockpilings of agricultural products, a feature of the autarchic economy from the late 1930s, were meant to make unnecessary any recourse to a black market in wartime. But these were administered poorly, sometimes corruptly and speculatively, and became part of the problem they were set up to pre-empt. Farmers basically lost confidence in the operation of these *ammassi*, disaffected by the disproportionate difference between consignment and sale prices, and attracted by the money to be made in supplying the unofficial market. Evasion of their legal obligation to consign goods to the *ammassi*, widespread in 1942–43, set off a counterproductive cycle of forcible requisitioning and more hiding of produce, alienating farmers and further reducing supply to the consumer.

Finally, Allied bombings of industrial cities intensified in the second half of 1942, disrupting production, causing homelessness and mass evacuations to rural areas, a dislocation which strained urban and country populations alike. The cumulative effects of rationing, high prices, bombings and evacuation, and the longer working hours and tighter factory discipline of wartime production, together with a by-now noticeable revival of organised anti-Fascist activity, sparked in March 1943 the first great strikes by industrial workers for nearly twenty years.

Perhaps unavoidably in these wartime circumstances, the regime's 'capillary' organisation, the party, could not hold the disintegrating home front. By late 1942 Mussolini was privately and publicly acknowledging that the nation had failed its ultimate test, reflecting what he rationalised as the endemic mental laziness of the Italian people only superficially touched by the process of 'fascistisation'. This was unwitting self-criticism as much as contempt for his inadequate human raw material, and to a party audience he condemned the inactivity of a PNF of his own making: 'There are 4 million members of the *fasci*, 8 million in GIL.... The regime controls something like 25 million individuals.... Well what are all these people doing? I ask myself what are they doing?'[1]

The sheer weight of numbers was part of the problem, and Mussolini rather futilely pined for a streamlined élite party where membership denoted faith in Fascism. This was rich coming from a leader who had endorsed Party Secretary Ettore Muti's decisions in 1939–40 to open PNF membership to the ex-combatants of all Italy's recent wars and to the 25–35 age group. Membership of male and female *fasci* swelled from 3.5 million in late 1939 to 4.25 million in March 1940 and 4.75 million in June 1943. This showy attempt to match the party to the young and not quite so young soldier-patriots posed an enormous administrative burden to the provincial PNF federations, forcing them to digest an army of new members.

This came just at a time when war placed the party in the same contradictory position as during the 'going to the people' campaign of the Great Depression. Mobilised to face the national emergency and involve itself even more in society, the party's capacity to cope with such an enhanced role was stretched by the extraordinary wartime conditions. Being at war put a premium on the PNF's functions of control, exhortation and surveillance. Together with responsibilities for organising civil defence, the welfare of combatants and evacuees and their families, and the direction and policing of price controls and the *ammassi*, these required extra human and material resources. Yet conscription and absence on military service of members, staff and leaders at all levels destabilised party organisation and reduced the regular income from subscriptions. The shortfall was not easily made up when other normal contributors to the funding of party activities, such as banks, companies and syndical organisations, were feeling the financial squeeze themselves because of the impact of war.

The PNF's involvement in the official price setting of basic consumer goods and the requisitioning of foodstuffs, unhappily not matched by its ability to do much about spiralling living costs and worsening shortages, took the party into areas of concrete disaffection with the war and made it and its activities unpopular. Fatally the party's capacity to carry the nation through the war and defend the regime was corroded by the perceptibly worsening course of the war on both the home and fighting fronts. It was difficult and ultimately pointless to counter 'defeatism' in all its forms and seek to maintain popular morale, when the regime's pretensions and propaganda were made incredible in contact with the awful reality of the war's impact. Hitler's scathing indictment in September 1943 of a Fascism melting away like snow under the sun at the time of Mussolini's fall from power in July underestimated the demoralisation and isolation which party men and organisation experienced as a result of that unbridgeable gap between aspiration and reality opened up by the war. The appointment in April 1943 of the old squadrist lag, Scorza, as the PNF's fourth Secretary in four years, promised 'a relaunching of the Party with a strong hand, intervening in all branches of public life'.[2] It was too late to mean much by then. But this desperate last-ditch evocation of squadrist methods, the imposition by force of the will of an armed minority, captured the siege mentality of the PNF's successor in the even more untenable situation of Mussolini's Social Republic in 1943–45.

3. THE FALL OF MUSSOLINI

Italy's war had gone badly almost from the start. But the military situation had been retrieved by German intervention and there was some hope that Fascist Italy could achieve a Mediterranean empire under the cover of German victories. But the war finally turned against the Axis in autumn 1942, with successful Allied landings in North Africa resulting in the loss of Libya in May 1943 and the start of huge Russian offensives. There was a real prospect of an Allied invasion of Italy itself, which occurred in July 1943, and this made the Anglo-Americans an influence on Italian political developments. The Allies talked of unconditional surrender, and it was evident that they would not negotiate a separate peace with Mussolini. He was more clearheaded than his ministers about the significance of this. In his view there was no possibility of disengagement from the Axis. A separate peace with the Allies, a renunciation of the German alliance, would mean the removal of Mussolini and the end of Fascism, while the Germans would occupy Italy if it tried to leave the Axis.

Mussolini's stance closed down the options of those who realised the war was lost, invasion imminent and wanted to find a way out of the war. Since Mussolini would not leave the German alliance, the only possible way out of the Axis and the war was his removal as Head of Government and commander of the armed forces, and the king's resumption of his power over these positions. Here, the incompleteness of the Fascist constitutional arrangements of the late 1920s proved fatal for the regime. Although the king had been reduced to a political cipher, the monarchy was still an alternative focus of legitimate political authority. Even under Fascism's own 1928 law on the attributes of Head of Government, the king could dismiss Mussolini, and he certainly could do so under the still-unrepealed constitutional statute. It was this Fascist-monarchist dyarchy which made Mussolini's fall in July 1943 as constitutionally ambiguous as his coming to power in 1922.

The loss of confidence in the regime and Mussolini's leadership was almost general as a result of the impact of the war and the near-certainty of Axis defeat. It extended to Fascists like Grandi, Bottai and Ciano, who were the main movers behind the calling of the Grand Council meeting in July, the first that Mussolini had allowed since December 1939.

Other conservative interests stood back from a now-discredited system. Industrialists had enjoyed high wartime profits, even the initial prospect of taking advantage of territorial gains, but by late 1942 the war was destroying their factories and interrupting production. The strikes of March 1943, involving over 100 000 workers in Piedmont and Lombardy, re-created the situation of organised labour agitation and left-wing political activity, the suppression of which had been one of the major reasons for their support-cum-connivance of Fascism over the past twenty years. Industrialists, whether individually or through Confindustria, probably took no direct part in the royal conspiracy to overthrow Mussolini. But the regime had clearly outlived its usefulness for them, and the eventual outcome of a military-bureaucratic government appointed by the king excluding both Fascists and anti-Fascists certainly best suited their concern to preserve their businesses under private management. Again, the Vatican could hardly go further officially than keeping to its traditional neutrality and pacifism in wartime. But its contacts with the American government were one of the channels through which it was made known to the king that a royal-nominated anti-Axis and anti-Communist government was an acceptable premise for a separate peace, again a solution suiting the church.

If it was clear that only the monarchy, backed by the army, could and would take Italy out of the war, the king himself was hesitant in taking the initiative. Soundings between the king's advisors, army generals including Badoglio and police chiefs began in early 1943 on the practicalities of a royal coup. But the final decision to act was probably only taken a week before the Grand Council meeting arranged on 25 July. As much as the church and the industrialists, he realised that as in 1924 during the Matteotti crisis, removing Mussolini raised the prospect of a civil war if the Fascists resisted and an anti-Fascist and left-wing succession, which would hardly forget or forgive his involvement with Fascism. Dismissing Mussolini was a judgement of the fellow-travellers as well as of the regime. The Grand Council meeting at least gave the king some kind of constitutional setting to which he could respond. Time was really pressing now that the country was being invaded, Rome being bombed, and German troops entering the country in force after the July Hitler–Mussolini meeting confirming the Axis alliance.

Grandi's resolution to the Grand Council, winning a 19:7 majority, urged the restoration of military command to the king and the proper functioning of the constitutional organs, the monarchy, Grand Council, government, corporations and parliament. This certainly amounted to the end of Mussolini's dictatorship and his running of the war. But there was no explicit reference to replacing Mussolini, and it seemed to suggest that there was life for some kind of more collegial Fascist government or at least one containing moderate Fascists. The genuine confusion over the meaning of the passing of Grandi's motion might go a little way to explaining why there was no immediate action to defend Mussolini by the Militia and Fascists. Both Mussolini and the Fascist Grand Council members were surprised by the suddenness with which the moderate Fascist conspiracy was overtaken by the plan of the king and the military. Mussolini was arrested, and Badoglio appointed head of a military government ruling by royal decree, which ordered the dissolution of all the organs of the Fascist regime, the PNF, Grand Council, Chamber of Fasces and Corporations, the Special Tribunal and the MVSN. The war would go on, but the Germans were not deceived by this formal reaffirmation of the Axis alliance, and their move into Italy and Italian-occupied Europe both before and after the September 1943 armistice was the basis of the temporary resurrection of Mussolini's political career.

8 The Italian Social Republic, 1943–45

1. THE GERMAN OCCUPATION OF ITALY AND MUSSOLINI'S RETURN

As Mussolini had realised, the first price to pay for leaving the Axis was his own fall from power. The second – German occupation of Italy and her territory – was completed speedily in September 1943 on the news of the Italian armistice with the Allies and her official changing of sides. The leisurely maladroit way in which Badoglio's royal government had opened its contacts with the Allies after July, and the king's irresponsible flight to the Allied-occupied south effectively delivered the whole of Italy's armed forces, men and equipment, to the invading Germans.

Mussolini was sprung from his prison in September and taken to Germany to join other Fascist leaders who had survived the July coup. The Germans obviously intended to fight in Italy to defend their own country from invasion, and exploit Italy's labour and resources for the German war effort. Against the advice of many in the Nazi and military leadership, who now regarded Italy as a traitorous enemy country to take revenge on, Hitler decided to set up a Mussolini government in northern Italy. This was some confirmation of the personal and ideological basis to the Axis. It would indicate that fascism was not in decline and that it could be revived under German patronage as an expression of confidence in the ultimate victory of the Axis.

Being an 'occupied ally'[1] was an odd and ambiguous status for Mussolini's Italy, or what remained of it. But a depressed and resigned Mussolini just seemed to go with the rapid sequence of events, from his imprisonment by the king, his release by the Germans, to his return to Italy, recognising that his fate was being decided by others. It is difficult to detect any sign of a 'double game' in Mussolini's passive acceptance of Hitler's decision to relaunch his political career as a fascist. There has been an attempt to portray Mussolini as the Italian equivalent of

Marshal Pétain in defeated and occupied France, setting up a regime which would be a buffer between the Italians and the German occupier, and Italy's 'shield' against the effects of a full, unmitigated German occupation. Mussolini, however, unlike Pétain, was a fascist and remained one. Even when the war went badly for Italy, Mussolini never wavered from the alliance with Nazi Germany, and his return was entirely consistent with his chosen position as the Nazis' fascist ally. Even if he had wanted to, Mussolini could do little, anyway, to prevent Northern Italy suffering the full rigours and demands of German occupation, and his regime was complicit in that occupation. In these senses, at least, Mussolini's government resembled that of Pétain in occupied France after 1942.

The anti-Fascist and anti-Nazi Resistance movement effectively began with the German occupation of Italy and the installation of a new Fascist government in September 1943. It was marked by the appearance of armed bands of escaping officers and soldiers reacting to the German invasion and the disbanding of Italy's army. They were basically loyal to the monarchical government of Badoglio, which from early 1944 was given jurisdiction over those parts of the south coming under Allied military administration and control. More generally, the Resistance was also the outcome of action by the anti-Fascist parties which had been driven underground or into exile after 1926, and painfully formed or reconstituted themselves in the late 1930s and especially during the later stages of Italy's Axis war in 1942-43.

The Communists, Socialists and a new liberal-socialist group, the Action Party, were the first to translate opposition to Fascism into armed struggle. Behind their participation in an increasingly nasty civil war within the war was the desire to determine the shape of Italy on the collapse of Fascism. A broad alliance of anti-Fascist parties constituted the Committee of National Liberation for Northern Italy (CLNAI), founded in January 1944 to co-ordinate the activities of the armed Resistance and to act as *a de facto* clandestine government in German-occupied Italy. These same parties were also represented in the Bonomi-led government which succeeded that of Badoglio in June 1944, after the Allied liberation of Rome and on the subsequent military advance, by the winter, to a line running across Italy from the Ligurian Riviera to Rimini on the Adriatic. The important point was that what united the Resisters, irrespective of their political complexion, was the determination to defeat Fascism and its occupying Nazi patron. The Resistance could credibly stand as an anti-Fascist and patriotic force, and contest the Fascist claim to be the true nation.

2. 'A RETURN TO THE ORIGINS'?

The reality of German control of Mussolini's government was inescapable and killed the *Repubblica Sociale Italiana* (Italian Social Republic or RSI) on the ground. As in the rest of occupied Europe, the Nazis exported their own competitive jungle of administration to Italy, overlaying and countermanding the Republic's ministries and offices at central and local level. Exploiting the tensions and rivalries within the Nazi system might have provided the RSI with some room for manoeuvre, but there was precious little of that actually available. All the Republic's actions and measures had to be filtered through and approved by Rudolf Rahn, German ambassador to Salò and as Reich Plenipotentiary Hitler's direct representative in Italy, and SS General Karl Wolff, responsible for police and internal security. The German occupying forces and German police were given a free hand to repress partisan Resistance activity in 1944, which led to a policy of reprisal and deterrent killings and forcible displacement of civilian populations 'suspected' of harbouring resisters. The RSI's own police and military co-operated in the occupier's methods of repression, just as before 1943 Fascist authorities had done in occupied Yugoslavia. So it was no joke that Mussolini had remarked to Hitler in their first meetings after his release, 'I have come to receive my orders.'[2] German control was so palpable that the Fascists, although claiming to restore national honour by sticking to the Axis alliance reneged on by Badoglio and the king, could no longer with any real authority portray themselves as the only national and patriotic force.

Worse still, and undermining the RSI's claim to embody the nation even more than the Allied occupation of the south, was the German reversal of Italy's territorial gains of the First and Second World Wars. Without consulting Mussolini, two Italian-held provinces, Zara and Ljubljana, were handed over to Croatia and eight in the South Tyrol, Venetia and on the Adriatic were 'provisionally' annexed to Germany and placed under Gauleiter administration.

The Republic's programme was agreed at the unruly congress of the *Partito Fascista Repubblicano* (Republican Fascist Party or PFR), the reconstituted successor to the PNF, held in Verona in November 1943. It was an attempt to give a meaning and content to the Republic, other than doing the Germans' business, and to win the support of the population nominally under its jurisdiction, whose loyalties were contested by the anti-Fascist and anti-German Resistance movements. It called for a constituent assembly to replace the monarchy with a social Republic, an elected head of state based on the US model, a scarcely credible charter of citizens' rights, a single party for the political education of the people, socialisation of the economy, treating the Jews as enemy aliens, and a foreign policy whose talk of 'living space' and European federation was a rehash of the former regime's New Order wartime propaganda.

The abolition of the monarchy and socialisation were both a rejection of and an alibi for Fascism's past. The desire for revenge and scapegoating was brutally evident in the extraordinary Special Tribunal's trial and execution of those of the July 1943 Grand Council 'traitors' who could be found, including Ciano. It was they, in league with the king and conservative bourgeois and capitalist interests, who were charged with not only bringing about Mussolini's fall and the Allied invasion but also subverting and sidetracking the Fascist Revolution during the twenty years of the regime. Now shorn of its conservative fellow-travelling elements and liberated from the 'pluto-monarchical compromises of 1922',[3] Fascism could 'return to the origins' and enact the national syndicalist and republican strands of the revolutionary interventionism and early Fascism of 1915–19. This was myth-making in the grand style, and to justify it Salò's propaganda evoked the legacy of Giuseppe Mazzini, D'Annunzio and Fiume.

Socialisation owed as much to the 'Third Way' corporatist rhetoric of the 1930s and of the Fascist New Order as to national syndicalism, at least in the proposals put together by the Republic's Ministry of Corporations. The principle of private property was still sacrosanct, but the state could regulate it in the context of a national economic plan and would take over or retain the running of essential national utilities and services. What the measure approved by the government in February 1944 proposed was a kind of socialisation of management, not capital, to create that collaborative and productivist 'community of producers'. The running of state and private firms was to be shared between an elected assembly of employees and shareholders, a management council of representatives of capital and labour, and an executive director elected by the assembly or chosen by the government.

But the Republic could decide on anything and enact little to nothing. Making 'labour ... the foundation of the Social Republic'[4] in this abortive 'return to the origins' cut across the two unavoidable realities of the Republic's tenuous existence: German control of Italy for the exploitation of its economy, and the worsening civil war between the Fascists and the Resistance. Hitler was mystified by the RSI's social policy but thought it irrelevant and innocuous. The German authorities on the ground intervened to nullify it. Hans Leyers, the head of the Italian arm of the German Ministry of Armaments and War Production, regarded socialisation as 'sabotage'[5] of the Italian industries working for the German war effort and co-operated with the industrialists themselves to exclude or obstruct its implementation in key areas. By April 1945 perhaps 60–80 firms with about 130 000 employees had been 'socialised', mainly newspapers and publishers under the auspices of the Ministry of Popular Culture, which took the measure seriously. The decree of February 1945 for the socialisation of large industries was a dead letter, not only because of German-inspired procrastination by employers but also because most workers boycotted the council elections. Industrial workers had enough experience of the Fascist regime not to trust in this false dawn or twilight of labour reforms. The left-wing Resistance movements certainly warned them off, as they did employers. Fascism's attempt to redefine itself could not escape the taint of its past.

What was left of the 'return to the origins' was squadrism and the tone of fanaticism it conveyed, and a partial replay of some of the most important intra-Fascist disputes of the early 1920s. The PFR Secretary Alessandro Pavolini's report to the Verona congress of an alleged membership of 250 000 was greeted by cries of 'too many' from delegates who were the old squadrists and Militiamen responsible for the spontaneous reconstitution of some *fasci* in September and October. The question as to whether the PFR should be an élite squadrist party or a mass, all-talents party was soon lost in the RSI's understandable concern to attract whom it could.

Much the same outcome marked the divergent conceptions of the formation and recruitment of the Republic's army, the emergence of which as a proper fighting force on the German side Mussolini regarded as crucial to the RSI's independence and credibility. In the light of the earlier events of 1943, the Germans were reluctant to allow this and refused to release interned Italian troops *en bloc* for a new Italian army. They trained four divisions in Germany drawn from internees, volunteers and conscripts, who were repatriated in the second half of 1944. These men were the core of what Rodolfo Graziani, the RSI's military commander and Minister of Defence, had hoped would be a national apolitical army. In this he was opposed by Ricci, the MVSN commander who wanted to take up Mussolini's initial inclination to reorganise the armed forces around the Militia, a party-army. Again, the Republic got both kinds of force, out of its need to recruit whom it could. Ricci organised an armed police force of ex-policemen and ex-Militiamen, the Republican National Guard, some of whom then moved into the Black Brigades, formed by Pavolini in summer 1944 as the party-in-arms specifically for anti-partisan operations. These regular and hybrid forces existed alongside freelance criminal bands whose savage policing and anti-Resistance activity was covered by German or Fascist political protection.

In the circumstances of war and civil war the PFR could hardly avoid being a squadrist party in leadership and function. Only men of the committed old guard and the young fanatics were prepared to come out into the open when it cost something to declare oneself a Fascist, and there was need for violent repression of the Republic's enemies among their fellow Italians. Repression, in the end, was all there could be with continuing popular discontent at wartime controls and shortages, the Resistance being fed by men evading the Republic's own coercive measures of conscription to the armed forces and labour service in Germany, and an escalating cycle of violence and counter-violence between Fascism and Resistance worsening from mid-1944. Significantly, only once did Mussolini leave the mundane bureaucratic chores of his office at Salò, a pattern of ordinary administration showing his own sense of resigned and depressed impotence, to address a public rally. This was not only an indication of the Germans' control of his movements, but also of the futility of trying to revive a popular rapport in favour of a man and a Republic which lacked standing and authority. Moving to Milan in April 1945, Mussolini was caught between partisan insurrections in the major northern cities and the German military's attempts to arrange a surrender with the advancing Allied forces. Fleeing north with a German military detachment, he was stopped, recognised and killed by partisans on 27–28 April 1945.

3. THE ITALIAN CIVIL WAR

The long running De Felician-inspired reinterpretation of Mussolini and Fascism has concentrated on the 1943–45 period in the late 1980s and early 1990s. Despite De Felice's apparent concern to write objective, non-partisan history, the 'revisionist' preoccupation with the war years clearly related to Italy's contemporary political upheavals, the collapse of the country's post-war party political framework mentioned in the introduction. The current Italian Prime Minister, Berlusconi, as well as De Felice, has suggested that as a result of the disintegration of the old party system, Italy has moved on to a 'post-Fascist' phase. Here, the old political divisions between Fascism and anti-Fascism, which in De Felice's view have compromised the post-war historiography of Fascism, are finally redundant, and Fascism can now become something in Italy's past, even Italy's 'heritage'.

In particular, the De Felician school has challenged the democratic and national credentials acquired by the Italian Communist Party, the PCI, through its participation in the armed Resistance against Nazi occupation and the Salò Republic. The PCI has been portrayed as the faithful stooge of Stalin's USSR, and in a complementary exercise, the RSI has been rehabilitated as a popular and patriotic Italian regime. In general, the 'revisionists' wanted to destroy what became the founding 'myth' of Italy's post-war democratic Republic, and for them the distorting 'myth' of post-war historiography, the 'myth' of the Resistance as a mass popular movement of national liberation from Fascism and its German Nazi ally and patron.

Some of the results of this renewed 'historians controversy' in Italy have been productive and illuminating. It is now respectable, even among anti-Fascist historians, to accept the idea that the 1943–45 period was to be seen not so much as a single anti-Fascist struggle to liberate the country from foreign occupation and its local Fascist collaborators, but more as a civil war between Italians, a conflict of competing patriotisms, that of the anti-Fascist Resistance and that of the Fascist Salò Republic. Whether this makes the forces of the Resistance and the forces of Salò moral equivalents, as De Felice suggests, is another matter.

In this recent controversy, Italian historians are playing catch-up, at last drawing on the historical insights and analogies of the nature of German occupation and the local responses to it which had already been made by historians of the war years in other Nazi-occupied countries in Northern and Western Europe. It was scarcely a surprise for historians of occupied France or the occupied Netherlands for De Felice to point out that the active supporters of the RSI and of the anti-Fascist Resistance were minorities competing, as it were, for the loyalties of a majority of people who were *attentiste*, waiting on events, not wanting to get involved, trying to survive as best they could in dangerous and straitened wartime conditions. War, and the civil war within it, increasingly made it very difficult for Italians to live a quiet life. Sometimes, their involvement, willy-nilly, in the wars being waged around them led them to respond in untidily human ways, both 'collaborating' and 'resisting', or perhaps, neither 'collaborating' nor 'resisting'. Italian peasant families offered refuge and food to the many displaced people of wartime, Allied airmen who had been shot down over them, Italian Prisoners of War (POWs) trying to get home from Germany, the Balkans and the Soviet Union, local lads dodging the German and Salò labour drafts, at the same time as they clearly resented the presence of partisan Resistance formations in their areas, because it was bound to draw on to them both German and RSI police raids and reprisals. Under the 'cover' of Resistance, though the protagonists would have seen their actions as part and parcel of Resistance, bands of landless peasants attacked and killed landowners and estate managers in the Po Valley provinces, in a replay of the bitter agricultural class war of the early 1920s. These attacks and reprisals in a so-called geographical 'triangle of death' continued into the immediate post-war period.

Of course Resistance was a minority activity; it was too dangerous to be otherwise. But it is scarcely credible to regard something involving over 200 000 people as anything other than a popular mass 'movement'. 'Resistance' and 'collaboration' were often choices forced on people in unpalatable and even incidental or accidental circumstances. But resisters were resisters also because of a basic political or ideological choice, of being against fascism, and a basic 'patriotic' choice, to get rid of the German occupier.

We are now able to take on a new orthodoxy, though again it would not be new to historians of occupied France, that 1943–45 in Italy was the arena for three conflicts in one, a patriotic war, civil war and class war.[6] But what kind of 'patriotism', and which 'nation'? It was understandable enough for Italians to wonder where they were in 1943–45, and certainly to wonder whether they had a country at all, since the war had quite literally divided Italy into areas invaded and occupied by opposed foreign powers, and led to the North and the Centre being fought over by the supporters of two very different ideas of the Italian nation. In a quite chilling compression of historical events, De Felice and the rest saw the whole idea of the 'patria', of Italian national feeling, dying in the period running from the king's changing of sides in September 1943 to the 'national liberation' of April 1945, and regarded this apparent 'death' of the nation as the war years' and the Resistance's most dire and pernicious legacy to the post-war Italian democratic Republic.

The logical conclusion to draw from this reading of the war years is that it would have been 'better' for Italy as a nation to have won the war. What was really at stake in 1943–45 was what kind of nation Italy would be. The 'Italy' that started 'dying' in September 1943, though the death throes probably began earlier than this, was not the 'nation' as such, but the Fascist version of it, statist and aggressively nationalistic, and by extension, the 'nation' as defined and embodied in its 'national' institutions, the monarchy and the armed forces, which were discredited both by their collusion and co-existence with Fascism and their quite shameful behaviour at the point of the armistice with the Allies in September 1943. In this highly charged debate over national identity in the war years, the 'objective' and 'scientific' historian, De Felice, revealed himself in his own true 'ideological' colours, as an historian of a conservative, nationalist tradition. What De Felice lamented was the passing of one kind of national patriotism. An alternative democratic republican citizens' 'patriotism' emerged, or re-emerged, during the anti-Fascist Resistance and was, indeed, the foundation of Italy's post-war political system.

Conclusion

Fascism was dead as a functioning independent regime from late 1942. It is futile to argue retrospectively that Fascism would have survived but for the external factor of the Second World War. It might have done, but it would not have been Fascism. War was essential not incidental to Fascism. The Fascist movement emerged as an extreme and violent political response to a perceived national crisis, consequent on the social and political strains set up by the impact and outcome of the First World War and expressed in what appeared to be Socialist revolution. It became a new mass movement of the middle classes, united in a heterogeneous anti-socialist coalition with important organised sectional interests and members of liberal Italy's political, economic and military establishment. These probably inescapable compromising alliances with the old order were built into the system of power evolving by the late 1920s, corrupting the implementation of a new socio-economic corporative order which Fascism alleged was its distinctive and innovative contribution to managing the social conflicts of modern society.

What was really new was the 'totalitarian' state, Fascism's resolution of the national crisis, which Fascists rooted in the weakness, inefficiency and divisiveness of parliamentary government, and the idea of the single mass party bridging the state to the population. The regime was built around the attempt to create through totalitarian mobilisation and control a national community and solidarity among a people notoriously divided by class and locality, which would progressively transcend the old order. The overriding aim of national unity was consciously linked to and a premise for territorial expansion and empire. War was means and end, the way of subverting both the existing internal and international order, effecting both conquest and 'fascistisation'.

This was Fascism's huge gamble, because wars can be lost as well as won. The great re-educative process of making Italians, based on organisation, propaganda and control, needed time. War was meant to accelerate things, but it destroyed any basis of rapport and support the regime had achieved, however imperfect and superficial it was. The lost war ruined the illusions and livelihood of the Italian middle classes, and detached the fellow-travelling conservative interests from the regime. This loss of popular consent, active, passive or lukewarm, was irretrievable in the period of the so-called Salò Republic, because everyone knew, Fascists, non-Fascists and anti-Fascists alike, that the Axis could never win the war. Throughout its short existence the Italian Social Republic was constantly and fruitlessly attempting to establish its legitimacy, in respect of the foreign powers occupying the country and the 'other' Italys located in the monarchical south and the anti-Fascist Resistance movements. The death of the Fascist regime was confirmed in the Social Republic's lack of credibility. Without any future prospects, Mussolini and the other Fascists of Salò were more concerned with the legacy of the past and putting the record straight. The Republic was seen as a kind of memorial to a Fascism which might have been.

The debate over the 'legacy' of Fascism, what it 'left' to Italy's post-war Republic, was revived in the 1990s, with the crisis and collapse of the country's party system. One suspects that some of the dubious linkages between Fascism and what came after would not have been made, but for the opportunity to rake over the ashes of Italy's 'failed' post-war political system. The Fascist regime, self-evidently, 'failed' against its own chosen measurement of 'success', which was war. Fascism's immediate legacy was, then, military defeat and the foreign occupation of Italy, which was bound to discredit both the system of rule and the aggressive nationalism which Fascism embodied. The 'legacy' of Fascism was anti-Fascism.

Defeat, occupation and the part played in the liberation of the country by the anti-Fascist Resistance movements between 1943 and 1945 seemed to mark the final defeat of Fascism and make possible a clean break with the Fascist period. In a real sense, this actually happened. The political system changed from a Fascist dictatorship to a democratic parliamentary republic, formally brought into being with the 1948 constitution. As political parties re-formed during and after the war, the basis of co-operation and unity between them for the country's post-war reconstruction was anti-Fascism. The constitution banned and made illegal the reorganisation of a Fascist Party, and the Socialist, Communist and Catholic Christian Democrat parties worked together in coalition governments between 1945 and 1947. The Italian Communist Party, which became one of the largest in Western Europe, consistently gaining between a quarter and a third of the popular vote, built its post-war political strategy around anti-Fascism. It did not seek to carry out a

Bolshevik-style revolution, but decided to build on the 1943–45 experience when it had fought alongside other groups in the political and military Resistance against the Fascists of the Salò Republic and their German allies, and to work with the democratic parties to install and defend a progressive, reforming republican and parliamentary system of government.

The Communist Party was, in effect, permanently excluded from government in 1947, with the onset of the Cold War in Europe, and thereafter coalition governments were dominated by the Christian Democrats. Even though anti-Communism became the cement of the coalition governments which were formed in the late 1940s and 1950s, the Cold War climate did not provide the opportunity for a Fascist revival. The Christian Democratic Party was conservative and anti-Communist, but was still committed to the parliamentary republic, and the dominant party's stance left little room for the neo-Fascist Party which had been formed in 1946, the Italian Social Movement or MSI (*Movimento Sociale Italiano*). In 1960, a right-wing Christian Democrat-led government won a vote of confidence in parliament with the support of the MSI deputies, but fell shortly after in the wake of popular and political outrage at what had happened, a confirmation that the anti-Fascist political agreement still existed.

The rebuilding of domestic politics on an anti-Fascist foundation was matched by changes to Italy's external relations. Nationalism, imperialism and autarky were no longer the inspiration for a foreign policy of greatness and expansion. Under its post-war democratic governments, Italy stopped even pretending to be an aspiring great power and found a place in international (NATO) and European (EEC) networks and in a capitalist global economy dominated by others. As for the countries of Southern and now Eastern Europe, post-war Italy saw its involvement in European integration as both a way back from a Fascist or 'totalitarian' recent past and a guarantee of its present and future democratic credentials.

The MSI was the most evident sign that Fascism still lived on in some form, though its relatively weak electoral performance convinced many that it was a spent force. The MSI took its name and inspiration from the so-called Italian Social Republic, the Fascist statelet in German-occupied Northern and Central Italy in 1943–45, but was never prosecuted as a Fascist organisation under the terms of the 1948 constitution. Within the MSI were groups who wanted a more authoritarian form of government and were prepared to use violence to achieve it, as well as groups who wanted to work in the parliamentary system and make the MSI a respectable conservative party. The anti-system neo-Fascists had a big hand in the so-called 'strategy of tension' in the 1970s when, in response to student and worker protest and unrest in the late 1960s, acts of terrorism aimed to make the country unstable and support the case for the introduction of 'strong government' to put an end to the instability. By the 1980s, however, the MSI was positioning itself as a conservative constitutional party. With the collapse of Communism in Eastern Europe, the end of the Cold War, and the break up of the Christian Democrat Party, it actually became a party of government again in the early 1990s, renamed as the National Alliance.

Recently, more attention has been given to the alleged hidden continuities between the Fascist period and the post-1945 period, which has led some commentators starting from very different historical and political viewpoints to deny that any real break between Fascism and anti-Fascism occurred in 1943–48. The De Felician school, for example, has argued that the anti-Fascist Resistance consensus of 1945–48 was 'responsible' for the emergence of the now discredited 'partyocracy' (*partitocrazia*) which characterised democratic republican politics after 1945. This line is really an extension of the same school's view of the 'death' of the 'nation' in 1943–48, where apparently the idea of the national state gave way to a reprehensible 'party state' of the anti-Fascist parties. The implication was clearly that any sense of national or collective good was lost in the pursuit of partial and sectional interests represented by these parties and inherent in a system of political parties, and the parties' sole concern with the simple retention of power. This view is open to the same objection as before that it takes one version of nationhood as the only possible version of nationhood. Such a view also seriously compresses historical events and reasoning, since the 'partyocrcay' was not actually there in the real period of anti-Fascist consensus between 1945 and 1948, but emerged in the 1950s when the Christian Democrats were politically dominant. The 'partyocracy', in other words, was how democratic politics in Italy evolved, not the dire legacy of the transition from Fascism to anti-Fascism in the 1940s.

The political hegemony of the Christian Democrats in the post-war republic is taken by some historians occupying different ideological ground to De Felice to be the post-war equivalent of the one-party 'total-itarian rule' of the PNF in the 1930s. Both the PNF and Christian Democracy were cross-class catch-all anti-Communist parties. They employed the same corrupt clientelistic and patronage networking to gain and retain their wide-ranging electoral support, exploiting their positions as the parties of power to 'park' their supporters in state agencies and so 'buy' political support with public money. As with the debate over Fascism as 'political religion', one wonders whether the comparisons between the PNF and Christian Democracy are to be taken literally or analogously. Did Christian Democracy actually model its politically hegemonic and hegemonising practices in the 1950s and 1960s on those of the PNF in the 1930s? Are we to assume from this comparison that Italy once again in the 1950s and early 1960s was a one-party state? The respective historical contexts seem all-important, here. The Christian Democratic Party was operating in a democratic and pluralist polity; even when it had an absolute parliamentary majority, it chose to form government coalitions with other democratic parties. The PNF was operating as the only legally permitted political organisation of the Fascist regime, and its job was to use this monopolistic position to 'fascistise' the Italian people and prepare them for war. The comparison between Christian Democracy and the PNF should serve to highlight the break between Fascism and anti-Fascism, not the continuity between the Fascist and post-Fascist periods.

The same argument can be applied to another area of apparent institutional continuity. The 1948 constitution did not commit itself one way or another to the kind of economic system Italy should have after the war, and certainly the idea of wholesale nationalisation and state control looked too much like the Fascist state's attempted regulation of the economy. The flow of American money to pay for Italian post-war economic reconstruction and Italy's place in the Western bloc during the Cold War division of Europe, ensured that it would be a capitalist economy. But the mixed part privately-run and part publicly-run economy carried on, and that included the state-owned or state-controlled economic agencies and enterprises which survived until the Thatcherite re-privatisations of the 1990s. But though IRI continued as a state holding company and a means of state involvement in the economy, its function had, nevertheless, qualitatively changed. It was no longer used, as it was under Fascism, to further Fascist goals of autarky, empire and war, but rather to promote economic modernisation, growth and prosperity in a global capitalist economy. So, again, an apparent demonstration of institutional continuity is really a mark of the fundamental break between a Fascist regime and a democratic one.

Having said this, one can scarcely deny that continuities existed. The monarchy was the one big institutional victim of the change from Fascism to democracy and paid for its co-existence with Fascism in the special referendum of 1946, when Italians voted narrowly to abolish the monarchy. But other institutions survived unreformed and prospered after 1945. Judges continued to apply the codes of civil and criminal law which had been drawn up by the Fascist government in the 1930s, and proposals for revising them were finally made only in the 1960s.

The neo-Fascist groups involved in the terroristic acts of the 1970s had some support from and connections with the state's civilian and military officials, especially senior men in the country's secret police and armed forces intelligence services. Some have seen this kind of complicity of some state officials in subversive activity as a sign of Fascism's hidden legacy to the post-war parliamentary republic. This was a reactionary and authoritarian 'culture' persisting among senior civil servants, judges and armed forces officers whose careers and those of their immediate predecessors had developed during the Fascist period and in the service of the Fascist state. It is difficult to measure the extent of such a set of attitudes among Italy's public employees. But while there was in 1945–46 every intention of getting rid of state officials compromised by their service of the Fascist state, such a large-scale purge never occurred. This was partly because so many civil servants had joined the Fascist Party as a matter of course, making it too difficult to determine the quality of their involvement with the Fascist regime, partly because many officials had gone South with the king after September 1943 and not been complicit in the RSI, and partly because after war and occupation the government needed an experienced state administration to get the country through post-war reconstruction. So the post-war democratic governments of Italy continued to be serviced by a state machine which had done its duty by the preceding Fascist regime.

The single most important national institution to make the transition from Fascism to democracy was the Catholic church. The Pope thought that the 1929 Concordat both protected and advanced the position of the church in Italian society and within the Fascist state, in a way which would probably be impossible to justify in a democratic system. It was expected that the Concordat would be abolished after the defeat of Fascism. But the Concordat, giving the Catholic church a privileged position in Italian life, was included in the 1948 constitution. The left-wing parties and, above all, the Communist Party, felt that abolishing the Concordat risked church–state conflict and could undermine the unity of anti-Fascist forces which had been behind the Resistance and was now the basis of the new republic. Essentially, the PCI backed the retention of the Concordat in order to ensure that Catholics and the Christian Democratic Party would back democracy.

The Catholic church, because it was the only non-Fascist body allowed to operate in the 1930s, had become by the fall of Fascism the one nationwide institution capable of replacing the mass organisations of the Fascist Party. Most of the leaders of post-war Christian Democracy and of the network of Catholic bodies which supported the political dominance of the party after 1948 had been educated in Catholic colleges and universities and were members and leaders of Catholic Action during the 1930s and early 1940s. The Concordat had allowed the Church to fence off a generation of Catholics from whose ranks came the political class of post-war Italy. In a very concrete way, this was one of Fascism's most significant handovers to the Italian post-war republic.

But the Catholic church's hold over many aspects of Italian life was a temporary one, eroding steadily from the 1960s as religious practice declined and society became more secular, a consequence of the so-called 'economic miracle' of the late 1950s and 1960s and the Christian Democratic Party's own commitment to state welfarism and US-style material well-being in post-war Italy. No Concordat, whether made in a Fascist or democratic context, could protect the Catholic church from the secularisation of society, and post-war Italy's economic growth and prosperity completed what the Fascist 'political religion' of the 'totalitarian' state had tried to initiate.

Notes

INTRODUCTION: LOCATING FASCISM

1. R.J.B. Bosworth, *The Italian Dictatorship. Problems and Perspectives in the Interpretation of Mussolini and Fascism* (London: Arnold, 1998). See also his earlier historiographical works, *Explaining Auschwitz and Hiroshima: History Writing and the Second World War, 1945–1990* (London: Unwin Hyman, 1990), and *Italy and the Wider World, 1860–1960* (London: Routledge, 1996).

2. R. Lamb, *Mussolini and the British* (London: John Murray, 1997).

3. J. Whittam, *Fascist Italy* (Manchester: Manchester University Press, 1995).

4. A. De Grand, *Italian Fascism. Its Origins and Development*, 3rd edn (Lincoln: University of Nebraska Press, 2000).

5. M.A. Ledeen (ed.), *R. De Felice. Intervista sul fascismo* (Bari: Laterza, 1975).

6. R. De Felice, *Rosso e Nero* (Milan: Baldini e Castoldi, 1995).

1. THE WAR, THE POST-WAR CRISIS AND THE RISE OF FASCISM, 1915–22

1. R.A. Webster, *The Cross and the Fasces. Christian Democracy and Fascism in Italy* (Stanford, Calif.: Stanford University Press, 1960) p. 56.

2. Quoted in A. Tasca (pseud. A. Rossi), *Nascita e avvento del fascismo. L'Italia dal 1918 al 1922* (Florence: La Nuova Italia, 1963) p. 10. English version is *The Rise of Italian Fascism* (London: Methuen, 1938).

3. Socialist propaganda in 1917, quoted in E. Ragionieri, *Storia d'Italia*, vol. 4:3, *La storia politica e sociale* (Turin: Einaudi, 1976) p. 2031.

4. Quoted in E. Ragionieri, *La storia politica e sociale*, p. 2051.

5. Article in *Il Popolo d'Italia*, 15 December 1917, in E. and D. Susmel (eds), *Opera Omnia di Benito Mussolini*, vol. 10 (Florence: La Fenice, 1952) p. 141.

6. From the text of Mussolini's speech at the inaugural Milan meeting, March 1919, in C.F. Delzell (ed.), *Mediterranean Fascism, 1919–1945* (London: Macmillan, 1971) p. 9.

7. Mussolini, speaking of the 1919 movement, as quoted in E. Gentile, *Storia del Partito Fascista 1919–1922. Movimento e Milizia* (Bari: Laterza, 1989) p. 236.

8. From Mussolini's speech, March 1919, in Delzell, *Mediterranean Fascism*, p. 10.

9. C.S. Maier, *Recasting Bourgeois Europe. Stabilization in France, Germany and Italy in the Decade after World War 1* (Princeton, NJ: Princeton University Press, 1975) p. 128.

10. Quoted in P.P. Attore, 'Gli agrari bolognesi dal liberalismo al fascismo', in L. Casali (ed.), *Bologna 1920. Le origini del fascismo* (Bologna: Cappelli, 1982) p. 138.

11. R. Vivarelli, *Il dopoguerra in Italia e l'avvento del fascismo (1918–1922)*, vol. 1, *Dalla fine della guerra all'impresa di Fiume* (Naples: Mondadori, 1967) p. 552.

12. Quoted in A. Tasca, *Nascita e avvento del fascismo*, p. 78.

13. Quoted in R. De Felice, *Mussolini il fascista*, vol. 1, *La conquista del potere 1921–1925*, 3rd edn (Turin: Einaudi, 1966) p. 186.

14. All quotations from the PNF 1921 programme in Delzell, *Mediterranean Fascism*, pp. 27–37.

15. Quoted in P. Corner, *Fascism in Ferrara 1915–1925* (London: Oxford University Press, 1975) p. 209.
16. From Delzell, *Mediterranean Fascism*, p. 41.
17. From ibid., p. 40.
18. A. Lyttelton, *The Seizure of Power: Fascism in Italy 1919–1929* (London: Weidenfeld and Nicolson, 1973) p. 86.

2. BETWEEN 'NORMALISATION' AND REVOLUTION', 1922–25

1. The phrase was coined by Farinacci in October 1925 when he was Party Secretary. Quoted in A. Aquarone, *L'organizzazione dello stato totalitario* (Turin: Einaudi, 1965) p. 63.
2. Mussolini said of his political opponents that he would 'pluck them like a chicken, feather by feather'. Quoted in D. Mack-Smith, *Mussolini* (London: Weidenfeld and Nicolson, 1982) p. 66.
3. The words of the Liberal, Amendola, quoted in A. Lyttelton, *The Seizure of Power. Fascism in Italy* (London: Weidenfeld and Nicolson, 1982) p. 126.
4. From extracts of the speech in C.F. Delzell (ed.), *Mediterranean Fascism* (London: Macmillan, 1971) pp. 45–6.
5. Quoted in A.J. De Grand, *The Italian Nationalist Association and the Rise of Fascism in Italy* (Lincoln, Nebr. and London: University of Nebraska Press, 1978) pp. 155–6.
6. M. Canali, *Il delitto Matteotti: affarismo e politica nel primo governo Mussolini* (Bologna: Il Mulino, 1997).
7. Quoted in P. Melograni, *Gli industriali e Mussolini. Rapporti fra Confindustria e Fascismo dal 1919 al 1929* (Milan: Longanesi, 1972) p. 45.

3. THE CONSTRUCTION OF THE TOTALITARIAN STATE, 1925–29

1 F.. and D. Susmel (eds), *Opera Omnia di Benito Mussolini*, vol. 21 (Florence: La Fenice, 1952) p. 362.
2. Gentile's speech of 8 March 1925, in G. Gentile, *Che cosa è il fascismo? Discorsi e polemiche* (Florence: Vallechi, 1925).
3. Mussolini's speech in Milan, 28 October 1925, in *Opera Omnia*, vol. 21, p. 425.
4. Article in Farinacci's newspaper, *Regime Fascista*, 31 August 1926.
5. From text in C.F. Delzell (ed.), *Mediterranean Fascism* (London: Macmillan, 1971) p. 65.
6. The circular is reproduced in A. Aquarone, *L'organizzazione dello stato totalitario* (Turin: Einaudi, 1965) pp. 485–8.
7. Both quotations from Mussolini's speech to PNF rally, 14 September 1929, in *Opera Omnia*, vol. 24, p. 141.
8. Quoted in B. Uva, 'Gli scioperi dei metallurgici italiani del marzo 1925', *Storia Contemporanea*, 1 (1970) p. 1028.
9. Archivio Centrale dello Stato (ACS), *Mostra della Rivoluzione Fascista* (MRF), Pt. 1, busta 9, 'Rapporto del Duce ai segretari federali (febbraio 1930)', 'Venezia Euganea'.
10. G. Miccoli, 'La chiesa e il fascismo', in G. Quazza (ed.), *Fascismo e società italiana* (Turin: Einaudi, 1973) p. 191.
11. *Opera Omnia*, vol. 22, pp. 37–8.
12. Mussolini's speech in Rome to a conference of FISA, 30 July 1925, in *Opera Omnia*, vol. 21, p. 377.
13. The Grand Council resolution of March 1937, quoted in C. Ipsen, *Dictating Demography. The Problem of Population in Fascist Italy* (Cambridge: Cambridge University Press, 1996) p. 178.

14. *Opera Omnia*, vol. 22, p. 384.
15. A. Lyttelton, *The Seizure of Power. Fascism in Italy* (London: Weidenfeld and Nicolson, 1982) p. 352.

4. THE YEARS OF THE GREAT DEPRESSION, 1929–34

1. Mussolini's speech at Naples, 25 October 1931. in E. and D. Susmel (eds), *Opera Omnia di Benito Mussolini*, vol. 25 (Florence: La Fenice, 1952) p. 50.
2. Mussolini's speech to the Senate, 25 May 1929, in *Opera Omnia*, vol. 24, p. 101.
3. Quoted in A. Aquarone, *L'organizzazione dello stato totalitario* (Turin: Einaudi, 1965) p. 267.
4. As quoted in P. Morgan, 'Italian Fascist Social Welfare Policy, 1927–37', *Tuttitalia*, 4 (1991) p. 5.
5. Quoted in G. Turi, 'Fascismo e cultura ieri e oggi', in A. Del Boca, M. Legnani and M.G. Rossi (eds), *Il Regime fascista. Storia e storiografia* (Bari: Laterza, 1995) p. 539.
6. Quoted in T. Benton, 'Speaking without Adjectives. Architecture in the Service of Totalitarianism', in D. Ades, T. Benson, D. Elliott and I. Boyd-White (eds), *Art and Power. Europe under the Dictators, 1930–1945* (Hayward Gallery: London, 1995) p. 39.
7. Quoted in J.T. Schnapp, 'Epic Demonstrations. Fascist Modernity and the 1932 Exhibition of the Fascist Revolution', in R.J. Golsan (ed.), *Fascism, Aesthetics and Culture* (London: University Press of New England, 1992) p. 2.
8. Quoted in D. Ghirardo, *Building New Communities: New Deal America and Fascist Italy* (Princeton, NJ: Princeton University Press, 1989) p. 18.
9. See E. Gentile, *Il culto del littorio: la sacralizzazione della politica nell'Italia fascista* (Bari: Laterza, 1993), in English, *The Sacralisation of Politics in Fascist Italy* (Cambridge, Mass: Harvard University Press, 1996); and M. Burleigh, *The Third Reich. A New History* (London: Macmillan, 2000).
10. Quoted in E. Gentile, 'Fascism as Political Religion', *Journal of Contemporary History*, 25 (1990) p. 237.
11. C. Burdett, 'Journeys to the Other Spaces of Fascist Italy', *Modern Italy*, 5 (2000) p. 10.
12. ACS, *MRF*, Pt. 1, busta 9, 'Rapporto del Duce', 'Liguria'.
13. Taken from the text in P. Scoppola, *La Chiesa e il fascismo. Documenti e interpretazioni* (Bari: Laterza, 1971) p. 269.
14. From the text of the agreement in Scoppola, *La Chiesa e il fascismo*, p. 280.
15. Scorza's report to Mussolini, 11 July 1931, in ACS, *Segretaria particolare del Duce, carteggio riservato (1922–43)*, fascicolo 242/R, 'Direttorio del PNF', sottofascicolo 2, inserto A.
16. Quoted in V. De Grazia, *How Fascism Ruled Women. Italy, 1922–1945* (Berkeley: University of California Press, 1992) p. 161.
17. From text in C.F. Delzell (ed.), *Mediterranean Fascism* (London: Macmillan, 1971) p. 127.
18. G. Salvemini, *Under the Axe of Fascism* (London: Gollancz, 1936) p. 114.

5. THE CREATION OF THE FASCIST EMPIRE, 1935–36

1. Mussolini's speech in Milan, 28 October 1925, in E. and D. Susmel (eds), *Opera Omnia di Benito Mussolini*, vol. 21 (Florence: La Fenice, 1952) pp. 423, 426.
2. Quoted in B. Vigezzi, *Politica estera e opinione pubblica in Italia dall'Unità ai giorni nostri. Orientamenti degli studi e prospettive della ricerca* (Milan: Jaca, 1991) p. 111.
3. Quoted in G. Candeloro, *Storia dell'Italia moderna*, vol. 9, *Il fascismo e le sue guerre* (Milan: Feltrinelli, 1981) p. 342.
4. Mussolini's speech in Rome, 9 May 1936, in *Opera Omnia*, vol. 27, p. 268.
5. Quoted in Candeloro, *Storia dell'Italia moderna*, vol. 9, p. 343.

6. THE AXIS CONNECTION AND THE 'FASCISTISATION' OF ITALIAN SOCIETY, 1936-40

1. From text in C.F. Delzell (ed.), *Mediterranean Fascism* (London: Macmillan, 1971) p. 201.
2. From the speech reproduced in R. De Felice, *Mussolini il Duce*, vol. 2, *Lo stato totalitario 1936-1940* (Turin: Einaudi, 1981) pp. 321-5.
3. Mussolini's speech to a rally of squadrists, 26 March 1939, in E. and D. Susmel (eds), *Opera Omnia di Benito Mussolini* (Florence: La Fenice, 1952) p. 251.
4. From text in De Felice, *Lo stato totalitario*, pp. 918-19.
5. Entry of 7 September 1939 in G.B. Guerri (ed.), *Giuseppe Bottai, Diario 1935-1944* (Milan: Rizzoli, 1982) p. 164.
6. Quoted in R.J.B. Bosworth, *Mussolini* (London: Arnold, 2002) p. 291.
7. Quoted in A. Del Boca, *Gli Italiani in Africa Orientale*, vol. 3, *La caduta dell'impero* (Milan: Mondadori, 1992) p. 147.
8. From text of Charter in Delzell, *Mediterranean Fascism*, p. 149.
9. Reported in M. Gallo, *Mussolini's Italy. Twenty Years of the Fascist Era* (London: Abelard-Schuman, 1974) p. 281.
10. Entry of 10 July 1938, in R. De Felice (ed.), *G. Ciano. Diario 1937-1943* (Milan: Rizzoli, 1980) p. 156.
11. Mussolini's speech to the National Assembly of Corporations, 23 March 1936, in *Opera Omnia*, vol. 27, p. 244.
12. M. Donosti, *Mussolini e l'Europa. La politica estera fascista* (Rome: Leonardo, 1945) p. 166.
13. Mussolini's remarks to Ciano, entry of 29 January 1940, in *Diario*, p. 391.
14. From Mussolini's secret report to the king, quoted in B. Vigezzi, *Politica estera e opinione pubblica in Italia dall'Unita ai giorni nostri* (Milan: Jaca, 1991) p. 107.

7. FASCIST ITALY AT WAR, 1939-40

1. Mussolini's speech to the PNF Directorate, 26 May 1942, in E. and D. Susmel (eds), *Opera Omnia di Benito Mussolini*, vol. 31 (Florence: La Fenice, 1952) p. 73.
2. G.B. Guerri (ed.), *Rapporto al Duce: Il testo stenografico inedito dei colloqui tra i federali e Mussolini nel 1942* (Milan: Bompiani, 1978) p. 371.

8. THE ITALIAN SOCIAL REPUBLIC, 1943-45

1. Quoted in C. Lévy, 'Historians and the "First Republic" ', in S. Berger, M. Donovan and K. Passmore (eds), *Writing National Histories. Western Europe since 1800* (London: Routledge, 1999) p. 270.
2. Quoted in G. Bocca, *La repubblica di Mussolini*, 3rd edn (Bari: Laterza, 1977) p. 23.
3. Letter to Mussolini, 11 October 1943, from the ex-socialist and communist leader, Bombacci, who rallied to the regime in the 1930s and then to Salò, quoted in S. Setta, 'Potere economico e Repubblica Sociale Italiana', *Storia Contemporanea*, 8 (1977) p. 260.
4. From the text of the Verona Manifesto of November 1943 in R. De Felice (ed.), *Autobiografia del Fascismo. Antologia di testi fascisti 1919-1945* (Bergamo: Minerva Italica, 1978) p. 583.
5. Quoted in Bocca, *La repubblica di Mussolini*, p. 178.
6. See C. Pavone, *La guerra civile. Saggio storico sulla moralità della Resistenza* (Turin: Bollati Boringheri, 1991).

Select Bibliography

The number of books and articles written on Fascism is endless. This book adds to the pile. Any bibliography is therefore necessarily selective, even idiosyncratic. This one broadly follows the structure of the book. Works are listed once under the period where they are most useful, but many of them are also relevant to the other periods. Good bibliographies can be found in G. Quazza *et al.*, *Storiografia e fascismo* (Milan: Franco Angeli, 1985) and in G. Candeloro, *Storia dell'Italia moderna*, vols 8–10 (Milan: Feltrinelli, 1978–84).

1. DOCUMENT COLLECTIONS AND COMMENTARIES

R. DE FELICE (ed.), *Autobiografia del fascismo: Antologia di testi fascisti 1919–1945* (Bergamo: Minerva Italica, 1978).

C.F. DELZELL (ed.), *Mediterranean Fascism 1919–1945* (London: Macmillan, 1971).

G.B. GUERRI (ed.), *Rapporto al Duce: Il testo stenografico inedito dei colloqui tra i federali e Mussolini nel 1942* (Milan: Bompiani, 1978).

A. LYTTELTON (ed.), *Italian Fascisms from Pareto to Gentile* (London: Cape, 1973).

P. SCOPPOLA (ed.), *La chiesa e il fascismo: Documenti e interpretazioni* (Bari: Laterza, 1971).

E. and D. SUSMEL (eds), *Opera Omnia di Benito Mussolini*, 36 vols (Florence: La Fenice, 1951–63).

2. BIOGRAPHIES AND MEMOIRS

R.J.B. BOSWORTH, *Mussolini* (London: Arnold, 2002).

G. BOTTAI, *Vent'anni e un giorno* (Milan: Garzanti, 1977).

F. CORDOVA (ed.), *Uomini e volti del fascismo* (Rome: Bulzoni, 1980).

R. DE FELICE (ed.), *G. Ciano. Diario 1937–1943* (Milan: Rizzoli, 1980).

G.B. GUERRI (ed.), *Giuseppe Bottai, Diario 1935–1944* (Milan: Rizzoli, 1982).

D. MACK-SMITH, *Mussolini* (London: Weidenfeld and Nicolson, 1982).

C.G. SEGRÈ, *Italo Balbo. A Fascist Life* (Berkeley, Calif.: University of California, 1987).

3. GENERAL WORKS

M. BLINKHORN, *Mussolini and Fascist Italy* (London: Methuen, 1984).

M. BLINKHORN (ed.), *Fascists and Conservatives: The Radical Right and the Establishment in 20th Century Europe* (London: Unwin Hyman, 1990).

R.J.B. BOSWORTH, *The Italian Dictatorship. Problems and Perspectives in the Interpretation of Mussolini and Italian Fascism* (London: Arnold, 1998).

R.J.B. BOSWORTH and S. ROMANO (eds), *La politica estera italiana 1860–1985* (Bologna: Il Mulino, 1991).

G. CANDELORO, *Il movimento cattolico in Italia*, 3rd edn (Rome: Editori Riuniti, 1974).

G. CANDELORO, *Storia dell'Italia moderna*, vols 8–10 (Milan: Feltrinelli, 1978, 1981 and 1984).

P.V. CANNISTRARO (ed.), *Historical Dictionary of Fascist Italy* (Westport and London: Greenwood Press, 1982).

G. CAROCCI, *Italian Fascism* (Harmondsworth: Pelican, 1975).

V. CASTRONOVO, *Storia d'Italia*, vol. 4:1, *La storia economica* (Turin: Einaudi, 1973).

M. CLARK, *Modern Italy 1871–1982* (London: Longman, 1984).

A.J. DE GRAND, *Italian Fascism: Its Origins and Development* (Lincoln, Nebr. and London: University of Nebraska Press, 2000).

A. DEL BOCA, M. LEGNANI and M.G. ROSSI (eds), *Il regime fascista. Storia e storiografia* (Bari: Laterza, 1995).

A.A. KALLIS, *Fascist Ideology. Territory and Expansionism in Italy and Germany, 1922–1945* (London: Routledge, 2000).

C.J. LOWE and F. MARZARI, *Italian Foreign Policy 1870–1940* (London and Boston, Mass.: Routledge Kegan, 1975).

D. MACK-SMITH, *Italy and its Monarchy* (New Haven, Conn. and London: Yale University Press, 1989).

J. POLLARD, *The Fascist Experience in Italy* (London: Routledge, 1998).

G. QUAZZA, *Resistenza e storia d'Italia* (Milan: Feltrinelli, 1976).

E. RAGIONIERI, *Storia d'Italia*, vol. 4:3, *La storia politica e sociale* (Turin: Einaudi, 1976).

L. SALVATORELLI and G. MIRA, *Storia d'Italia nel periodo fascista* (Turin: Einaudi, 1971).

E. SANTARELLI, *Storia del movimento e del regime fascista*, 2 vols (Rome: Editori Riuniti, 1967).

R. SARTI, *Fascism and the Industrial Leadership in Italy 1919–1940* (Los Angeles and London: University of California, Berkeley, Press, 1971).

L. SCHAPIRO, *Totalitarianism* (London: Macmillan, 1972).

C. SETON-WATSON, *Italy from Liberalism to Fascism 1870–1925* (London: Methuen, 1967).

Storia della società italiana, vols 21–2 (Milan: Teti, 1982–3).

A. TAMARO, *Venti anni di storia*, 3 vols (Rome: Volpe, 1971–5).

E.R. TANNENBAUM, *Fascism in Italy. Society and Culture 1922–45* (London: Allen Lane, 1973).

G. TONIOLO, *L'economia dell'Italia fascista* (Bari: Laterza, 1980).

G. TONIOLO (ed.), *L'economia italiana 1861–1940* (Bari: Laterza, 1973).

B. VIGEZZI, *Politica estera e opinione pubblica in Italia dall'Unità ai giorni nostri* (Milan: Jaca, 1991).

R.A. WEBSTER, *The Cross and the Fasces: Christian Democracy and Fascism in Italy* (Stanford, Calif.: Stanford University Press, 1960).

'The Aesthetics of Fascism', whole issue, *Journal of Contemporary History*, 31 (1996).

E. GENTILE, 'The Problem of the Party in Italian Fascism', *Journal of Contemporary History*, 19 (1984).

E. GENTILE, 'Fascism in Italian Historiography: in Search of an Historical Identity', *Journal of Contemporary History*, 21 (1986).

E. GENTILE, 'Fascism as Political Religion', *Journal of Contemporary History*, 25 (1990).

R. GRIFFIN, 'The Sacred Synthesis: the Ideological Cohesion of Fascist Cultural Policy', *Modern Italy*, 3 (1998).

MACGREGOR KNOX, 'Conquest, Foreign and Domestic, in Fascist Italy and Nazi Germany', *Journal of Modern History*, 56 (1984).

D. MACK-SMITH, 'Mussolini: Reservations about Renzo De Felice's Biography', *Modern Italy*, 5 (2000).

4. THE CONQUEST OF POWER, 1919–29

A. AQUARONE, *L'organizzazione dello stato totalitario* (Turin: Einaudi, 1965).

M. BERNABEI, *Fascismo e nazionalismo in Campania 1919–1925* (Rome: Edizioni di Storia e Letteratura, 1975).

M. CANALI, *Il delitto Matteotti: affarismo e politica nel primo governo Mussolini* (Bologna: Il Mulino, 1997).

A.L. CARDOZA, *Agrarian Elites and Italian Fascism. The Province of Bologna 1901–1926* (Princeton, NJ: Princeton University Press, 1982).

L. CASALI (ed.), *Bologna 1920. Le origini del fascismo* (Bologna: Cappelli, 1982).

S. COLARIZI, *Dopoguerra e fascismo in Puglia 1919–1926* (Bari: Laterza, 1971).

F. CORDOVA, *Le origini dei sindacati fascisti 1918–1926* (Bari: Laterza, 1974).

P. CORNER, *Fascism in Ferrara 1915–1925* (London: Oxford University Press, 1975).

R. DE FELICE, *Mussolini il rivoluzionario 1883–1920*, 3rd edn (Turin: Einaudi, 1965): *Mussolini il fascista*, 1: *La conquista del potere 1921–1925*, 2: *L'organizzazione dello stato fascista 1925–1929* (Turin: Einaudi, 1966 and 1968).

A.J. DE GRAND, *The Italian Nationalist Association and the Rise of Fascism in Italy* (Lincoln, Nebr. and London: University of Nebraska Press, 1978).

F.J. DEMERS, *Le origini del fascismo a Cremona* (Bari: Laterza, 1979).

G. DE ROSA, *Il Partito Popolare Italiano*, 3rd edn (Bari: Laterza, 1974).

C. DUGGAN, *Fascism and the Mafia* (New Haven, Conn.: Yale University Press, 1989).

E. GENTILE, *Le origini dell'ideologia fascista 1918–1925* (Bari: Laterza, 1975).

E. GENTILE, *Storia del Partito Fascista 1919–1922: Movimento e Milizia* (Bari: Laterza, 1989).

C. IPSEN, *Dictating Demography. The Problem of Population in Fascist Italy* (Cambridge: Cambridge University Press, 1996).

A. KELIKIAN, *Town and Country under Fascism The Transformation of Brescia 1915–1926* (Oxford: Oxford University Press, 1986).

P. LAVEGLIA (ed.), *Mezzogiorno e fascismo: atti del convegno nazionale di studi promosso dalla regione Campania, 1975* (Naples: Edizioni Scientifiche Italiane, 1978).

A. LYTTELTON, 'Fascism and Violence in Postwar Italy: Political Strategy and Social Conflict', in W.J. MOMMSEN and G. HIRSCHFELD (eds), *Social Protest, Violence and Terror in 19th and 20th Century Europe* (London: Macmillan, 1982).

A. LYTTELTON, *The Seizure of Power. Fascism in Italy 1919–1929* (London: Weidenfeld and Nicolson, 1973).

C.S. MAIER, *Recasting Bourgeois Europe. Stabilization in France, Germany and Italy in the Decade after World War I* (Princeton, NJ: Princeton University Press, 1975).

P. MELOGRANI, *Gli industriali e Mussolini: Rapporti fra Confindustria e fascismo dal 1919 al 1929* (Milan: Longanesi, 1972).

J. PETERSON, 'Elettorato e base sociale del fascismo negli anni venti', *Studi Storici*, 16 (1975).

F. PIVA, *Lotte contadine e origini del fascismo. Padova-Venezia: 1919–1922* (Venice: Marsilio, 1977).

L. RAPONE, 'Il sindacalismo fascista: temi e problemi della ricerca storica', *Storia Contemporanea*, 4–5 (1982).

D.D. ROBERTS, *The Syndicalist Tradition and Italian Fascism* (Manchester: Manchester University Press, 1979).

G. RUMI, 'Mussolini e il "programma" di San Sepolcro', *Movimento di Liberazione in Italia*, 71 (1963).

G. SABBATUCCI, *I combattenti nel primo dopoguerra* (Bari: Laterza, 1974).

G. SABBATUCCI (ed.), *La crisi italiana del primo dopoguerra. La storia e la critica* (Bari: Laterza, 1976).

G. SALVEMINI, *Under the Axe of Fascism* (London: Gollancz, 1936).

G. SAPELLI, 'Per la storia del sindacalismo fascista: tra controllo sociale e conflitto di classe', *Studi storici*, 19 (1978).

F.M. SNOWDEN, 'On the Social Origins of Agrarian Fascism in Italy', *Archives Européens de Sociologie*, 13 (1972).

F.M. SNOWDEN, *The Fascist Revolution in Tuscany 1919–1922* (Cambridge: Cambridge University Press, 1989).

F.M. SNOWDEN, *Violence and the Great Estates in the South of Italy: Apulia 1900–1922* (Cambridge: Cambridge University Press, 1986).

Z. STERNELL, M. SZNAJDER and M. ARHERI, *The Birth of Fascist Ideology. From Cultural Rebellion to Political Revolution* (Princeton: Princeton University Press, 1994).

A. TASCA (pseud. A. ROSSI), *Nascita e avvento del fascismo. L'Italia dal 1918 al 1922* (Florence: La Nuova Italia, 1963). English version, *The Rise of Italian Fascism 1918–1922* (London: Methuen, 1938).

N. TRANFAGLIA, *Dallo stato liberale al regime fascista. Problemi e ricerche* (Milan: Feltrinelli, 1973).

P. UNGARI, *Alfredo Rocco e l'ideologia giuridica del fascismo* (Brescia: Morcelliana, 1963).

B. UVA, 'Gli scioperi dei metallurgici italiani del marzo 1925', *Storia Contemporanea*, 1 (1970).

R. VIVARELLi, *Il dopoguerra in Italia e l'avvento del fascismo 1918–1922*, vol. 1, *Dalla fine della guerra all'impresa di Fiume* (Naples: Mondadori, 1967).

R. VIVARELLI, *Il fallimento del liberalismo. Studi sulle origini del fascismo* (Bologna: Il Mulino, 1981).

P.G. ZUNINO, *L'ideologia del fascismo. Miti, credenze e valori nella stabilizzazione del regime* (Bologna: Il Mulino, 1985).

5. THE FASCIST REGIME, 1929-36

D. ADES, T. BENSON and I. BOYD-WHITE (eds), *Art and Power. Europe under the Dictators* (London: Hayward Gallery, 1995).

A. AQUARONE and M. VERNASSA (eds), *Il regime fascista* (Bologna: Il Mulino, 1974).

M. BEREZIN, *Making the Fascist Self* (Ithaca and London: Cornell University Press, 1997).

G. CAROCCI, *La politica estera dell'Italia Fascista 1925–1928* (Bari: Laterza, 1969).

A. CASSELS, *Mussolini's Early Diplomacy* (Princeton, NJ: Princeton University Press, 1970).

S. CASSESE, *La formazione dell stato amministrativo* (Milan: Giuffré, 1974).

A. CENTO BULL, *Capitalismo e fascismo di fronte alla crisi: industria e società bergamasca, 1923–1937* (Bergamo: Il Filo di Aranna, 1983).

R. DE FELICE, *Mussolini il Duce*, 1: *Gli anni del consenso 1929–1936* (Turin: Einaudi, 1974).

A.J. DE GRAND, *Bottai e la cultura fascista* (Bari: Laterza, 1978).

V. DE GRAZIA, *The Culture of Consent. Mass Organization of Leisure in Fascist Italy* (Cambridge: Cambridge University Press, 1981).

V. DE GRAZIA, *How Fascism Ruled Women. Italy, 1922–1945* (Berkeley: University of California Press, 1991).

S. FALASCA ZAMPONI, *Fascist Spectacle. The Aesthetics of Power in Mussolini's Italy* (Berkeley: University of California Press, 1997).

G. GERMANI, 'The Political Socialization of Youth in Fascist Regimes', in S.P. Huntington and C.H. Moore (eds), *Authoritarian Politics in Modern Society: The Dynamics of Established One-Party Systems* (New York: Basic Books, 1970).

T.H. KOON, *Believe, Obey, Fight. Political Socialization of Youth in Fascist Italy 1922– 1943* (Chapel Hill, NC and London: University of North Carolina Press, 1985).

M.A. LEDEEN, *Universal Fascism. The Theory and Practice of the Fascist International 1928–36* (New York: Howard Fertig, 1972).

G. NENCI (ed.), *Politica e società in Italia dal Fascismo alla Resistenza: Problemi di storia nazionale e storia Umbra* (Bologna: Il Mulino, 1978).

M. PALLA, *Firenze nel regime fascista 1929–1934* (Florence: Olschki, 1978).

J. PETERSON, *Hitler e Mussolini: La difficile alleanza* (Bari: Laterza, 1975).

J.F. POLLARD, *The Vatican and Italian Fascism 1929–32: A Study in Conflict* (Cambridge: Cambridge University Press, 1985).

D. PRETI, *Economia e istituzioni nello stato fascista* (Rome: Editori Riuniti, 1980).

G. QUAZZA (ed.), *Fascismo e società italiana* (Turin: Einaudi, 1973).

G. QUAZZA et al., *Storiografia e fascismo* (Milan: Franco Angeli, 1985).

L. ROSENSTOCK-FRANCK, *L'économie corporative fasciste en doctrine et en fait. Ses origins historiques et son évolution* (Paris, 1934).

G. RUMI, *Alle origini della politica estera fascista 1918–1923* (Bari: Laterza, 1968).

G. SAPELLI (ed.), 'La classe operaia durante il fascismo', in *Annali della Fondazione Feltrinelli*, 20 (1979–80).

R. SARTI (ed.), *The Axe Within: Italian Fascism in Action* (New York: New Viewpoints, 1974).

M.S. STONE, *The Patron State. Culture and Politics in Fascist Italy* (Princeton, NJ: Princeton University Press, 1998).

D. THOMPSON, *State Control in Fascist Italy. Culture and Conformity 1925–1943* (Manchester: Manchester University Press, 1991).

P. TOGLIATTI, *Lezioni sul fascismo* (Rome: Editori Riuniti, 1976).

La Toscana nel regime fascista 1922–1939, 2 vols (Florence: Olschki, 1974).

A. AQUARONE, 'Italy: the Crisis and the Corporative Economy', *Journal of Contemporary History*, 4 (1969).

A. AQUARONE, 'Violenza e consenso nel fascismo italiano', *Storia Contemporanea*, 10 (1979).

S. ROGARI, 'Azione Cattolica e fascismo', 1: 'Come la chiesa si difese da Mussolini', *Nuova Antologia*, 533 (1978).

N. TRANFAGLIA (ed.), *Fascismo e capitalismo* (Milan: Feltrinelli, 1976).

C. VALLAURI, *Le radici del corporativismo* (Rome: Bulzoni, 1971).

6. FASCIST EXPANSIONISM, 1936–1943

P.V. CANNISTRARO, *La fabbrica del consenso. Fascismo e mass media* (Bari: Laterza, 1975).

F. CATALANO, *L'economia italiana di guerra 1935–1943. La politica economica-finanziaria del fascismo dalla guerra di Etiopia alla caduta del regime* (Milan: INSMLI, 1969).

A. DEL BOCA, *Gli Italiani in Africa Orientale*, 4 vols (Milan: Mondadori, 1992).

R. DE FELICE, *Mussolini il Duce*, 2: *Lo stato totalitario 1936–1940; Mussolini l'alleato 1940–1945*, 1: *L'Italia in guerra 1940–1943*, 2 vols (Turin: Einaudi, 1981 and 1990).

R. DE FELICE (ed.), *L'Italia fra tedeschi e alleati. La politica estera fascista e la seconda guerra mondiale* (Bologna: Il Mulino, 1973).

E. DI NOLFO, R.H. RAINERO and B. VIGEZZI (eds), *L'Italia e la politica di potenza in Europa 1938–1940* (Milan: Marzorati, 1986).

MACGREGOR KNOX, *Mussolini Unleashed 1939–1941. Politics and Strategy in Fascist Italy's Last War* (Cambridge: Cambridge University Press, 1982).

G. MAIONE, *L'imperialismo straccione. Classi sociali e finanza di guerra dall'impresa etiopica al conflitto mondiale 1935–1943* (Bologna: Il Mulino, 1979).

T.M. MAZZATOSTA, *Il regime fascista tra educazione e propaganda 1935–1943* (Bologna: Cappelli, 1978).

M. MICHAELIS, *Mussolini and the Jews. German–Italian Relations and the Jewish Question in Italy 1922–1945* (Oxford: Clarendon Press, 1978).

P. MORGAN, 'The Italian Fascist New Order in Europe', in M.L. SMITH and P.M.R. STIRK (eds), *Making the New Europe. European Unity and the Second World War* (London: Pinter, 1990).

A. SBACCHI, *Ethiopia under Mussolini: Fascism and the Colonial Experience* (London: Zed Books, 1985).

Operai e contadini nella crisi italiana del 1943–1944 (Milan: Feltrinelli, 1974).

P.V. CANNISTRARO and E.D. WYNOT, 'On the Dynamics of Anti-Communism as a Function of Fascist Foreign Policy', *Il Politico*, 4 (1973).

A.J. DE GRAND, 'Cracks in the Facade: The Failure of Fascist Totalitarianism in Italy 1935–9', *European History Quarterly*, 21 (1991).

M. FULLER, 'Wherever You Go, There You Are: Fascist Plans for the Colonial City of Addis Abeba and the Colonising Suburb of EUR "42" ', *Journal of Contemporary History*, 31 (1996).

M. LEDEEN, 'The Evolution of Italian Fascist Anti-Semitism', *Jewish Social Studies*, 37 (1975).

A. LYTTELTON, J. PETERSON and G. SANTOMASSIMO, 'Il Mussolini di Renzo De Felice', *Passato e Presente*, 1 (1982).

MACGREGOR KNOX, 'The Fascist Regime, its Foreign Policy and its Wars: an "anti-anti-Fascist Orthodoxy" ', *Contemporary European History*, 4 (1995).

S. ROGARI, 'Azione Cattolica e fascismo', 2: 'La crisi del 1938 e il distacco dal regime', *Nuova Antologia*, 534 (1978).

S. ROGARI, 'L'opinione pubblica in Toscana di fronte alla guerra 1939–1943', *Nuova Antologia*, 557 (1987).

L. ROSENSTOCK-FRANCK, *Les étapes de l'économie fasciste italienne. Du corporatisme à l'économie de guerre* (Paris, 1939).

M. SARFATTI, 'Fascist Italy and German Jews in South Eastern France in July 1943', *Journal of Modern Italian Studies*, 3 (1998).

C.G. SEGRE, 'Italo Balbo and the Colonisation of Libya', *Journal of Contemporary History*, 31 (1996).

D.C. WATT, 'The Rome-Berlin Axis. Myth and Reality', *Review of Politics*, 22 (1960).

7. THE ITALIAN SOCIAL REPUBLIC, 1943–5

R. ABSALOM, *A Strange Alliance: Aspects of Escape and Survival in Italy, 1943–1945* (Florence: Olscki 1991).

G. BOCCA, *La Repubblica di Mussolini* (Bari: Laterza, 1977).

F.W. DEAKIN, *The Brutal Friendship: Mussolini, Hitler and the Fall of Mussolini* (London: Weidenfeld and Nicolson, 1962).

R. DE FELICE, *Mussolini l'alleato, 1940–1945*, 2: *La guerra civile, 1943–1945* (Turin: Einaudi, 1997).

D. ELLWOOD, *Italy 1943–1945* (Leicester: Leicester University Press, 1995).

L. KLINKHAMMER, *L'Occupazione tedesca in Italia, 1943–1945* (Turin: Bollati Boringheri, 1993).

C. PAVONE, *La guerra civile. Saggio storico sulla moralità nella Resistenza* (Turin: Bollati Boringheri, 1991).

S. SETTA, 'Potere economico e Repubblica Sociale Italiana', *Storia Contemporanea*, 8 (1977).

CONCLUSION

C. DUGGAN, 'Italy in the Cold War Years and the Legacy of Fascism', in C. DUGGAN and C. WAGSTAFF (eds), *Italy in the Cold War. Culture and Society, 1948–1958* (Oxford: Berg, 1995).

E.A. MILLAR (ed.), *The Legacy of Fascism* (Glasgow: Glasgow University Press, 1989).

Index

and anti-Fascism, 1926–43, 151
and Resistance, 1943–5, 225, 234
before First World War, 14–16
during First World War, 20, 21,
22, 23, 26
Somalia, 166, 188, 191
Sorel, Georges, 17, 18, 22
South Tyrol, 70, 184, 226
Southern Italy:
1943–5, 224, 234
Fascism in, 1925–43, 148
politics in, 1870–922, 13–16, 31,
32, 33, 37, 39–40, 51–2
politics in, 1922–5, 88–90
Soviet Union, *see* Russia
Spain, 150, 186, 207
Spanish Civil War (1936–9), 181,
185, 200, 207, 208
Special Tribunal for the Defence of
the State, 100, 223
sport, 105, 129, 130, 135, 148,
149, 194
squadrism and squads, Fascist, 30,
50, 52, 54, 55, 57, 58, 60, 62,
66–8, 69, 72, 77, 81, 83, 84, 85,
87, 96, 99–100, 102, 193, 197,
198, 220, 228
Starace, Achille, 128, 129, 131, 132,
134, 137, 197
State, the Fascist, *see* Fascist regime,
'totalitarian'
Steinbeck, John, 139
Sternell, Zeev, 17, 19
Strapaese, 'Super-provincial', 140
Stresemann, Gustav, 184
students, 131–2
Sturzo, Luigi, 34, 35, 36, 56, 86, 87
Sudan, 191
Suvich, Fulvio, 205
Sweden, 119
Switzerland, 211
syndicalism and syndicates, Fascist,
69, 77, 83–4, 86, 105–7, 108,
146, 157, 159, 227
in agriculture, 52–3, 54, 60, 61, 65
in industry, 56, 77, 83–4, 105–6,
108, 109, 135, 146; *see also*
corporations

teachers, 63, 130–1
Teruzzi, Attilio, 188, 192
'totalitarian', 'totalitarian' state,
'totalitarianism', 28, 96–8,
99–100, 101, 104, 114, 115–16,
120, 129, 137–8, 148, 154, 167,
168–9, 174–5, 186, 193, 197,
214, 233
trade unions:
catholic, *see Confederazione Italiana
del Lavoro*
Fascist, *see* syndicalism
socialist, *see Confederazione Generale
del Lavoro, Federterra,
Federazione Italiana Operai
Metallurgici*
trasformismo, 'transformism', 14–16,
37, 57, 59, 90
Trento, 70
Treviso, 62
Trieste, 50
trincerocrazia, 'trenchocracy', 27
Triple Alliance, 20, 164
Tunisia, 183
Turati, Augusto, 61, 83, 101,
104, 105, 117, 127, 128,
132, 135, 144
Turin, 83, 188
Tuscany, 51, 54, 55, 57, 58, 60, 61,
89, 95, 98, 103

Udine, 74
Umbria, 40
United States of America (USA), 44,
116, 117, 167, 169–70, 205, 206,
222, 237; *see also* Allies
'universal' fascism, *see* international
fascism
universities, *see Gioventù Universitaria
Fascista*, students
Ustasha movement, Croatia, 165

Vatican, 34, 36, 86–7
and Fascist government, 1922–6,
86–7
and Fascist regime, 112, 113, 114,
150, 152, 204, 210, 211, 222;
see also church, catholic